New Approaches to Religion and Power

Series Editor

Joerg Rieger
Vanderbilt University Divinity School
Heidelberg, Germany

While the relationship of religion and power is a perennial topic, it only continues to grow in importance and scope in our increasingly globalized and diverse world. Religion, on a global scale, has openly joined power struggles, often in support of the powers that be. But at the same time, religion has made major contributions to resistance movements. In this context, current methods in the study of religion and theology have created a deeper awareness of the issue of power: Critical theory, cultural studies, postcolonial theory, subaltern studies, feminist theory, critical race theory, and working class studies are contributing to a new quality of study in the field. This series is a place for both studies of particular problems in the relation of religion and power as well as for more general interpretations of this relation. It undergirds the growing recognition that religion can no longer be studied without the study of power.

More information about this series at
http://www.springer.com/series/14754

Nami Kim • Wonhee Anne Joh
Editors

Critical Theology against US Militarism in Asia

Decolonization and Deimperialization

palgrave
macmillan

Editors
Nami Kim
Spelman College
Atlanta, Georgia, USA

Wonhee Anne Joh
Garrett-Evangelical Theological Seminary
Evanston, Illinois, USA

New Approaches to Religion and Power
ISBN 978-1-137-48012-5 ISBN 978-1-137-48013-2 (eBook)
DOI 10.1057/978-1-137-48013-2

Library of Congress Control Number: 2016958034

Printed on acid-free paper

This Palgrave Macmillan imprint is published by Springer Nature
The registered company is Nature America Inc.
The registered company address is: 1 New York Plaza, New York, NY 10004, U.S.A.

Introduction: Critical Theology Against US Militarism in Asia: Decolonization and Deimperialization

Nami Kim and Wonhee Anne Joh

US Militarism in Asia

The year 2015 marked the seventieth anniversary of the end of World War II, the seventieth memorial of atomic bombings of Hiroshima and Nagasaki in Japan, and the fiftieth anniversary of US Immigration and Nationality Act of 1965 that had reopened the US borders for immigrants from Asia. The year 2015 also was fortieth anniversary of the end of the Vietnam War, or what some call the American War, which passed the US Indochina Migration and Refugee Assistance Act of 1975 that permitted war refugees from Vietnam and Cambodia to enter the US. For the past 60 years, the US has engaged in various wars, including the Korean War, the Vietnam War, the first Gulf War (aka Operation Desert Storm), war in Afghanistan, and war against Iraq (aka Operation Iraqi Freedom) under the banner of freedom, democracy, liberation, and human rights. Asia has long been a first, key stage for the US's global fight against communism, and recently against terrorism. Part of the deadly genius of the fundamental logic of "War on Terror" is its rootedness in a logic of preemption that allows for wars without ends. This logic is simple yet lethal. As lethal as the deterrence of the Cold War, the logic of preemption relies on the affective perception of the US for any and all possible and potential threats. If the US "feels" there is a possible threat to the security of the US or to its interests around the world, it has given itself license to wage war based on that perception of possible impending threat with a preemptive strike. The US has now sanctioned itself to go to war anywhere and anytime for any reason it deems a threat. While the "official" Cold War may have ended,

US interventions have not, and in fact, scholars, like Brian Massumi, argue that the US is now and has been since 9/11 in the throes of what he terms "ontopower," where deterrence is not the justification for war but rather an ideology of "preemption." Such ontopower is generated through "a mutually assured destruction" that is "equilibrium seeking." It tends toward the creation of a "balance of terror."[1] What we experience today is the unprecedented "global omnipresence and unparalleled lethality of the US military, and the ambition with which it is being deployed around the world."[2] As Zillah Eisenstein has noted, "War is our cultural metaphor. We war on drugs, AIDS, on cancer, on poverty, on terrorism...War is a danger to democracy because it justifies and therefore normalizes secrecy, deception, surveillance, and killing." Since the fall of the Soviet Union, and especially after 9/11, the US has been able to take aim at mastery of all being, pressing even further the Pentagon claims of Bill Clinton's regime to pursue "full spectrum dominance." This war metaphor has mapped on now to the everyday and ordinary life.[3] US military presence in Asia has been justified over the years as a protection of the region from potential military aggression of the communist states, such as former Russia, China, North Vietnam, and North Korea and, in recent times, from terrorist attacks. For instance, military bases in the Philippines were considered key sites for US global defense, especially during the Vietnam War and the first Gulf War. The increase of US military bases is also closely linked to the rise of sex tourism in various Asian cities. As Rita Nakashima Brock and Susan Thistlethwaite show in their book *Casting Stones*, Thailand's sex tourism enormously increased in the 1970s and 1980s largely due to the Vietnam War. Bangkok became a major city for US soldiers' "Rest and Recuperation (R & R) breaks, which the GIs called I & I (Intoxication and Intercourse)." Manila was also a favorite city for US troops returning home at the end of the Gulf War.[4]

Now, one third of US military bases overseas are located in so-called Islamic countries, a marked increase compared with less than 1 percent of bases there during the Cold War.[5] By 2008, the US had SOFA (Status of Forces Agreement) with more than 100 nations, which does not include "undisclosed SOFAS with Islamic countries."[6] The expansion of the US military–industrial complex and the global network of US military bases brought changes in racial relations and configurations both inside and outside US borders. The consequence of this militarism is noted even to the extent that it is a "structuring force of (im)migrations, displacements, and diasporas," and, indeed, now the ways that the diaspora operates has become a specific modality of neocolonialism.[7] The Korean War was the first US-involved war that had racially integrated army units, signaling the changes to come in US racial relations during the era of the Civil Rights Movement. The relationship between US soldiers and women in US war-torn regions as well as in camptowns around US military bases overseas revealed unequal power relations not only between them but also between white US GIs and black/brown US GIs.[8] As Asian American studies scholar Nadia Y. Kim shows in her *Imperial Citizens*, the US "racially 'Americanizes' other countries by way of its White-over-Black order."[9] One of the enduring consequences of this is that immigrants' understanding of race and white racism is already constituted even before their migration to the US.

As immigration reform activist Jose Antonio Vargas has aptly put it, "We're Here Because You Were There." This phrase reminds us that (im) migration of Asians to the US needs to be understood within the context of US military involvement in Asia that is ongoing. In other words, US militarism in Asia and Asian immigration in the US are intrinsically related to each other. As Lisa Lowe states, "'becoming a national citizen' cannot be the exclusive narrative of emancipation for the Asian American subject. Rather, the current social formation entails a subject less narrated by the modern discourse of citizenship and more narrated by the histories of wars in Asia, immigration, and the dynamics of the current global economy."[10] This means that any critical understanding of Asian America and how Asian North American subjectivity is constituted must take account of the long and complex histories of geopolitical, cultural, social, and economic interactions between the US and the diverse expanse of Asia and, most critically, the theater of war by the US in Asia.[11]

When it comes to Asians, the US immigration policy changed as US armed forces brought their "war brides" and children from overseas under the War Brides Acts, which was passed in 1945. For instance, referring to the Korean immigrants in the US as a population formed "in large part by women-centered kin Korean migration,"[12] Nadia Y. Kim says that "the history of this migration network began with US intervention in the Korean War of 1950–1953, as US soldiers came home with their Korean wives, and then sponsored kin through the family reunification clause."[13] Around 6500 Korean military brides entered the US between 1951 and 1964, and as of 2003, there are more than 100,000 military brides living in the US.[14] As Grace Cho poignantly states in her critical work *Haunting the Korean Diaspora*, the story of how Korean military brides came to be in the US remains in the shadows like the long-forgotten Korean War itself. From 1975 until early 1990s, war refugees from Vietnam and Cambodia also arrived on the shores of the empire, of which military action was justified "precisely in the name of a threatened humanity" that each refugee person embodies.[15] These "strangers and their multiplicities" have been incorporated into "the racialization of liberalism's powers" under the banner of what Mimi Thi Nguyen calls transnational multiculturalism that demands "their highest allegiance to a transnational America as an empire of humanity."[16] Those who show their "flags" become the "good refugees," and their stories, as Yen Le Espiritu argues, "valorizes capitalism, equating 'freedom' with economic access and choice, upward social mobility, and free enterprise."[17] In doing so, the distance between "the free world" and the "enemies of freedom" is discursively constructed through the "collapsing of capitalism into freedom and democracy," and this perceived distance justifies continued US military actions as a way to defend and give freedom.[18] One of the compelling critiques against US militarism by Espiritu is her exposure of militarized violence as often undergirding and accompanying humanitarian ideas.[19] We might recall that frequent and more notable so-called humanitarian move by which colonizers often claimed to be providing "education" to the local peoples. This legacy continues in another significant dimension of militarism, in which it facilitates the adoption of infants and young children.[20]

There seems no end to the US's desire to conquer more land and to dispossess more peoples. In the wake of 9/11, as William Spanos put it, "the limited geographical frontier metamorphosed into an illimitable temporal frontier."[21] In other words, when the US's frontier extended to the Pacific and Southeast Asia, it was not only making a transformation of "the spatial (frontier)"—a new transoceanic geographical move—but also launching a "temporal metaphor (the unending 'war on terror')."[22] 9/11, which was perceived to be the first time that "Americans" felt vulnerable in their own lands. But this erased experiences of many immigrants and US people of color, for whom "'America' has been a site of potential or realized violence for all of their lives."[23] Nevertheless, 9/11 not only revitalized American nationalism, but also prompted and sought to legitimate the US's project called Global War on Terror (GWOT).[24] As was demonstrated by Richard Slotkin's work, unless we come to understand the violence that is at the heart of the history of US violent expansion, we will not be able to stop from making more war. Taiwanese cultural critic Kuan-Hsing Chen's notion of "imperialist desire" is also helpful in understanding the works of imperialism. According to Chen, imperialist desire is "the imperialist expansionist mentality" that justifies all kinds of exploitation. It also "generates hardships and long-term resentment among other peoples which may become the seeds of future regional conflicts."[25] As Chen rightly argues, the elimination of imperialism cannot be done without "lessening our own imperial desire."[26]

The Myth of American Exceptionalism

> Just as Asia is critical to America's future, an engaged America is vital to Asia's future. The region is eager for our leadership and our business—perhaps more so than at any time in modern history. We are the only power with a network of strong alliances in the region, no territorial ambitions, and a long record of providing for the common good. Along with our allies, we have underwritten regional security for decades...As we move forward to set the stage for engagement in the Asia-Pacific over the next 60 years, we are mindful of the bipartisan legacy that has shaped our engagement for the past 60.[27]

Former US Secretary of State Hilary Clinton's reference to "America" (i.e. the US) as "the only power" with "no territorial ambitions, and a long record of providing for the common good" is another expression of the enduring myth of American exceptionalism. Not only does the ideology of American exceptionalism define America as a model for the rest of the world, but it also "argues for boundless expansion, where national particularism and international universalism converge."[28] The narrative of American exceptionalism obfuscates the fact that US military bases have been "an integral part of American empire building, going back to America's westward expansion."[29] The massacre and genocide of indigenous peoples of the Americas is founded through the violence of settler colonialism. It is no wonder then that wars waged against the Native Americans could not be assuaged once the "frontier" seemed to end. In fact, much of linguistics, metaphors and cultures, "camps," "calvary," and references to "enemy" territory as "Indian Country" circulated during the wars in Korea, the Philippines, and Vietnam, and had their roots in militarized culture of violence against the indigenous peoples of the US. The language that was used in the genocidal violence of settler colonialism can be found in military language and metaphors used by soldiers and military leaders, for example, referring to the "enemy territory" as "Indian territory" in places like Korea and Vietnam.[30]

There is a direct link between the massive military spending and intensification of US militarism around the world with the continuation of the logics of the Cold War but under the new rhetoric of War on Terror. US penchant for war should not be surprising given the extent of militarized violence present in its own founding. The power behind settler colonialism was the genocide and dispossession of indigenous peoples and colonization of land through diverse methods, to be sure. But at the core of its driving force was militarism and the numerous rationales that were produced to justify such violence. According to Richard Slotkin, various myths constructed to justify violence were at the heart of the US myth of the frontier, manifest destiny as well as its exceptionalism underpinned by Christian theological ideas. Slotkin's main argument is that these founding myths never came to a stop with the expansion of the US once it reached the West Coast but that the "frontier" was extended across the Pacific when faced with the closing of the continental frontier. The myth of the frontier and its rootedness in the idea that violence was necessary continued through history and through present wars. Another example is the racist trope of the other as "savages" or "barbarians" that need civilization. Many of the orientalist and colonialist rhetorics that have been unpacked by numerous postcolonial scholars were present not only in justifications for US war participation but also in its production of war today. Slotkin's reference to the US as the "gunfighter nation" is rooted in the ways that the language, metaphors, and myths justifying violence against the other are part of the US's founding myth. This myth did not end or become relegated to a historical past. Rather, it continues today. The logic of such myths needs violence to regenerate its strength, its understanding of itself as a morally bound nation. In Slotkin's carefully traced history, the construction of regeneration through violence in this sense is always explained as defensive and a reaction against the other. The US becomes the hapless victim who cannot but help lash back in face of primitive savagery of the other. Wars including the Spanish–American War, wars against the indigenous, the two World Wars, and the wars in Korea, Vietnam, Iraq, and Afghanistan are and have been interpreted mostly as a defensive violence.[31] In other words, as Slotkin summarizes, the US's addiction to militarized violence is difficult to halt because its existence feeds off more and more violence. It has no other life than to create and make violence to justify itself.[32] The legacy of indiscriminate attacks on civilians harkens back to the massacred indigenous peoples and this is now a US tradition such that, as critical social and political theorist Carl Boggs argues,

> [s]aturation bombings, the dropping of nuclear weapons, sustained attacks on urban centers, destruction of life-support systems, introduction of chemical warfare, widespread use of napalm, white phosphorous, depleted uranium, anti-personnel bombs—all amounts to a criminal legacy no other group or nation has even remotely duplicated.[33]

While the US had paved its way to world's super military power by winning the war against Spain and annexing the Philippines, Guam, and Puerto Rico as well as the Hawaiian Islands in 1898, it is widely understood and accepted that the US military–industrial complex emerged after World War II. Actually, that "military–industrial complex" was only famously named as such by US President Dwight D. Eisenhower in his 1960 farewell address. Although the US has expanded its military empire for the past 60 years through the Cold War and the recent GWOT, it is commonly understood that the US, unlike colonial empires of the past centuries, "has developed and maintained a wide range of flexible relationships with host countries in the form of defense treaties and security arrangements."[34] However, as sociologist Seungsook Moon points out, the US instituted its rights to base as "an occupying force in South Korea, Germany, and Japan (mostly Okinawa), the three hubs of its global military deployment during the entire span of the postwar era."[35] In other words, US military bases that have been built in over 150 countries do "territorialize U.S. empire."[36] Furthermore, as Moon argues, if viewed from the standpoints of people who are living in the areas that host US military bases, "the U.S. empire has never been deterritorialized."[37] Many Americans are either unaware of the sheer magnitude of US militarism abroad or sincerely believe that the US military presence abroad is always-already justified. Catherine Lutz observes that ordinary US citizens' perception of US militarism might be rooted in the beliefs (1) that the presence of US military bases is of material value to the peoples who live in proximity to the military vicinity, (2) that the presence of US military bases is at the invitation of the hosting local governance, (3) that the presence of US military bases is on a benevolent mission as the most civilized form of militarism, and (4) that the always-already militarized notions of "threat," "enemy," and "security"[38] warrant militarized response resonate with "peace and security" motif long found in US logic of domination. Even when a closure of a military base seems to point toward a decrease in militarism, we would do well to remember that, most often, one base closure often means increased militarism elsewhere. For example, in 1992, bases were closed in the Philippines. However, the troops from that site were transferred instead to Okinawa and South Korea. Years after this, when the US presence was decreased in Okinawa, there was a significant increase in Guam. All this is to say that a decrease in US military presence in one place does not mean an overall reduction worldwide, but it does point to the mobility of US military and the ease with which it travels through various local sites.

The Cold War ideology was rooted in the logic of colonialism, with its notions of civilizing mission of the West for the rest of the world. Christianity aided and abetted in this so-called civilizing mission of US imperialism in ways that it found equivalence in democracy, the West, and civilization, while communism was construed as the East, barbaric, other, totalitarian, undemocratic, and in opposition to Christian values. The Cold War, which was "marketed as a Christian enterprise,"[39] *officially* ended with the collapse of the Soviet Union in 1991. However, the effects of the Cold War in Asia still remain. As some scholars have pointed out, contrary to what the dominant script tells about the end of the Cold War, there are "the diverse and locally specific ways in which the cold war is coming to an end." In other words, the Cold War is not a "single and globally identical phenomenon."[40] The continuing presence of US military bases in South Korea and Okinawa is one of the "undeniable markers of the continuation and extension of the cold war."[41] And the Korean Peninsula still remains as the region that was divided by the Cold War politics, with North Korea standing as the only remaining communist country in hostile relations with the US after the US has restored its relations with Cuba and removed it from the list of state sponsors of terrorism. Furthermore, there has been a noticeable acceleration of military buildup in Asia since the emergence of US War on Terror. Then, what would US engagement in Asia over the next 60 years look like when what Chen calls the "de-cold-war process" has hardly been completed yet in Asia?[42]

Chen maintains that to "urge that the de-cold-war process be a priority on the intellectual agenda is to insist on the continuity of the process with the work of decolonization."[43] And the work of decolonization in the former colonies should also proceed together with the work of deimperialization in the imperial center, without which the former cannot be completed. Yet, the work of decolonization, deimperialization, and de-cold-war in Asia will be further complicated with the resurgence today of Japan as a dominant military force in alliance with the US in Asia and the rise of China and India as major military and economic powers. The ongoing strain in East Asia over Japan's colonial legacy, the rising tension between Japan and China over a disputed territory, North Korea's suspected possession of nuclear weapons, the unfathomable level of violence in West Asia (aka Middle East)—all of these have created waves of refugees. The continuing armed conflicts in various regions in Asia will further help the US to justify and consolidate its powerful military presence in Asia, ironically in the name of peace and security. At the same time, resistance against US militarism will also persist in various regions in Asia through multiple anti-war movements and peace-building efforts, however small in scope and number. It is plausible that global geopolitical outlook for the next 60 years may unfold in ways that cannot be foreseen. Nonetheless, as shown in the above statement by previous US Secretary of State Hillary Clinton, it is doubtful that the US will voluntarily relinquish its military superpower status in Asia as well as in other parts of the world. There is no evidence that US militarist imperialism will decrease. Rather, ample evidence points to the increase and intensification of US militarism around the world. President Barack Obama's willingness to increase US military improvements on nuclear weapons with more precision than ever before will cost over $1 trillion dollars over the next three decades.[44] Indeed, Obama's Trans-Pacific Partnership (TPP) trade agreement linking Latin American and Asia to US economic and geopolitical interests entails a strong militarizing component to strengthen what has been termed the Obama administration's "Asia Pivot."

The history of US militarization today as continuation of the Cold War could be pursued in numerous theaters of operations.[45] Here, though, this volume asks, if the Cold War is, as Tobi Siebers describes, "in part a history of false endings"[46] and how does critical Christian theology engage the de-cold-war process, decolonization, and deimperialization? The contributors to this book seek to address these questions at this historical juncture.

Why Critical Christian Theology?

We begin by noting a significant lacuna in theological studies. In assessing the steady increase of academic attention and literature on the relationship between Christianity and empire from theological, historical, biblical, ethical, and interdisciplinary approaches, one can notice that there is no substantive discussion of the US as a military empire from the perspectives of scholars of Asian descent. In response, we here name and call for a "critical

Christian theology" that considers the tasks of Christian theology in relation to critical studies of US imperialist militarism in Asia. According to the Pew Research Center (July 19, 2012), the highest religious affiliation among Asian North Americans was with Christianity, some 42 percent. While the research indicates a diversity of religious beliefs and affiliations among Asian North Americans, with the greatest number affiliating with Christianity, a key question must not be avoided: How are their religious affiliations, and also accompanying religious beliefs, shaped to a large extent by the US military presence in Asia? Prior to coming to the US, many of the Asian immigrant communities experienced intense conflict with the US, or still continue to do so, because of a US military presence. As we have indicated earlier, much of US militarist expansionism has been rationalized through specifically Christian language that further buttresses notions like the white man's burden, manifest destiny, and the civilizing mission by the West.

While there are groundbreaking texts addressing some of these issues emerging out of Asian American Studies, a critical interrogation of these issues in Christian theology is still not available. Thus, this volume seeks to address the current paucity of work in this area. When we say "Christian theology," we seek to theorize a broad range of work falling under this general name, be it theological, ethical, historical, or biblical, which demonstrates critical theoretical commitments such as feminist, postcolonial, critical race, Asian American, and cultural studies. The critical Christian theology recognizes the role of Christianity in empire building.[47] This volume is grounded in the idea that Christianity, through its theological, ethical, historical, biblical, and liturgical engagement, is necessarily linked to the US military presence in Asia—East and West Asia, North and South/Southeast Asia. One of the goals, then, is to begin a conversation around the ways that Christianity's many complex relations with empire have left distinct marks on the lives of both Asians and Asian North Americans. Furthermore, critical Christian theology of US imperialist militarism is invaluable for those who seek different ways of engaging Christianity within the academy and the church in the midst of ongoing militarism, militarized violence, and militarization, locally and globally. Christian theology is rooted in the emergence of the Jesus movement. As many scholars now agree, it is inconceivable to understand the Jesus movement apart from its historical context of Roman imperialism. The context of the Roman imperialism in Palestine and Judea involved not only political, religious, social, and economic forces, but also militarist ones. It is within militarized violence that the formation of the Jesus movement and the emergence of Christianity took place. As a movement that was, at its heart, a response to the legacy of militarized violence, it is critical that Christian theology offer an account of its relationship to militarized violence today. The word "critical" is related to Christian in that "critical" is etymologically related to the words crisis and cruces, which also relate to the cross. Etymological relationships are significant in this regard. A critical Christian theology, we hope, is one that offers a crucial critique at a critical point of crisis. We believe that militarized violence proffered by the US all over the world is a condition of crucial crisis that needs theological reflections to end violence.

We believe that militarized violence will not lessen but rather intensify and further escalate given various invested ways that militarism is connected to economic flows globally. We are also mindful that with the escalation and intensification of militarized violence, it is conceivable that religious rhetoric will continue to justify and sanction state violence. It is then critical that religious scholars continue to interrogate the ways that religious ideas fuel militarized violence as well as explore how it may be that religious ideas might also intervene and contest militarized violence from anywhere.

Scope of the Volume

Drawing on cultural studies scholar Chen's threefold notion of decolonization, deimperialization, and de-cold-war, this volume provides analyses of the interrelated issues—what we might call three "thematics"—concerning the relationship between Christianity and US militarism in Asia: (1) militarized subject formation, which focuses on effects of US imperialist militarism on the formation of Asian and Asian North American collective subjectivity and inter/intra-subjectivity; (2) Christian ideological reinforcements, which analyze ways in which Christianity (broadly defined) in its own complexity has been complicit in maintaining and reinforcing US military agendas in both national and international contexts; and (3) Christian practices of resistance, identifying various sites where Christianity has been a force of resistance against US militarism.

This volume assembles essays from a diverse range of scholars in the field of Christian theology (broadly defined), all of whom can be said to be working from Asian/Asian North American perspectives. The volume highlights important contributions made by scholars covering a wide range of topics: from memory, trauma, and conditional citizenship to transnational conservative Christian human rights advocacy for North Koreans, and from Guam as a site of mourning and the US military mission in the Philippines to feminist analysis of transnationalized US militarism. A caveat in this volume is that "Asia" in this volume does not encompass the entire workings of US militarism in Asia. We hope that future discussion on US militarism in Asia will be able to incorporate and further expand to bring in critical theological work that discuss the effects of US militarism on various regions in Asia that are not discussed in this volume, on various racial formations, including Asian North American Muslims, in relation to anti-Muslim racism and Christian hegemony as well as the lasting consequences of current US war on terror in Asia. The volume has been organized to reflect the three thematics that we identified above. The chapters begin with rethinking Asian and Asian North Americans' multiple and fluid identities and discuss effects of US imperialist militarism on the formation of collective subjectivity and inter/intra-subjectivity of Asian and Asian North Americans, with focus on citizenship, masculinity, the circulation of unmourned loss and grief in the aftermath of war, and transnational adoptees. The second thematic portion of each chapter addresses ways in which Christianity in its complexity still colludes, at times, with maintaining and reinforcing US military agendas in both national and international contexts, with particular attention to Korea, Vietnam, and the Philippines. Finally, the third thematic addresses the various sites where Christianity has been a critical force of resistance against militarized violence, with specific focus on Guam and Jeju Island.

As noted earlier, imperialism cannot be eliminated without eliminating our own imperial desires. Imperial and colonial violence are coterminous and create histories of violence as well as resistance to it. When examining militarized violence in Asia, we explore the ruins left by US militarism. However, we are also mindful that such ruins often do the work of recreating other ruins. One such complex legacy can be that of South Korea. According to Chen, previously devastated places like South Korea now serve the role of being a "subimperial" nation. As a subimperial nation, South Korea mimics the transnational neoliberalism of the US as well as its military imperial desires. How, then, is decolonialization even possible under histories of relationship with the US that have been inevitably designed to foster imperial desires in subordinated peoples and nations? Perhaps decolonization and deimperialization become possible when we are able to examine the intricate ways that conditions of possibility in one context are often premised upon different conditions for another group of people. For example, the US nuclear bombings of Hiroshima and

Nagasaki must be addressed as war crimes along with Japanese colonization of places like Korea even as Koreans must address their role in assisting the US war in Vietnam and the atrocities they have committed against the Vietnamese people during the Vietnam War. All of these, of course, must also be examined in relation to other histories such as the genocide of Native Americans, along with the Middle Passage and chattel slavery of African Americans. Furthermore, what is the militarized imperial desire embedded in the TPP trade agreement and the so-called "Asia Pivot" of the Obama administration? What if US Christians in particular begin to make these connections of imperial militarized desire with violence against African Americans, Native Americans, along with Palestinians under Israeli occupation as well as anti-immigrant violence? What if Christians begin to make the connections between Roman imperial desires during times of its emergence in confrontation with the beliefs held by the Jesus movement? If the Jesus movement began with confrontation and contestation in the ruins of Roman imperialism, where is such contestation and confrontation against imperial desires today? How might Christianity today contest the romance of imperial desires as well as imperial memory?[48] How might Christian memory that is counter-imperial shape the future of Christianity in its relation to imperial desires especially rooted in militarism?

We offer this introductory volume with hopes that it will generate further conversations around the legacy of US militarism and Christianity in Asia and elsewhere. This collection is far from definitive. We offer our appreciation to the contributors of this volume for their chapters and for their critical scholarship. The scarcity of Christian theological scholars working directly on issues of militarism in Asia, in addition to conflicting schedules, however, meant that we were not able to procure contributors who could offer in-depth analysis and theological reflection on places like Okinawa, which has been and continues to be a critical site for US militarism and resistance for demilitarization.[49] Deimperialism, decolonization, and de-cold-war are possible when the force of resistance against the proliferation of militarized terror and its attending structures of support results in a significant dismantling of US militarist formations. Such forces of resistance must be built through collaboration and coalition among the peoples of the world, who know so well the legacy of militarized violence springing from imperial desires for exploitation and domination. The ends of militarized violence and terror are nowhere in sight and produce despair and hopelessness. Yet for Christians whose tradition emerged as a resistance to imperial structures of domination with hopes for a better future, we anticipate this volume as only one of many starting points for critical theological reflection on US militarism and Christianity.

Notes

1. Brian Massumi, *Ontopower: War, Powers, and the States of Perception* (Durham: Duke University Press, 2015), 7.
2. Catherine Lutz, ed., *The Bases of Empire: The Global Struggle Against U.S. Military Posts* (New York: New York University Press, 2009), 1.
3. Zillah Eisenstein, "Resexing Militarism for the Globe," in Robin L. Riley and Chandra Talpade Mohanty and Minnie Bruce Pratt, ed., *Feminism and War: Confronting U.S. Imperialism* (New York: Zed Books, 2008), 29.
4. Rita Nakashima Brock and Susan Thistlethwaite, *Casting Stones: Prostitution and Liberation in Asia and the United States* (Minneapolis, MN: Augsburg Fortress, 1996), 5. See also, Sealing Cheng, *On the Move for Love: Migrant Entertainers and the U.S. Military in South Korea* (Philadelphia: University of Pennsylvania Press, 2010).
5. Kent Calder, *Embattled Garrisons: Comparative Base Politics and American Globalism* (Princeton, NJ: Princeton University Press, 2007), 51. Quoted in Maria Höhn and Seungsook Moon, "Empire at the Crossroads?" in *Over There*, 401.
6. Maria Höhn and Seungsook Moon, "The Politics of Gender, Sexuality, Race, and Class in the U.S. Military Empire" in *Over There*, 14–15. Höhn and Moon argue that SOFAS "are primarily concerned with guarding the 'rights and privileges' of American soldiers stationed abroad (Mason 2008, 1–2)." (Höhn and Moon, 15). See also, Ji-Yeon Yuh, *Beyond the Shadow of Camptown: Korean Military Brides in America* (New York: New York University Press, 2002) as well as, Katharine H.S. Moon, *Sex Among Allies: Military Prostitution in U.S.-Korea Relations* (New York: Columbia University Press, 1997). Also, Sandra Pollock Sturdevant and Brenda Stoltzfus, *Let the Good Times Roll: Prostitution and the U.S. Military in Asia* (New York: The New Press, 1992).
7. Setsu Shigematsu and Keith L. Camacho eds., *Militarized Currents: Toward A Decolonial Future in Asia and the Pacific* (Minneapolis University of Minnesota Press, 2010), xxvi.
8. Cf., Cynthia Enloe, *Bananas, Beaches and Bases: Making Feminist Sense of International Politics* (Los Angeles, CA: University of California Press, 1990). See also Ji-Yeon Yuh, *Beyond The Shadow of Camptowns: Korean Military Brides in America* (New York: New York University Press, 2002). Also, Cheng, *On the Move for Love*. Also, Vernadette Vicuña Gonzalez, *Securing Paradise:*

Tourism and Militarism in Hawai`i and the Philippines (Durham: Duke University Press, 2013).

9. Nadia Y. Kim, *Imperial Citizens: Koreans and Race from Seoul to LA* (Stanford: Stanford University Press, 2008), 8.
10. Lisa Lowe, *Immigrant Acts: On Asian American Cultural Politics* (Durham: Duke University Press, 1996), 33.
11. See also, Sylvia Shin Huey Chong, *The Oriental Obscene: Violence and Racial Fantasies in the Vietnam Era* (Durham: Duke University Press, 2012).
12. Kyeyoung Park, *The Korean American Dream: Immigrants and Small Business in New York City* (Ithaca: Cornell University Press, 1997), Quoted in Nadia Y. Kim, *Imperial Citizens*, 41.
13. Kim, *Imperial Citizens*, 41.
14. Ibid.
15. Mimi Thi Nguyen, *The Gift of Freedom: War, Debt, and Other Refugee Passages* (Durham: Duke University Press, 2012), 140.
16. Ibid., 154.
17. Yen Le Espiritu, "Thirty Years Afterward: The Endings That Are Not Over." *Amerasia Journal* 31, no. 2 (2005), xv.
18. Ibid.
19. Yen Le Espiritu, *Body Counts: The Vietnam War and Militarized Refuge(es)* (Los Angeles: University of California Press, 2014), 175.
20. Cf., Arissa H. Oh, *To Save the Children of Korea: The Cold War Origins of International Adoption* (Stanford: Stanford University Press, 2015). Also Eleana J. Kim, *Adopted Territory: Transnational Adoptees and the Politics of Belonging* (Durham: Duke University Press, 2010) and Kim Park Nelson, *Invisible Asians: Korean American Adoptees, Asian American Experiences, and Racial Exceptionalism* (New Brunswick: Rutgers University Press, 2016).
21. William V. Spanos, *American Exceptionalism in the Age of Globalization: The Specter of Vietnam* (New York: State University of New York Press, 2008), 199.
22. Ibid., 198.
23. Paola Bacchetta, Tina Campt, Inderpal Grewal, Caren Kaplan, Minoo Moallem, and Jennifer Terry, "Transnational Feminist Practices against War." (October 2001). www.geocities.com/carenkapalan03/transnational-statement.html. Quoted in Gargi Bhattacharyya, *Dangerous Brown Men: Exploiting Sex, Violence and Feminism in the War on Terror* (New York: Zed Books, 2008), 9.
24. Ibid.
25. Kuan-Hsing Chen, *Asia as Method: Toward Deimperialization* (Durham: Duke University Press, 2010), 20.
26. Ibid., 198.

27. Hillary Clinton, "America's Pacific Century," *Foreign Policy* (November 2011). Available at March 16, 2012 http://www.foreignpolicy.com/articles/2011/10/11/americas_pacific_century.
28. Amy Kaplan, *The Anarchy of Empire in the Making of U.S. Culture* (Cambridge: Harvard University Press, 2002), 16.
29. Maria Höhn and Seungsook Moon, "The Politics of Gender, Sexuality, Race, and Class in the U.S. Military Empire" in *Over There: Living with the U.S. Military Empire from World War Two to the Present*, ed., Maria Höhn and Seungsook Moon (Durham: Duke University Press, 2010), 5.
30. Cf., Roxanne Dunbar-Ortiz, *An Indigenous Peoples' History of the United States* (Boston: Beacon Press, 2014).
31. Cf., John Tirman, *The Death of Others: The Fate of Civilians in America's Wars* (Oxford: Oxford University Press, 2011), 350–353.
32. Cf., Richard Slotkin, *Gunfighter Nation: The Myth of The Frontier in Twentieth-Century America* and also, *Regeneration through Violence: The Mythology of the American Frontier 1600–1860.*
33. Carl Boggs, *The Crimes of Empire: Rogue Superpower and World Domination* (New York: Pluto Press, 2010), 86.
34. Seungsook Moon, "In the U.S. Army But Not Quite of It: Contesting the Imperial Power in a Discourse of KATUSAs" in *Over There*, 233.
35. Moon, "In the U.S. Army But Not Quite of It," 233.
36. Ibid.
37. Ibid.
38. Catherine Lutz, ed. *The Bases of Empire: The Global Struggle against U.S. Military Posts* (New York: New York University Press, 2009), xi–xii.
39. Mark Edwards, (2009). "'God Has Chosen Us': Re-Membering Christian Realism, Rescuing Christendom, and the Contest of Responsibilities during the Cold War." *Diplomatic History* 33, no. 1 (2009: 67–94), 85.
40. Heonik Kwon, *The Other Cold War* (New York: Columbia University Press, 2010), 25–26.
41. Chen, *Asia as Method*, 119.
42. Ibid., 120.
43. Ibid., 123.
44. "In Hiroshima Obama Calls for World Without Nukes, Contradicting New $1 Trillion Weapon Upgrade Plan." *Democracy Now* (May 27, 2016). Accessed May 28, 2016 http://www.democracynow.org/2016/5/27/in_hiroshima_obama_calls_for_world. Cf. Lisa Yoneyama, *Hiroshima Traces: Time, Space, and the Dialectics of Memory* (CA: University of California Press, 1999).
45. Joseph Masco, *The Theater of Operations: National Security Affect from the Cold War to the War on Terror* (Durham: Duke University Press, 2014).

46. Tobi Siebers, *Cold War Criticism and the Politics of Skepticism* (New York: Oxford University Press, 1993), 29.
47. Joerg Rieger mentions the importance of studying the role of religion and theology in empire building, especially the role of Christianity. See Joerg Rieger, "Liberating God-Talk: Postcolonialism and the Challenge of the Margins" in *Postcolonial Theologies: Divinity and Empire*, ed., Catherine Keller, Michael Nausner, and Mayra Rivera (St. Louis: Chalice Press, 2004).
48. On the notion of imperial memory, a brief discussion is found in Jodi Kim's *The Ends of Empire: Asian American Critique and the Cold War* (Minneapolis: University of Minnesota Press, 2010).
49. Cf. Kozue Akibayashi and Suzuyo Takazato, "Okinawa: Women's Struggle for Demilitarization" in Catherine Lutz, ed., *The Bases for Empire: The Global Struggle Against U.S. Military Posts* (New York: New York University Press, 2009), 243–269.

Spelman College
Atlanta, GA, USA
Nami Kim

Garrett-Evangelical Theological Seminary
Evanston, IL, USA
Wonhee Anne Joh

Contents

Author Biographies

Amy R. Barbour is a doctoral student in systematic and constructive theologies at Garrett-Evangelical Theological Seminary. Among her other studies, she received her MDiv (Master of Divinity) from Union Theological Seminary in the City of New York and completed graduate studies at Bossey, the Ecumenical Institute of the World Council of Churches. She is a Woman of Color Scholar (The United Methodist Church), consults the US military special operations chaplaincy community as a subject matter expert in moral injury and suicide, and works for the Henry M. Jackson Foundation for the Advancement of Militarized Medicine.

Michael Sepidoza Campos is the founding member of Emerging Queer Asian-Pacific Islander Religion Scholars and researches at the intersection of Filipino-American diaspora, postcolonial theory, queer theory, and critical pedagogy. His writings on queer life and religion include "Embracing the Stranger: Reflections on the Ambivalent Hospitality of LGBTIQ Catholics" in *More Than A Monologue: Sexual Diversity and the Catholic Church—Inquiry, Thought, and Expression* (Fordham University Press, 2014); "The Baklâ: Gendered Religious Performance in Filipino Cultural Spaces" in *Queer Religion: LGBT Movements and Queering Religion* (Praeger, 2012); and "In God's House: Of Silences and Belonging," in *Theology and Sexuality*, vol. 17.3 (Equinox, 2011). Campos co-edited *Queering Migrations Towards, From, and Beyond Asia* (Palgrave Macmillan, 2014) with Hugo Córdova Quero and Joseph N. Goh. He served as steering committee co-chair for the Asian North American Religion, Culture, and Society Group at the American Academy of Religion.

Wonhee Anne Joh is Associate Professor of Theology at Garrett Evangelical Theological Seminary and affiliate faculty in Asian American Studies and Department of Religious Studies at Northwestern University. Joh's areas of research interests are at the intersection of critical theories on race, gender, trauma, affect, postcolonialism, and militarism in relation to transpacific Asian America. She is the author of *Heart of the Cross: A Postcolonial Christology* (Westminster John Knox Press, 2006) as well as of chapters in edited volumes. Forthcoming is *Terror, Trauma and Loss: A Postcolonial Theology of Hope*.

Mimi Khúc is a Vietnamese American scholar, teacher, and writer on race and religion, queer of color politics, mental health, and Asian American motherhood. She is a lecturer in Asian American Studies and Religious Studies at the University of Maryland College Park, and the guest editor of a special issue of the *Asian American Literary Review* on Asian American mental health.

Nami Kim is Associate Professor of Religious Studies at Spelman College. She is the author of The Gendered… (Palgrave Macmillan, 2016). Kim serves on the editorial board of the *Journal of Feminist Studies in Religion* and the *Journal of Race, Ethnicity, and Religion*.

Tat-siong Benny Liew is currently Class of 1956 Professor in New Testament Studies at the College of the Holy Cross (Worcester, MA). He is the author of *Politics of Parousia* (Brill, 1999) and *What Is Asian American Biblical Hermeneutics?* (University of Hawaii Press, 2008). In addition, he is the editor of the *Semeia* volume on "The Bible in Asian America" (with Gale Yee, Society of Biblical Literature [SBL], 2002), *Postcolonial Interventions* (Sheffield Phoenix, 2009), *They Were All Together in One Place?* (with Randall Bailey and Fernando Segovia, SBL, 2009), and *Reading Ideologies* (Sheffield Phoenix, 2011). Liew is currently also the Executive Editor of the journal, *Biblical Interpretation* (Brill) and Series Editor of the *Sheffield Phoenix Guide to the New Testament*.

Keun-Joo Christine Pae is an Episcopal Priest and Associate Professor of Religion/Ethics at the Religion Department and Women's and Gender Studies at Denison University. Her teaching and research interests include ethics of peace and war, transnational feminist ethics, interfaith peace activism, and Asian/Asian American feminist theology and ethics. She has published various articles and book chapters, and is currently working on the manuscript titled *Sex and War: U.S. Military Prostitution and a Feminist Ethic of Peace*. In 2010–2012, she was a co-convener of Asian American Ethics Working Group at the Society of Christian Ethics. She is currently serving on the steering committees of the Pacific, Asian and Asian North American Women in Theology and Ministry Association of Asian North American Educators, and the Women and Religion Session of the American Academy of Religion.

Jeremy Posadas is Assistant Professor of Religious Studies and a core faculty member in Gender Studies at Austin College (on the Texas–Oklahoma border). He teaches and researches in the area of religion and society, and is currently focused on the theological interpretation of work in conversation with the field of new working-class studies.

Jonathan Tran is Associate Professor of Religion at Baylor University, where he also serves as Faculty Master of the Honors Residential College. He is author of *The Vietnam War and Theologies of Memory* (Wiley, 2010) and *Foucault and Theology* (T&T Clark, 2011).

CHAPTER 1

Postcolonial Loss: Collective Grief in the Ruins of Militarized Terror

Wonhee Anne Joh

> Open grieving is bound up with outrage, and outrage in the face of injustice or indeed of unbearable loss has enormous political potential...Whether we are speaking about open grief or outrage, we are talking about affective responses that are highly regulated by regimes of power and sometimes subject to explicit censorship.
>
> —Judith Butler, *Frames of War: When Is Life Grievable?*[1]

> Theological inquiry...bespeaks a deep affective attitude toward a historical process on the part of the human being.
>
> —Walter Benjamin, *The Arcades Project*

The military empire of the US can be called the "dynamic engine of American history."[2] The Korean War is an important part of this engine of history. To deny this would be to foreclose and also deny that American military empire is a global and transnational reality across geopolitical space and time. Recognizing the breadth of this spectrum opens spaces for transnational work to address connective sites of transnational histories,

W.A. Joh (✉)
Garrett-Evangelical Theological Seminary, Evanston, IL, USA

N. Kim, W.A. Joh (eds.), *Critical Theology against US Militarism in Asia*,
DOI 10.1057/978-1-137-48013-2_1

which are generated as a result of US imperial militarism across such sites as Laos, Cambodia, Vietnam, the Philippines, Guam, Hawai'i, Okinawa, and numerous others in Asia, West Asia, and the Pacific.[3]

This chapter's critical Christian theology engages US militarism by first turning to the context of the Korean War and its ongoing traumatic aftermath. This requires acknowledgment of loss in the postcolonial plight of contemporary Koreans and Korean Americans.[4] Thus, in subsequent sections, I explore that plight and loss with the aid of trauma theory before bridging into key related notions of affect theory (grief, grievability, mourning). This is no mere trafficking in negativity and despair. It is, as Butler writes in the above quote, "to tap the enormous political potential" unlocked by what she also calls "open grieving bound up with outrage, and outrage in the face of injustice."[5] I will also show how a critical Christian theology engaging US militarism can unlock this "enormous political potential" by theorizing the spectral power of the cross in distinctive ways. In this sense, this chapter is an exercise in critical Christian theology, and thus is like the "theological inquiry" that Benjamin describes above, one bespeaking "a deep affective attitude toward a historical process." The chapter, then, follows an arc of interpretation of the Korean War and its aftermath, to postcolonial perspectives on collective trauma and affective registers like grief, rage, and mourning, and then to the ways a spectral theory of the cross catalyzes resistance to the ways of the US imperial state today.

The Korean War and Aftermath

I begin my commentary on the Korean War with a quote from *Ends of Empire* by Jodi Kim, "What does it mean to want to represent or 'remember' a war that has been 'forgotten' and erased in the U.S. popular imaginary, but that has been also trans-generationally seared into the memories of Koreans and Korean Americans, and experienced anew everyday in a still divided Korea?"[6] For Kim, the Korean War signals not only the traumas and arbitrary and violent separations of self, family, and state in addition to other forms of loss, but also displays that the Korean War is a problem of "Cold War knowledge that saturates both American nationalist discourse and Korean America's public or 'admitted' knowledge about the conditions of possibility for its very formation in the post-1945 conjuncture."[7] The significance of Kim's analysis of the Korean War is that it surfaces counter-narratives, indeed an entire "unsettling hermeneutic of Korean

War" that not only shows a naïve retrieval of glorious war memories, but also inscribes an epistemological project that seeks to foreclose knowledge about how Cold War discourse continues imperial projects of the US. Kim's analysis questions all this, and in so doing reveals a counter-imperial narrative that is radically different from the usual Cold War discourse that privileges imperial power.[8]

Because in the US the Korean War is often "the forgotten war," let us consider some of its basic features. It is estimated that the Korean War resulted in 4 million casualties, of which 2 million were civilians. The numbers are staggering, and they represent a higher percentage of population lost by Koreans than what the US lost in World War II. Historian Bruce Cummings notes that a total of 36,940 Americans lost their lives in the Korean War. Some 92,134 Americans were wounded in action, and even now, more than 8176 are still reported missing. South Korea sustained 1 million deaths, 312,836 casualties, including nearly a half-million dead. These are in addition to deaths suffered by other US allies. Estimated North Korean casualties were approximately 2 million, including 1 million civilians and half-million soldiers. Another 900,000 Chinese soldiers lost their lives in combat.[9] After three years, in 1953, a cease-fire agreement was signed and brought forth the "demilitarized zone" (DMZ) that separates the Koreas as North and South. Of course, these numbers do not really point to a more holistic picture of who/what was lost as a result of this war. These figures are premised on discrete identifiable figures but do not account for other unseen, unaccounted, and obscured "side-shows." As Viet Thanh Nguyen notes, there are "human losses, financial costs, and capital gains," and points to ways that a war neither knows nor respects borders and boundaries.[10] No peace treaty has yet been signed and Korea is technically still in a state of war.[11] It has been over 60 years now and still no end in sight. In the ruins of devastation, unprecedented economic reconstruction, militarized alliances, and compromises have followed. Further, if it is indeed the case that Korea has become what Kuan–Tsing Chen refers to as now a "sub-imperial" nation in Asia ("sub-" vis-à-vis the imperial power of the US), it is crucial that we explore questions of critical memory and works of mourning and the practices of hope that also often have been foreclosed for South Korea, which is given this "sub-imperial" role.

In 2001 I visited Korea and went to the DMZ after 25 years in the US. Little did I realize then that my visit to the DMZ also was an event of witnessing the traumas of the Korean War. As Suk-Young Kim notes,

"...the zone between two Koreas stands as a monument to stalemate; an anachronism that memorializes not only the prolonged separation of a once-unified nation but also a longing for the lost other half...For both South and North Koreans, one of the reasons the DMZ figures so prominently as national trauma is that so few are able to cross it."[12] In this, the DMZ figures in the lingering war traumas. While distanced by time and space from the Korean War, it became clear in my visceral response that the Korean War and its subsequent aftermath continue to haunt even those whose formation is in the diaspora.[13] Edwidge Danticat's observation accurately describes my own experiences in the US and in Korea:

> There are many ways that our mind protects us from present and past horrors. One way is by allowing us to forget. Forgetting is a constant fear in any writer's life. For the immigrant writer, from home, memory becomes an even deeper abyss. It is as if we had been forced to step under the notorious forgetting trees, the *sabliyes,* that our slave ancestors were told would remove their past from their heads and dull their desire to return home. We know we must pass under the tree, but we hold our breath and cross our fingers and toes and hope that the forgetting will not penetrate too deeply into our brains.[14]

To return to Korea and find myself at the DMZ was to witness the persistent wounds of "scorched earth" policy that had been deployed against the land and its peoples doing the Korean War. The visit enabled my better understanding of the flight by many South Koreans to the US, which some people dismiss as simply a matter of pursuing "the American Dream" and fleeing to the "Promised Land."[15] Not only did the policies during the war indiscriminately scorch the land and left it in "smoldering ruin" by several players[16] and the peoples but they also left searing marks indicating the legacy of war's afterlife.[17] Affective life shaped by destructions of war haunts even the generations distanced through space and time from that historical event. I will say more about this later. The aftermath of my experience at the DMZ and its haunting affective remainder continue to allow me to link both the intimate and the familial with political and historical vectors, and to restore connections suspended by time, place, and politics. I understand this familiar memory that circulates in many Korean and Korean American people as "wounded identification," of which Palestinian American scholar Lila Abu-Lughod speaks. This form of "wounded identification" allows me to enter provisionally into not only the world/s of those who directly experienced the Korean War but also the worlds of its aftermath and also the world that I now inhabit.[18] Perhaps it is *because* of my positioning within the diaspora,[19] distanced by time and space from Korea and the Korean War yet living in the heart of the US empire, that it is possible to begin to articulate the complex interaction "between the affects of belonging and the politics of entitlement in a diasporic world, rethinking and retheorizing the complex interactions between loss and reclamation, mourning and repair, departure and return."[20] It is critical for each of us interested in questions of belonging, of roots and routes, to examine the affective aftermath and the continuing effects of the Korean War as well as the continuous and inextricably intimate relation between Korea, the US, and Korean America. Only then will we be able to create space for the persistent power of nostalgia and the magnetism of the idea of belonging, and even the obsession with roots in relation, always in relation, to our geopolitical historical convergences. Rather, this dual recognition—the war is simultaneously significant but also not exceptional—forges a way toward an ethical commitment that takes seriously the differential effects of war and dispossession, of migration and the new hegemonies and power structures that are "formed within diasporic communities and gendered and raced conceptions of the relationships between routes and roots in the self conception of displaced peoples."[21]

So, why does the Korean War still matter today? Why should the Korean War still be significant for the work that remains when it comes to war? Perhaps because the Korean War is what really set in motion the Cold War ideology that morphed into the War on Terror. All the while, the division of Korea and cease-fire still remain. The Korean War, technically, is still the longest war and may provide a critical lens for understanding the dynamic and complex ways that war makes for alliances that are difficult to disentangle. While for many Americans it is known as the Forgotten War, for Koreans, it is known as the Unending War or the Unforgotten War. This war matters because it has not ended and because of the haunting presence as well as the recent Obama administration's "Pacific Pivot" or "rebalance" strategy toward Asia-Pacific region. Beginning in the fall of 2011 the Obama administration has issued a series of steps to expand and intensify the already significant presence of the US and explicitly identified the Asia-Pacific as a geostrategic priority for the US. By 2020, 60 percent of US naval capacity will be based in the Asia-Pacific, where 320,000 US troops are already stationed. The realignment will entail rebuilding and refurbishing former US facilities in the Philippines, placing 2500 marines in Australia, transferring 8000 marines and their families from Okinawa to Guam and Hawai'i, and building new installations like the one on the tiny Pacific island of Saipan. Meanwhile, the US military regularly stages massive joint military exercises involving tens of thousands of troops and nuclear-powered aircraft carriers with its key allies—and China's neighbors—that is, with Japan and South Korea.[22]

Therefore, the Korean War is hardly a discrete event. It is a geographical and historical phenomenon that calls forth a broader perspective, one, I suggest, that is provided by postcolonial studies. Let us therefore look more carefully at how a postcolonial paradigm might shift our understanding of collective trauma amid war and its aftermath.

A Postcolonial Perspective on Collective Trauma

In taking up a postcolonial approach to collective trauma, I want to first foreground a problem. Too often, trauma theory texts too marginalize "the traumatic experiences of non-western cultures, assume the definitions of trauma and recovery that the West has developed are universal and often favor a distinctively modernist form in order to 'bear witness' to trauma."[23] Consider, for example, the treatment of trauma in the studies by one of trauma theory's founders, Cathy Caruth. In her seminal book, Caruth engages trauma studies through discourses of psychoanalysis and deconstruction to argue that extreme events that defy interpretation and understanding can be represented through a textualist approach.[24] As Stef Crap has critiqued, in this approach, "textual 'undecideability' or 'unreadability' come[s] to reflect the inaccessibility of trauma."[25] What this suggests then is that, for many, history and the material conditions that produce collective trauma are elided in favor of the individual who is trapped in the terrors of unspeakable trauma, whose response is loss of articulation. There is a sophisticated theorization of trauma with respect to the individual, but what is missing is a careful examination of the broader political matrix of collective trauma produced by historical and material conditions of colonial and imperial power.

What is not brought forth in many trauma studies is trauma studies tendency to be discursively preoccupied with, indeed to "screen" or displace and repress, historical pasts like nuclear warfare, the genocide of Native Americans, slavery, segregation, and the many wars the US wages around the world. The neglect of these points to an unexamined Eurocentrism in trauma theory, and a Eurocentrism that conflates the West with the world.[26] This means that interpretations of trauma and following diagnosis like post-traumatic stress disorder (PTSD) are often rooted in unexamined universalization of modernist Western paradigms and practices. What is direly necessary are ways to distinguish historical and colonial suffering from other structural forms. Moreover, counter-narratives are needed to make sense of the aftermath of militarized violence and trauma. There is nothing self-evident that justifies any attempts to unproblematically transfer Eurocentric definitions and diagnosis of trauma to non-European contexts.[27] Trauma theories and diagnosis like that of PTSD have been universally applied as if there are no differences across time, space, cultures, and traditions.

Those of us working in Western traditions often feel that when there is a wrong or an injury done to another, then a knowable, calculable, and measureable recompense must take place for the sake of justice. However, what we often have not dealt with is the ambivalent and often heavy weight of nonequivalence. As Judith Butler notes, "…no utilitarian calculus can supply the measure by which to gauge the destitution and loss of such lives."[28] There are affective remainders that continue to haunt us even when we think that we have achieved justice.[29] There often remains a loss of language in experiences of trauma so deep and so long that it generates a grief that is unconsciously passed on to the next generation. How shall we interpret this work of grief? Grief resulting from war operates not only in individuals but also in the collective and public unconscious. Precluding possibilities of working through legacies of war is a way in which narratives of memories are often constructed from the dominant perspective and not from the perspectives of victims so that they are "[h]aunted by memories of pain and suffering, post-conflict communities paradoxically search to 'forget' the horror of war while simultaneously becoming emotionally fixated and constituted by it."[30] Many war victims live in a kind of recursive temporality that defers any sense of temporal belatedness that is often necessary to even engage in any form of trauma articulation.

Because of the limitations of early trauma studies, it is better to inscribe both trauma theory and affect theory within a broader postcolonial studies paradigm. Indebted to earlier anticolonial and decolonial movements taking place in the international arena from early 1950s and 1960s, postcolonial theory examined the complex ways that coloniality and decolonial movements were imbricated in various historical trajectories. In many ways postcolonial theory not only attempts to make sense of the persistent colonial divide but also examines various ways that colonial power gets circulated, generated, recuperated, and so regenerates itself. As a political discourse then, postcolonial theory critiques and problematizes inherent limits and failures of notions that sustain justification for colonial projects such as democracy, justice, freedom, war, civilization, rights, and even salvation. Addressing not only the colonization of lands, material resources, exploitation of peoples, and production of knowledge—to name a few sites of destruction—postcolonial theories of decolonization also name structural and systematized colonization made legible in the interior psychic space of those who come within the reach of the colonizer and his/her world.[31] This aggressive and unavoidably imperial reach also leaves in its wake worlds in ruins. While the colonial world may have ended, we continue to live in a world shaped and often overdetermined by the myriad of legacies left through histories of colonialism and ongoing imperialism. A most noticeable continuation of this legacy is the global presence of the US military empire. In the ruins of imperial militarism, imperial war leaves its devastation not only in the lands of peoples but also in their psyches.

It may be that affects circulate and produce what Raymond Williams describes as "structure of feeling."[32] These affects include, but are not limited to, shame, rage, guilt, and grief. The affective registers of militarized trauma produce grief, terror, and deep loss in postcolonial spaces that often are not mourned or remembered. Or as is often the case, what is remembered is yet another management by the state of selective remembering and forgetting. Affects like unmourned grief are unknowingly transmitted to the following generations. Affects are transmitted intergenerationally despite the overwhelming and often misleading belief that "justice" has been rendered and the assumption that grief has been worked through.[33] In the case of South Korea, the state fabricates if not people's outright denial of the ongoing state of war, then at least a perpetual myth that the two Koreas are only in a perpetual mode of cease-fire. This is perhaps why while a sense of loss circulates, so too does a certain terror and fear that now congeals as the new norm, persisting more than 60 years since "the ceasefire" and living as part of the ordinary everyday life of Korean peoples. It is to live with the terror of potential war at anytime.[34] Viet Than Nguyen's phrase "vertigo of sorrow and longing"[35] expresses powerfully the incredible weight of both sorrow and longing that are borne by so many traumatized people and which they live with and know so intimately. While vertigo is not a diagnosis, it is often common parlance for the loss of equilibrium, where the ground upon which one stands is always tilted, if not spinning out of control—a world turned upside down. There is no anchoring or balancing point, but one must learn to ride the waves of spinning and tossing sensations. With affects like sorrow, grief, shame, and rage, there are no beginning and ending points. They continue to stick and build around one and one's relations. Kelly Oliver notes that "affects move between bodies; colonization and oppression operate through depositing the unwanted affects of the dominant group onto those othered..." Thus, affects, especially negative affects, get "deposited into the bones" of the oppressed, and here I would add those whose oppression is marked by experiences of trauma.[36] These affects are not linear or singular but constantly and persistently build and morph unto other affects. It becomes difficult to know which affect is operative and from whence any of them may originate. Affects not only stick to us and travel from person to person but, as they travel, these affects also build intensity.

When affect is only understood as equivalent to the notion of "feeling," then there can simultaneously occur a reification of a false dichotomy that is so beloved by Western modernity, the binary of feelings/emotions and reason. Often the privileging of the latter is taken for granted. However, against this simplifying reification, it should be recalled that affects are also sites of knowledge re/productions. Feelings like terror, for example, are not discreet nor without rationale. Affects are somatic and thus affect the entire relations of corporeal bodies and are remembered and even transmitted through generations.[37] For example, we are unable to control the way that shame may make us blush or the way that terror makes our bodies clench and tremble. These trembling vibrations travel to touch and cause other bodies to tremble. Affects thus have long-term mental and physical consequences.[38] Grief when limited to dynamics pertaining only to individuals may lose a dialectical or recuperative dimension that enables a community to acknowledge, hold, and build resilience through loss. In contrast, without this dimension, grief is unending.[39] While affect circulates and abounds through diverse scenes of trauma and colonial relationality, here I want to specifically argue that colonization as a sustained source of violent forms of domination and conquest produces what many theorists term collective trauma. While trauma that privileges the individual experience of something "outside the range of the ordinary" breaking into the everyday has been the significant focus of much of trauma studies, my approach in this chapter requires exploring the collective experience of historical trauma, with particular attention to affective registers like grief and the absence of public mourning, especially subsequent to historical and collective trauma. I am here more interested in the social dimension of how affects like grief get transformed into the service of further state-sanctioned violence and in the managing of affects after violence as well as in the ways that affects like grief are denied public consciousness. For example, after the Korean War, affective registers like grief, sorrow, loss, shame, and terror do not get experienced as discrete and singular but rather as messily congealed with other affects like fear and rage. These affects conceal the ways that state violence continues with the public's complicity facilitated by this concealment. State violence, and here I mean both the US and the Korean state violence, thus, is left unexamined even while it saturates the collective cultural production of memory. To be sure, these affects at work in the public are intentionally harnessed by the state to reinvigorate the official narrative of potential threat of war. This in turn is used to justify US and South Korean (?) military build-up and presence in Korea. This is not to exonerate Koreans only as victims of the state, of their own or that of the US. Rather, this points to ways that affective politics manage social and collective feelings like terror and fear. This is especially evident in the US and South Korean continual demonization of North Korea. It is no surprise in context then that collective trauma "depends on collective processes of cultural interpretation."[40] In an era of perpetual unending wars, most especially those waged by the US through its War on Terror, there is much at stake in attending to ways that grief and other affects (terror, fear, etc.) saturate many communities traumatized by militarized violence.[41]

Exemplary of the more complex ways of attending to grief that are evident in postcolonial theory is Abraham and Torok's work on "trans-generational haunting." They suggest that trauma[42] does not die out with the person who first experienced it.[43] The aftermath of a traumatic event continues to whisper and hover through to the next generation—thus, in me, my family, our families, immigrant communities in the US—as it seeks/demands suturing, re-membering. The more we maintain silence, the stronger its whispers grow in the next generations. While Americans think of the Korean War as the "Forgotten War," it is rather an unending war and not forgotten, cannot be forgotten by Koreans and all those who had been involved in Korea because the specter of the Korean War is felt to be a threat that "some would like to believe is past and whose return it would be necessary again, once again in the future, to conjure away..."[44]

In other words, memories have histories. September 1945 marked the beginning of US military occupation of the Korean Peninsula and thus began Korea's entanglement with the US, which intensified and became increasingly ambivalent during the Korean War, and, as Grace Cho notes, "the subordinate relationship to the U.S. that was generated on the Korean peninsula through war and imperialism laid the ground on which Koreans could participate in the American dream."[45] What is often not mentioned is the fact that the Korean War is what set Korean migration into motion. War's devastation means displacement and dispossession. Terror and trauma and its affective remainder refuse foreclosure but continue to seek and demand redress and justice, and do not forget.

Trauma's affective remainder from the Korean War has been transgenerationally seared into our collective psyche. This affective remainder is the unmourned grief that continues to unmoor those who are dispossessed by the traumas of war from each other. Affective registers like grief articulate the damaged sense of future that peoples who know dispossession know well.[46] Approaching this unmourned grief is the crucial problem with which this chapter wrestles toward its conclusion.

Unmourned Postcolonial Grief

What and how do we respond and bear witness to the kind of loss that hunkers down and sits with us? The kind of grief and loss unbearably so heavy that it refuses to lift and dissipate but rather seeps into one's body and leaks into every cell and every minute of one's life? Grief where consciousness floats between reality and illusion, between form and content, incarnated in the body but disincarnating at the same time? The kind of grief that permeates us, to the very edges of everything we see, the bodily movements of everydayness in which feelings are filtered through the weight of a heavy fog of grief. What do we do with grief so heavy with the gravity of its weight pulling and pressing down on one where one cannot do more than lay prostrate under its weight? What and how do we respond theologically to unthinkable imposed suffering that literally takes one's *breath away or takes one into such darkness that one cannot see anything else*? How do we make sense of grief so shattering that language becomes inadequate and all we are left with are aching keens of fragile and unrelenting anguish of both lament and outrage? How are we to understand the melancholic remainder that stays and sticks to our very being?

Militarized violence leaves in its wake pervasive grief that can be transformed into postcolonial "critical melancholia." A critical melancholia that "cannot be seen as good or bad, because affect is not about judgment, even if it is about a form of demand for justice."[47] There is a "critical" maneuver here in that the heavy ache of melancholia, the weight of loss that persists amid and after war, is harnessed as a way to achieve not only survival and persistence in the aftermath of imperial war, but also a kind of resistance. This "critical melancholia" is what is needed to direct our desire for a better world from the aftermath of militarized terror. How might we understand postcolonial grief without claiming it in order to overcome it, pass it, and "get over it" but to work through and stay in it so that such affect might "annul the multitude of losses continually demanded by an unforgiving social world."[48] As Anne Cheng has argued, "…'getting over' something or 'moving on' is itself symptomatic of the culture's [American] attachment to coercive normality."[49] In many cases in Asia where militarized terror has been experienced, it is more often that remembering and working through the experience of terror, loss, and grief have been managed. Memorialization, if it takes place at all, often celebrates state powers' selected narratives of heroism, heroic sacrifices, and benevolence.[50] In the US, such celebrations are usually focused on the supposed benefits of US interventions. In this regard, state memorialization and practices of remembering are often acts of easy forgetting that dismiss or glossed over the injustice done. At the very least, this easy forgetting is a preemptive foreclosure of the mourning that is needed. Such foreclosure is often carried out by a state's continual manufacturing of "legitimate" memories that suppress any and all possible counter-narratives to the legitimacy of state power. In contrast, we might consider Butler's suggestion that there is something about tarrying with grief that actually helps us transform our sense of vulnerability in relation to others and in relation to the production of cycles of violence. Butler asks, "Is there something to be gained from grieving, from tarrying with grief, from remaining exposed to its unbearability and not endeavoring to seek a resolution for grief through violence?"[51] It is this sense of "tarrying" with grief that I want to recuperate in later sections of this chapter through an interpretation of the cross for our neocolonial times. As George Bonanno argues, "When we live with grief we live with dissonance…In the West, where scientific objectivity rules, we tend to recoil at the thought of communing with the dead. Yet, in many regions around the globe, this idea has long been sewn into the very fabric of people's lives."[52] Grief saturates our world today, yet we rush to foreclose the possibility of grieving with too much haste. The state's preemptive foreclosure of mourning unmoors us from one another and leaves unattended the unbearable loss and the pervasive terror that many in the world bear today. It leaves unnamed the losses and injustices that constitute the ruins of the past and makes endurance of our losses and resistance to the state difficult, if not impossible.

Trauma studies in general contend that traumatic experiences are often the type that are uninvited, outside our control, catastrophic, unexpected, sudden, unrecognizable, and impossible to integrate into ordinary systems of meaning and identity. They cannot adequately be put into words and constitute a fundamentally destabilizing event. Thus, bearing witness becomes an often ambivalent and complex process that relies much on intensely fractured or fragmented memory. Here, I want us to consider making a postcolonial turn to affect theory to help us revisit our interpretation of the cross through recognition of the powerful affect of grief. By doing so we may find that there is significance to trauma's affect of grief as a force generative of hope in the face of sufferings proffered by the countless crosses of then and now.

Although many people use the terms grief and mourning interchangeably, strictly speaking, they are not the same. Grief refers to the "feelings of sorrow, anger, guilt, and confusion which occur when one experiences the loss of attachment figure." Whereas mourning refers to "the culturally constructed social response to the loss of an individual." Grief is a painful emotion that is looking for a cure, while mourning is a ritual that "heals" the pain of grief. Peter Homans writes that grief is an emotion, mourning a grief-infused symbolic action.[53] In this section, which in some ways begins the work of a critical Christian theology against US militarism, I want to put forth a preliminary exploration on grief, grievability and mourning, by working at the core of Christian remembrance of the crucifixion and interrogating the limits and failures of mourning that its connection with imperialism may have hindered and compromised. I suggest then that the driving force for all postcolonial resistance work should entail learning rituals of mourning to help us face the overwhelming losses and social suffering meted out in our hyper-militaristic neocolonial world. As Butler notes, "If we are interested in arresting cycles of violence to produce less violent outcomes, it is no doubt important to ask what, politically, might be made of grief besides a cry for war."[54] Moreover, as Christians, we can be challenged to ask the following: Is grief for us also regulated so much so that there we often grieve only for those who are "like us" but do not extend the same grieving or even recognize the grievability of those constructed to be "unlike" us according to the various framing operations in structures domination? Or as Nguyen frames this, might it be possible to engage in a kind of just memory in which our remembering is inclusive of others, even our enemies? Is it possible to grieve and remember not only ours but others so that there is an "ethics of remembering one's own or remembering others."[55] Butler argues that in today's world, even affects are regulated to such an extent that our sense of horror and of outrage in the face of suffering and loss do not run equally for and on behalf of everyone. In fact, because our apprehensions of the world are constructed for us, it is inevitable that our feelings of loss, despair, empathy, and outrage are only directed against a particularly recognizable people who are "like us" while these affects are preemptively closed to those who are apprehended as the "other." Thus, we need ask why the moral horror in the face of violence and loss is differentially experienced.

One way to destabilize the now very familiar interpretation of the cross as a singular event that displaces all other experiences of suffering and loss then and now is to reframe the focus from one singular individual to encompass a broader experience of social suffering. An interpretation of suffering and loss as always-already within the matrix of the social allows us to redress the social memory that grief often generates. By expanding and reframing the scene of the cross, we have a broader picture of not only the direct victims of those who suffered torture and terror but also those who participated in carrying out the mandates of the empire as well as those who can make claims to eyewitness status or from a distance and merely heard of what took place. All experienced the overflow of social affect that generates both outrage and grief. So let us look more closely at potential reframing of the scene of the cross.

At the Cross: Trauma, Terror, Grief, and Mourning

"The central symbol of Christianity is the figure of a tortured man," so writes biblical scholar Stephen Moore.[56] Many scholars from Josephus to Cicero to Martin Hengel note just how horrific and wretched it was to die on the cross. According to Hengel, "…crucifixion was a punishment in which the caprice and sadism of the executioners were given full rein."[57] After going through the many gruesome technologies deployed while one is killed on the cross, Hengel notes that "the earliest Christian message of the crucified messiah demonstrated the 'solidarity' of the love of God with the unspeakable suffering of those who were tortured and put to death by human cruelty."[58] That this cruel mode of execution was a political act of an imperial and dominative state makes the cross a crucial starting place for critical Christian theologies engaging US militarism in Asia or elsewhere.

There are many interpretations of the cross, however, that more particularly turn our gaze away from the horror on the cross. Thus, we endorse the much easier alibi of God's love. The most familiar interpretation we have learned is that all this suffering finds equivalence and even justice because God's love exceeds the expanse and depth of suffering, especially that caused by human cruelty evidenced on the cross.

Prominent interpretations of both Abelard's moral exemplar theory of atonement and also of Anselm's theory of satisfaction turn their gaze away from the site of the tortured body, and then they also skitter away from those who witness its slow death and horror. Their gaze and thus our gaze for too long have been directed upward to a God's love that is expected to right the wrongs of such human cruelty. Perhaps the cross bears witness to human capacity for cruelty to another, but God's love neither condones nor stands as alibi to human capacity to impose suffering on another. Mixed with the horrific technology that carries out the tortuous public killing on the cross, I want to call our attention, particularly, to the affect of grief that hovers and thickly saturates the scene of the execution. There is some evidence of rituals of mourning by the tortured body on the cross as well as by those who bear witness to it from near and afar.[59]

What might it mean for us to turn our gaze straight into the horror of what happened before, during, and after the crucifixion and recognize that perhaps, while not valorizing suffering in and of itself, such horrific suffering needed to be redeployed. Theorist Rey Chow notes, "…to the Roman officials in occupied Judea, the execution of a political dissenter such as Jesus, too, probably meant little more than the routine extermination of 'lice,' but for the followers of Christianity, that execution (together with its iconic instrument, the cross) has carried a definitive symbolic significance of sacrifice over the centuries. For these followers, it is the subject that bears the cross, rather than the subject that has been crossed out, that remains noteworthy."[60] In Chow's take, a suffering subject cannot be "erased", "crossed" out by some other message of "God's love," "divine forgiveness," and so on.

The slow tortuous killing on the cross was one that not only Jesus but countless others before, after, and alongside him experienced. While the numbers make it seem as if dying on the cross might have been "normal" and "routine," we know from historians that such was not the case. Dying on the cross was preserved for a class of people who may have had absolutely no status and sovereign power. However, while their bodies had no value and could thus be easily subjected to one of the most humiliating and painful deaths, it was a form of death that extracted the maximum surplus value in producing terror for all from the perspective of the empire.[61] Again, this makes the cross a key discursive site in a critical Christian theology that arises from the ruins of US imperial wars and empire.

Thus, dying on the cross, or rather getting publicly tortured to a slow death, caused lasting trauma to those who bore witness to the event. Jesus' event of torture by crucifixion, any torture, is not just event for that individual subject. It is a collective subjectivity we must examine. But, if indeed, as Butler notes in the beginning epigraph, "Open grieving is bound up with outrage, and outrage in the face of injustice or indeed of unbearable loss has enormous political potential. Whether we are speaking about open grief or outrage, we are talking about affective responses that are highly regulated by regimes of power and sometimes subject to explicit censorship," is it possible that our open grieving as well as our outrage as affective responses have been censored and regulated by the regimes of power now, just as then in Jesus' time? If open grief and outrage against unbearable loss have political and thus theological potential to transform our world, how might we interpret the cross so that it continues to be the affective space that allows for both grief and outrage? In a world fraught with unbearable grief, what might Christian tradition offer by way of intersubjective mourning so that we may work through our grief?

Conclusion: The Specter of the Cross

I provide here one example of what I mean by reframing our tendency to connect the cross with one singular individual to a more social experience of suffering as well as social memory.[62] My example comes from Nancy Pineda-Madrid's work on the suffering of women, known as feminicide, in Ciudad Juarez, Mexico, just across the border from El Paso, Texas. While not the DMZ of Korea, Ciudad Juarez/El Paso is yet another borderland fraught with traumas of militarization, state terror, and gendered violence.[63] Pineda-Madrid writes, "The cross signals a past event, the execution of Jesus, that participants claim holds meaning for them now. It is a central symbol in the life of this gathered community...the event of Jesus and the contemporary execution of Juarez's daughters are linked in the use of this symbol."[64]

This too resonates with Kathleen Corley's work on funerary rituals in the early Christian movements. Corley's work examines the ways in which early followers of Jesus may have followed their elaborate funerary rituals to do the work of mourning with and on behalf of the loss experienced by their communities. However, later resurrection theologies tended to gloss over and even erase the work of lamentation that may have been done by mostly women to help their communities to remember the loss of loved ones as Corley notes that it was women's funerary rituals or the cult of the dead "that created community by creating continuity with the living and the deceased, in this case, Jesus. Jesus became the special dead of the community whose presence was memorialized and felt in women's and ordinary people's mortuary and meals and laments."[65] When we put Corley and Pineda-Madrid in conversation, we can do the work of reframing that I mentioned earlier. Notably as the mourning rituals allowed for the process of grieving through remembrance of the loved one, Pineda-Madrid's work with women of Ciudad Juarez clearly shows that the slain daughters too are like Jesus, who draws forth from us both wails of grief and shouts of outrage that such unthinkable acts take place and without the state being able or willing to hold the perpetrators accountable. What is particularly crucial, as Pineda-Madrid shows, is that both the grief and the rage draw forth, too, expression in collective action and organizing by the surviving women for redressive action for the whole of the community. Thus, resurrection in this rising resistance from ruin is evident again.[66]

In thinking of the cross for our neocolonial times, I fear that not much has changed since the Roman Imperial powers executed Jesus to the neoliberal militarized economic engines that solicit degradation and rage that target women in Ciudad Juarez and elsewhere around the world. If we juxtapose the tortured death of the one we have as the central figure of our belief and practices alongside the deaths of women of Ciudad Juarez as one example, Christians must grapple with disturbing and urgent questions: what experiences of suffering are differentially interpreted? Whose bodies really count? Whose sufferings elicit outrage and grief and which do not? What theological understanding of being human must be reimagined so that "their" suffering becomes our "suffering"? How do we theologically understand that the Jesus who ends up on the cross does so precisely because of his affect/ion for the world and for those who suffer with unbearable grief, loss, and outrage after his crucifixion?

Neither in Jesus nor in those who witnessed the vulnerable exposure to death of many in their communities do we find the violative tendencies toward a repressive amnesia. Those who know the terror and trauma of crosses strewn around this world, then and now, know them not simply as implements of torture and trauma, but as specters, continuing to haunt us, generating mourning and a critical melancholia that can produce resistance and counter-imperial faith. They return always seeking and demanding their suffering be remembered, be properly mourned, and that outrage on their behalf is never too late. As Derrida so aptly notes, "In this mourning work in process, in this interminable task, the ghost remains as that gives one the most to think about-and to do…A ghost never dies, it remains always to come and to come-back."[67] The postcolonial spectrality of the cross haunts our time for the times to come, in which we recognize that we are always-already vulnerable and undone in the face of the suffering other. In the ruins of colonial and neocolonial death-dealing projects, affect like grief exceeds our attempt to control, regulate, or discipline.

As I wrote in an earlier work, *The Heart of the Cross: A Postcolonial Christology*, there is another "cross"—a torturous yet also spectral border where pain and hope cross, as for Pineda-Madrid in the Ciudad Juarez city traumatized at the borderline of US imperial, economic, and misogynous hegemony. In *Heart of the Cross,* I stood and reflected at the DMZ, where US-backed South Korea borders a demonized North Korea, cycling and recycling a lament and rage among peoples in Korea and which continues intergenerationally into Korean-Americans in the US. Yet, as I showed in that book, our thinking and feeling from the Korean DMZ—another *es una herida abierta* "open wound" as Gloria Anzaldúa called the US/Mexican border—can generate hope and resistance.[68]

For Christians, the cross becomes a critical memory, giving evidence for the spheres of the affective in transforming this world, a world that extracts a "multitude of losses continually demanded by an unforgiving social world."[69] If affect is "sticky" and is what "sticks," then grief and love "stick" intimately.[70] To struggle with grief and let grief bring forth lament and outrage is to be stuck to "love [that] is to struggle, beyond solitude, with everything in the world that can animate existence."[71]

Notes

1. A brief portion of this chapter was previously published as "Grief and Grievability: A Postcolonial Spectrality of the Cross" in *Concilium: International Journal of Theology* (Spring, 2013).

2. Quoted in Maria Höhn and Seungsook Moon, eds., *Over There: Living with U.S. Military Empire from World War Two to the Present* (Durham: Duke University Press, 2010), 4.
3. Cf. Catherine Lutz, ed., *The Bases of Empire: The Global Struggle against U.S. Military Posts* (New York: New York University Press, 2009).
4. Much evidence shows that the phenomenal economic growth of Korea is significantly connected to Korea's relation with the US. Moreover, this relationship is built upon mutual militarized desires for not only economic growth but also regional dominance. However, there are fault lines and noticeable points of overreach that are presently evidenced in works by scholars like Jesook Moon, *South Koreans in the Debt Crisis: The Creation of Neoliberal Welfare Society* (Durham: Duke University Press, 2009). Also, Katharine H.S. Moon, *Protesting America: Democracy and the U.S.-Korea Alliance* (Los Angeles: University of California Press, 2012).
5. Judith Butler, *Frames of War: When Is Life Grievable?* (New York: Verso, 2009), 39.
6. Kim, Jodi. *Ends of Empire: Asian American Critique and the Cold War* (Minneapolis: University of Minnesota Press, 2010), 34. For Kim, "the Korean War appears not simply as a congealed historical episode that is given narrative form after-the-event, but also as a Cold War epistemology in the making." Foremost in this structuring narrative is the production and invention of North Korea.
7. Ibid., 145.
8. Ibid., 145.
9. Bruce Cummings, *The Korean War: A History* (NY: Random House, 2010), 35.
10. Viet Thanh Nguyen, *Nothing Ever Dies: Vietnam and the Memory of War* (Cambridge: Harvard University Press, 2016), 7.
11. Of course this list of deaths does not include other aspects of war's aftermath in Korea such as the deployment of Koreans in the Vietnam War, the growth of military camptowns and camptowns shadow cast even over the Pacific to the Korean diaspora in the US. It also does not include the aftermath of war and the emergence of transnational adoption, and because the war did not end and US militarism has continued to be present over 60 decades, we need to examine another phenomenon—that is, intergenerational circulations of US military soldiers deployed to Korea.
12. Suk-Young Kim, *DMZ Crossing: Performing Emotional Citizenship Along the Korean Border* (New York: Columbia University Press, 2014), 7.
13. Cf. Michael Rothberg, *Multidirectional Memory: Remembering the Holocaust in the Age of Decolonization* (Stanford: Stanford University Press, 2009). Rothberg offers a critique of competitive memory as a "notion of the public sphere as a pregiven, limited space in which already-established groups

engage in a life and death struggle." Rothberg proposes instead memory's multidirectionality as "a malleable discursive space in which groups do not simply articulate established positions but actually come into being through their dialogical interactions with others," 5.

14. Edwidge Danticat, *Create Dangerously* (Princeton: Princeton University Press, 2010), 65.
15. Ji-Yeon Yuh, *Beyond the Shadow of Camptown: Korean Military Brides in America* (New York: New York University Press, 2002), 37. Not only did the Korean War set in motion the flight of Koreans to the US, Latin America, and elsewhere, but it also set in motion local economic dependence in its direct relationships with, for example, military camptowns: "The U.S. military presence in South Korea has meant, for example, that whole towns have grown economically dependent on the local U.S. military base, their fortunes waxing and waning with the size of the troops. In short, towns such as Uijeongbu, Songtan…are economically dependent on decisions made thousands of miles away by the leaders of a foreign country."
16. For an excellent analysis of various American wars and what he terms as the epistemology of war, see an important work by John Tirman, *The Death of Others: The Fate of Civilians in America's Wars* (Cambridge: Oxford University Press, 2010), 91.
17. Cf. Bruce Cummings, *Dominion from Sea to Sea: Pacific Ascendancy and American Power* (New Haven: Yale University Press, 2009).
18. For more in-depth discussion on "vicarious trauma" and "empty empathy," see E. Ann Kaplan, *Trauma Culture: The Politics of Terror and Loss in Media and Literature* (New Brunswick: Rutgers University Press, 2005). Kaplan notes that there are degrees, spheres, and different positions through which trauma is experienced across time and space.
19. Memory and collective memory, over time and across space, undergo sedimentation and re-presentations and are reconstituted during different times. Cf. Ron Eyerman, *Cultural Trauma: Slavery and the Formation of African-American Identity* (Cambridge: Cambridge University Press, 2001). See also, Alison Landsberg's *Prosthetic Memory: The Transformation of American Remembrance in the Age of Mass Culture* (New York: Columbia University Press, 2004), 25. "Prosthetic memories are those not strictly derived from a person's own lived experience. Prosthetic memories circulate publicly, and although they are not organically based, they are nevertheless experienced with a person's body as a result of an engagement with a wide range of cultural technologies. Prosthetic memories thus become part of one's personal archive of experience, informing one's subjectivity as well as one's relationship to the present and future tenses." Cf. Maurice Halbwachs, *On Collective Memory* (Chicago: University of Chicago, 1992).

20. Hirsch, Marianne and Nancy K. Miller, ed., *Rites of Return: Diaspora Poetics and the Politics of Memory* (NY: Columbia University Press, 2011), 5.
21. Ibid., 6.
22. http://kpolicy.org/open-fire-and-open-markets-the-asia-pacific-pivot-and-trans-pacific-partnership/ "'The hidden hand of the market,' as *New York Times* columnist Thomas Friedman famously wrote in the 1990s, 'will never work without a hidden fist.' The Asia-Pacific Pivot, a one-two neoliberal-militaristic punch, packs both." Accessed September 20, 2015.
23. Gert Buelens, Sam Durrant and Robert Eaglestone, eds. *The Future of Trauma Theory: Contemporary Literary and Cultural Criticism* (New York: Routledge, 2014), 5.
24. Cathy Caruth, *Unclaimed Experience: Trauma, Narrative and History* (Baltimore: Johns Hopkins University Press, 1995).
25. Stef Craps, "Beyond Eurocentrism: Trauma Theory in the Global Age," in Gert Buelens, Sam Durrant and Robert Eaglestone, eds., *The Future of Trauma Theory: Contemporary Literary and Cultural* Criticism (New York: Routledge, 2014), 45.
26. For an excellent and one of the most carefully researched and crafted critiques of Eurocentrism that is part of the very structure of the discourse that is trauma studies in general, see Stef Craps, *Postcolonial Witnessing: Trauma Out of Bounds* (New York: Palgrave Macmillan, 2013).
27. Ibid., 48 See also, Ethan Waters, *Crazy Like Us: The Globalization of the American Psyche* (New York: Free Press, 2010).
28. Judith Butler, *Frames of War*, 54.
29. Ranjana Khanna, *Algeria Cuts: Women and Representation, 1830–Present* (Stanford: Stanford University Press, 2008). In her interrogation of postcolonial Algeria, Khanna offers a critical insight perhaps even for Korea. Her insight is that justice for trauma's "inassimilable remainders" must be sought outside the mechanisms of "virile wars," 242.
30. Emma Hutchinson and Roland Bleiker, "Grief and Transformation of Emotions After War" in Linda Ahall and Thomas Gregory, eds., *Emotions, Politics and War* (New York: Routledge, 2015), 210.
31. While I do not examine here the ways that the individual as part of the traumatized collective manages unmourned grief and loss, but suffice it to say that one significant area that needs further critical interrogation is that of sustained collective culture of addiction. Addiction becomes a collective effort to manage pain and loss for many who have experienced collective historical sense of loss and suffering. Cf. Angela Garcia, *The Pastoral Clinic: Addiction and Dispossession Along the Rio Grande* (Los Angeles: University of California Press, 2010).
32. R. Williams, *Marxism and Literature* (Oxford: Oxford University Press, 1977), 128–135.

33. Cf. Teresa Brennan, *The Transmission of Affect* (Ithaca: Cornell University Press, 2004). Also, D. Eng writes, "Historical traumas of loss, grief, and forgetting are passed down from one generation to another unconsciously…" in *The Feeling of Kinship: Queer Liberalism and the Racialization of Intimacy* (Durham: Duke University Press, 2010), 167.
34. The way that Koreans have lived in a state of terror and perpetual readiness for the breakout of another war has become a way of life for Koreans. In fact, one may say that it is like living in fear of a potential breakout of terror in a domestic violence context. One is trapped in a scene without end, and thus, problematic modes of survival become the new normal.
35. Viet Thanh Nguyen, *The Sympathizer* (New York: Grove Atlantic, 2015).
36. Kelly Oliver, *The Colonization of Psychic Space: A Psychoanalytic Social Theory of Oppression* (Minneapolis: University of Minnesota Press, 2004), xix.
37. For more on how the body becomes the site of memory, see Bessel van der Kolk, *The Body Keeps the Score: Brain, Mind, and Body in the Healing of Trauma* (New York: Penguin Books, 2014).
38. Cf. Arthur W. Frank, *The Wounded Storyteller: Body, Illness and Ethics* (Chicago: University of Chicago Press, 1995). Also refer to, Arthur Kleinman, *The Illness Narratives: Suffering, Healing and the Human Condition* (New York: Basic Books, 1988).
39. Eugenia Brinkema, *The Forms of the Affects* (Durham: Duke University Press, 2014). For Brinkema, whose focus is on individual loss, grief names "…that which resists the relational dimension of loss; the form for that suffering of a general economy in which not everything can be made to mean and things escape systematically without return, labor guarantees no profit… grief resists mediation and ongoing processual struggle. It takes a different form altogether, and it is undialectical," 71.
40. Jeffrey C. Alexander, *Trauma: A Social Theory* (New York: Polity, 2012), 3.
41. For explorations in ways that the neoliberal capitalism works against memory and remembering either through erasure or commodification, see various essays in Michael O'Loughlin, ed., *The Ethics of Remembering and The Consequences of Forgetting* (Maryland: Rowman & Littlefield, 2015).
42. In locating and extending sustained structural traumas as another form and distinct from a singular traumatic event, Dominick LaCapra explores the various ways that a singular event as definitive of trauma needs to be challenged. Cf. LaCapra, Dominick *Writing History, Writing Trauma* (Baltimore: Johns Hopkins University Press, 2001). In much of trauma studies, "trauma" has been defined as the event that is beyond the experience of everyday life. A trauma then is an extraordinary event in which the ordinary is breached. However, there are scholars now who offer critiques of this by arguing that some traumas cannot be encapsulated into a singular historical event. A trauma can be a sustained way in which the everyday and

the ordinary is violated, e.g., many women live within a reality that is saturated with gender-based violence. Many others live with racialized forms of violence that have become routine and the norm that defines and shapes everyday life.

43. Cf. Abraham, Nicholas and Maria Torok, *The Shell and the Kernel* (Chicago: University of Chicago Press, 1994).
44. Jacques Derrida, *Specters of Marx* (New York: Routledge, 1994), 48.
45. Grace M. Cho, *Haunting the Korean Diaspora: Shame, Secrecy and the Forgotten War* (Minneapolis: University of Minnesota Press, 2008), 13.
46. Judith Butler writes that the "predicament of being moved by what one sees, feels, and comes to know is always one in which one finds oneself transported elsewhere, into another scene, or into a social world in which one is not the center. And this form of dispossession is constituted as a form of responsiveness that gives rise to action and resistance..." How then do those in cultures that uphold the idea of sovereign self become dispossessed of the sovereign self and enter into forms of collectivity that oppose forms of dispossession that systematically exclude and atomize populations and peoples from collective belonging and justice?
47. R. Khanna, 'Hope, Demand and the Perpetual', in W. Anderson, D. Jenson, and R. C. Keller, eds., *Unconscious Dominions: Psychoanalysis, Colonial Trauma and Global Sovereignties* (Durham: Duke University Press, 2011), 257.
48. Eng, *Loss*, 366.
49. Anne Anlin Cheng, *The Melancholy of Race: Psychoanalysis, Assimilation and Hidden Grief* (Cambridge: Oxford University Press, 2001), 95.
50. Cf. Erika Doss, *Memorial Mania: Public Feeling in America* (Chicago: University of Chicago Press, 2010).
51. Judith Butler, *Precarious Life: The Powers of Mourning and Violence* (NY: Verso, 2004), 30.
52. George A. Bonanno, *The Other Side of Sadness: What the New Science of Bereavement Tells Us About Life After Loss* (New York: Basic Books, 2009), 203.
53. P. Homans, *Symbolic Loss: The Ambiguity of Mourning and Memory at Century's End* (Charlottesville: University Press of Virginia, 2000), 2.
54. Butler, *Precarious Life*, xii.
55. Nguyen, *Nothing Ever Dies*, 12.
56. Stephen Moore, *God's Gym: Divine Male Bodies of the Bible* (New York: Routledge, 1996), 4.
57. M. Hengel, *Crucifixion* (Minneapolis: Fortress Press, 1997), 87.
58. Ibid., 88.
59. K.E. Corley, *Maranatha: Women's Funerary Rituals and Christian Origins* (Minneapolis: Fortress Press, 2010).
60. Rey Chow, *The Age of the World Target: Self-Referentiality in War, Theory, and Comparative* Work (Durham: Duke University Press, 2006), 86.

61. For more detailed discussions on the spectacle of torture and killings as terrorizing forms of regulation, discipline, and punishment, see D.G. Kyle, *Spectacles of Death in Ancient Rome* (London: Routledge, 1998). Also, Richard A. Horsley, 'Prominent Patterns in the Social Memory of Jesus and Friends', in A. Kirk and T. Thatcher, eds., *Memory, Tradition and Text: Uses of the Past in Early Christianity* (Atlanta: The Society of Biblical Literature, 2005).
62. Cf. A. Kirk, 'Social and Cultural Memory,' in *Memory, Tradition, and Text.*
63. Kathleen Staudt and Zulma Y. Mendez, *Courage, Resistance and Women in Ciudad Juarez: Challenges to Militarization* (Austin: University of Texas Press, 2015).
64. N. Pineda-Madrid, *Suffering and Salvation in Ciudad Juarez* (Minneapolis: Fortress Press, 2011), 134.
65. Corley, 133.
66. On affective labor of women as a form of biopolitical labor for producing social relations of life, see M. Hardt and A. Negri, *Commonwealth* (Cambridge: Harvard University Press, 2009), 131–147.
67. Derrida, *Specters of Marx*, 123.
68. Gloria Anzaldúa, *Borderlands/La Frontera: A New Mestiza* (San Francisco: Aunt Lute Books, 1987), 25.
69. D. Eng and S. Han, 'A Dialogue on Racial Melancholia', in David Eng and David Kazanjian, eds., *Loss* (Berkeley: University of California Press, 2003), 362–363.
70. Sara Ahmed, 'Happy Objects', in Melissa Gregg and Gregory J. Seigworth, eds., *The Affect Theory Reader* (Durham: Duke University Press, 2010), 29.
71. A. Badiou, *In Praise of Love* (New York: The New Press, 2012), 104.

CHAPTER 2

Militarism, Masculinism, and Martyrdom: Conditional Citizenship for (Asian) Americans

Tat-siong Benny Liew

Introduction

"Serious historians...have often undervalued fiction, if only...because by convention history is concerned with the recovery of truth about the past. But for social history—for the history of culture, for the history of people's understanding of their own society—fiction occupies a privileged position."[1] Just as Keith Hopkins extends with these words the archive for the study of history, I would like to extend the meaning of *history* from a narrower understanding of it as something of the past to a broader—and longer—view that it also includes our present. In addition, I would like to expand Hopkin's category *fiction* to include movies, even or especially Hollywood blockbusters, as a resource to understand a society's ideologies (especially since many Hollywood productions are based on "bestselling" novels) by referring to various novels and movies.[2] A recent message

T.-S. B. Liew (✉)
Department of Religious Studies, College of the Holy Cross,
Worcester, MA, USA

N. Kim, W.A. Joh (eds.), *Critical Theology against US Militarism in Asia*,
DOI 10.1057/978-1-137-48013-2_2

from Hollywood, and hence, as Hopkins suggests, a potentially popular understanding of the people of the US, is this: "What are you going to do when the US is under threat of military or militarized attack by Asians in this, the second decade of the twenty-first century?" Let me give two examples.

Screen Messages from Hollywood

I begin by placing two Hollywood productions, which were released within the last three or four years, within a broader and longer view of history. First is the movie *Olympus Has Fallen* (2013). In the movie, the US President is taken hostage literally in his own house. In the words of the movie's director, Antoine Fuqua, "the religion of the White House [is] a cathedral that we all sort of worship."[3] In addition to the white male President, hostages include a Latino male Vice President and a white female Secretary of Defense. The main protagonist is a disgraced yet Rambo-like white male former Secret Service agent (Gerald Butler) who works with or, more accurately, helps the African American male Speaker of the House (Morgan Freeman) and the African American female Secret Service Director (Angela Bassett) to rescue the President and restore order. Although this seemingly diverse administration lacks any Asian American presence, the enemies, who infiltrate the White House with the help of a turncoat white agent, are all Asian—or, more accurately, North Korean.

The second movie is *Red Dawn* (2012), which is a remake of a 1984 movie by the same title. Instead of the White House, the target of attack and occupation is a town in the state of Washington: Spokane. The invaders in the 1984 version are Soviets and their allies from Cuba and Nicaragua, but in this remake, the invaders are—again!—North Koreans. A white male US marine (Chris Hemsworth), who happens to be home on leave, trains a small group of high schoolers to be a kind of guerilla resistance force against the North Korean occupiers, who are under the command of a Captain Cho (Will Lun Lee). Like the administration in *Olympus Has Fallen*, this band of high school students—who call themselves the Wolverines after their school mascot—includes both genders and non-whites, though, once again, no one is of Asian ancestry. In fact, the movie ends with one of the white male Wolverines calling people of his town to join and support their resistance efforts: "For them," he says, "this is just a place; for us, this is our home." This statement reinforces the stereotypical view of Asians as "perpetual foreigners" in the US and is an example of what Alain Milton calls a "relegation" status: Asian Americans in the US are "neither banned nor imprisoned...[but] in a unique situation, because [they are] inside without being able to belong fully."[4]

This chapter does not focus on why North Koreans were cast as invaders or perpetrators of US security in these two films. Instead, I want to situate these two films and other popular cultural works within a longer time frame and a broader context. By doing so, we can explore the cultural logics that pervade US society, especially its treatment of those who are of Asian ancestry within its national body and what that treatment might imply about the ethos *of* and *for* the population of the entire society.[5]

US entry into the Second World War was, in many ways, a very significant moment in its social history. With Japan's bombing of Pearl Harbor and the subsequent US declaration of war against Japan, Asia became an increasingly important focus of US national attention and intention. People of the US were by no means unaware of Asia and Asians before this point in time. Asians had been living and working in the US for a long time. In addition, many missionaries had already gone from the US to Asia in their global effort to "civilize" and Christianize. The role that the US played in the Second World War, however, fulfilled a promise made by Henry R. Luce. Luce was the son of a missionary to China and founder of *Time* magazine. In 1941 he promised that the US could create an "American Century" by entering the war and spreading its gospel of democracy.[6] With the US replacing Great Britain as the most dominant power in the world, the people of the US had to learn how to redefine themselves as a nation and as a society at the end of the Second World War. However, Great Britain's decline as an imperial power also meant that peoples and countries in Asia were emerging and engaging in a process of decolonization.[7] With the dynamics of the "Cold War" era, US military forces took the opportunity to extend their presence and power into various countries and regions in both East Asia and Southeast Asia. I put "Cold War" within quotation marks to signify that it might have multiple meanings. Heonik Kwon, for example, argues for a different understanding regarding the chronology, geography, and (moral) framework of the "Cold War."[8] The conventional view uses "Cold War" to signify a more or less peaceful—and hence "cold"—power struggle between the US and the Soviet Union; it did not have a clear beginning (despite George Orwell's coining of the term in 1945) but ended definitively when the Berlin Wall fell in 1989.[9] This view, for Kwon, is largely a European and North American perspective. By contrast, people in Asia might see the "Cold War" as a structure of domination and power differential which led to all kinds of physical and political violence and continues to have lingering effects. According to this latter version, the "Cold War" is not only still decomposing but also "a chapter in the ongoing process of globalization," which is being led by the US.[10]

Kwon's work provides a helpful lens to re-view *Olympus Has Fallen* and *Red Dawn*. *Olympus Has Fallen* can be seen to betray the characterization of the "Cold War" as peaceful. The North Korean terrorist leader, Kang Yeonsak (Rick Yune), demands that the US withdraw its military fleet from the Korean Peninsula. Kang plans not only to invade South Korea as a strategy to reunify Korea but also to detonate the nuclear missiles *of* the US *on* the US. Kang is motivated by a desire to avenge the deaths of his parents, who were killed during the "Cold War." One is therefore hard pressed to insist that the "Cold War" was "peaceful" or that it is wholly a matter of the past.

It is also telling that the portrayal of the attack on the US by North Koreans in both movies is reminiscent of the Japanese attack on Pearl Harbor, despite the difference in time and geography. Like the 1941 Japanese attack, the North Koreans in both movies mount an air assault—though, this time, the assault has moved to the continental US by targeting the White House and a town in Washington, respectively. In fact, some of the shots in both movies, especially those in *Red Dawn*, look eerily similar to footage of Pearl Harbor. This linkage with Pearl Harbor relates to Kwon's concern about the (moral) framework of the "Cold War" and its lingering effects, because it effectively presents the subsequent violence of the white male protagonists against North Koreans as self-defense.

It is important to note that both movies make a point to depict their respective white male protagonist as only a "counter puncher": neither Butler's nor Hemsworth's character initiates the fight. Both characters resort to violence only as a (moral) response to "foreign" aggression. Butler's character is a former US Army Ranger assigned to Special Operations and a former Secret Service agent who is working a *desk job* at the Treasury Department at the time of the attack on the White House. Hemsworth's character is an active duty US marine who is home *on leave* when the North Korean invasion descends from the sky. Before things turn violent in *Olympus Has Fallen*, the US President declares to his cabinet, in a message similar to the one given by President Franklin Roosevelt before Pearl Harbor, that he would not want the US to enter into war. By reading with the long view of the US's various exploits in Asia after the Second World War, one can see how these plot developments cover over the unequal power structure of the "Cold War," which Kwon discusses. These story lines are also part of what Mary Louis Pratt calls "anti-conquest" strategies, which work to "secure [one's own] innocence in the same moment as [one] assert[s]...hegemony" through violence.[11]

By placing these two movies within a longer time frame, I want to underscore the need to examine the larger cultural logics at work behind and through these movies rather than to focus on some immediate causes or isolatable events, like the terrorist attacks of 9/11. In fact, many Asian American scholars have helpfully drawn parallels between how people of Japanese ancestry were treated in the US after Pearl Harbor and how those of South Asian ancestry have been treated in the US since 9/11.[12] These works, once again, point to the need to attend to larger cultural continuity that may span decades.

Farewell Through Arms...Plus a (Red?) Badge of Citizenship

Both *Red Dawn* and *Olympus Has Fallen* basically depict US Americans and (North) Koreans or Asians as mutually exclusive but similarly militaristic peoples vying to win the "tough guy" battle and title. However, the films also share deeply ironic and telling casting choices. The actors who play the patriotic US American heroes in both movies are not US citizens: Hemsworth is Australian and Butler Scottish. In contrast, those actors who play the chief North Korean villains—Will Lun Lee and Rick Yune, respectively—are both native-born US citizens: Lee was born in Arlington, Virginia, and Yune in Washington, D.C. Race trumps everything, including nativity and even citizenship, in this country called the US.

However, there is one big difference between these two movies, which is equally telling. In the remake of *Red Dawn*, the small band of resisters hook up with some US marines. Most significantly, one of these marines, Corporal Smith, is played by an Asian actor of Korean descent, Kenneth Choi. Scholars have paid much attention to the citizenship question for Asian Americans. They use different arguments and adjectives, from "consuming,"[13] "economic,"[14] and "elusive"[15] to "imperial"[16] and "inhuman."[17] Without suggesting in any way that these proposals are wrong or inadequate, I do want to suggest that we can also think about this question—for a different emphasis, nuance, or purpose—in terms of a *conditional* or *contingent citizenship*. I suggest this because I agree with Denise Ferreira de Silva's proposal that racialization logics operate by selective inclusion rather than by blanket exclusion (2007).[18] The particular arrangement in *Red Dawn* of an Asian man in the US military with Smith as his last name—the casting choice and the last name for this role are both intentional changes from its 1984 original—reveals much about how US racialization logics work to create certain condition(s) for citizenship for Asian Americans.

"Smith" is generally known to be the most prevalent family name in the US, including among African Americans because of the history of slavery, during which masters named their slaves after themselves. Supposedly, the last name Smith originated in England for metal workers who had not only special skills but also the special task of forging armor, swords, and other weapons. I am not a scholar on family names and have done no research on the subject. What is important and pertinent to my argument is the existence and ubiquity of this popular perception. Corporal Smith in *Red Dawn*, with his Asian face and body in a military uniform, as well as a weaponry-associated, non-Asian but most prevalent US family name, signifies that the willingness to risk one's life for the love of country through military service is an essential and eventual evidence of an Asian's assimilability—and hence an important condition for citizenship.

We can actually trace this condition, contingency, or connection between military service and US citizenship for Asians back to (before) the Second World War. Many Chinese who resided in the US during the Second World War were ineligible for naturalization or citizenship because of the 1882 Chinese Exclusion Act. Not being US citizens, they could not enlist but could be drafted into US military service during the war. Without dismissing or denying the racial tension that existed for Chinese Americans during this time (such as being relegated to their own segregated units within the US military), it was their participation in the war, particularly their military service, that led to the repeal of the Chinese Exclusion Act in 1943. This repeal opened the door to naturalization, citizenship, and even new immigration for others from China.[19] Because of US militarism, the military uniform can help cover up different kinds of racial/ethnic bodies. In fact, the exchange of "expedited naturalization or even citizenship itself for honorable military service" was a practice as early as the Revolutionary War (1775–1783). This practice also enabled a small number of Chinese "aliens" to become US citizens after their military service in the First World War.[20] During the Second World

War, about 20 percent of the adult Chinese male population in the US (i.e., 12,000–15,000 men) served in the US military. These Chinese men served even though Chinese culture has traditionally frowned on such service, saying "good iron does not become nails, good guys don't become soldiers."[21] It is important to note that Chinese women, though of a much smaller number, were also recruited by the Women's Army Corps during the Second World War.[22] The irony of trading one's life to have a life in the US was (and is) not lost on Chinese Americans. In a 1943 letter to the State Department, a Donald L. Chu wrote, "Personally, I don't mind [joining the military] for I always want to do my part for America. However, I hate to think of this: I am given a chance to naturalization only at the risk of my life!"[23] What the Chinese American historian Mae Ngai calls "impossible subjects" is thus rather apt for this population.[24] The contradiction involved in this conditional citizenship—belonging by dying—implies something close to an impossibility.

To be clear, the willingness to risk or give one's life is not the only condition for citizenship that people of Chinese ancestry experienced during this time. Various scholars have shown that during the Second World War, the dominant US society used both the depiction of Chinese as the "good Asians" and the 1943 repeal of the Chinese Exclusion Act of 1882 to deflect and disavow US racism and imperialism. This deflection and disavowal enabled the US to enhance its national image during a time of immense and intense international warfare.[25] Later in the chapter I will say more about the place of religion in what I am calling *conditional citizenship*. For now, let me just say that if, according to John's Gospel, Jesus says that a grain of wheat has to fall into the earth and die to bear fruit and that those who love their life would end up losing it (John 12:24–25), the reality for Asian Americans is that the earth (dominant US society) has to be in a favorable condition to receive the grain or seed (Asians/Asian Americans) that is ready to fall and die in it. The required condition for Asian Americans to achieve citizenship in the US does not rest solely on their willingness to risk their lives through military service; something must also be happening in the US for the dominant society to value or demand that willingness.

The necessity of this other—or, more accurately, first or even prerequisite—condition is clearly illustrated in the experience of Filipino men. While in a time of war, the US Congress passed several conflicting laws. The first was a law passed in 1942, which gave Filipino men in US military service the option of becoming US citizens. The second and third laws passed in

1946, the Rescission Act and the Treaty of Manila, respectively, abruptly removed all benefits previously promised to Filipino servicemen, as well as their status as US nationals. However, the US–Philippines Military Base Agreement (1947) dropped the requirement of US immigrant credentials as a condition for US military service. This change enabled the US Navy to recruit and enlist Filipino men who were foreign nationals without having to offer the promise or even prospect of US citizenship in exchange for that service.[26]

US citizens of Japanese descent, who were seen at the beginning of the Second World War as enemies because of race and ethnicity, also had to prove their worthiness for US citizenship through military service. They were not only forcefully moved to internment camps but also asked at these camps two questions regarding military service. Those two questions have become rather well known, thanks to John Okada's novel, *No-No Boy*.[27] First, "are you willing to serve in the armed forces of the US on combat duty wherever ordered?" Second, "will you swear unqualified allegiance to the US and faithfully defend the US from any or all attack by foreign or domestic forces, and foreswear any form of allegiance or obedience to the Japanese emperor, to any other foreign government, power, or organization?" The way for a US American of Asian ancestry to demonstrate his or her allegiance and to have a chance to be accepted as almost white and on the right side—like Corporal Smith in *Red Dawn*—is through military service.

Like their Chinese counterparts, Japanese American citizens of the US, because of the changing needs and interests of the US nation, changed from being interned in camps and generally excluded from military service in 1942 to being displayed as US soldiers (first by enlistment and then by draft) and eventually to being freed from internment in 1944. Takashi Fujitani suggests that the move from what he calls "vulgar racism" to "polite racism" or "inclusionary racism"—that is, the movement of Japanese Americans during this time "from the outside to the inside of the American population"—was conditional upon both the US's desire to display its "benevolence" to the world (perhaps particularly to the countries and peoples of Asia?) and its need for "labor and lives" to win the war.[28] Referring to Michel Foucault's thought on *bio-power* and *governmentality*, Fujitani insightfully notes that while the dominant US society shifts its mode and show of power from a negative emphasis on taking life to a seemingly more positive emphasis on making life—that is, on studying and managing the welfare of its population—under conditions of "total war,"[29] these are but different forms of exercising power. Freeing Japanese Americans from internment camps might just mean, therefore, including or incorporating them within the state's technologies of management. For Fujitani, the (selective) inclusion of Japanese Americans "would also allow young men of this population to die for the national community."[30] This is similar to Foucault's statement that illustrates his understanding of *biopolitics* and *thanatopolitics* as two sides of the same governmentality coin: "Go get slaughtered and we promise you a long and pleasant life."[31] Military service as a condition for inclusion marks a population with a rather high likelihood for (premature) death.[32] Also referring to Foucault's bio-power and governmentality, Jin-Kyung Lee tellingly calls military service a type of *necropolitical labor*: "the 'fostering' of life...[is] premised on [one's] death or the disposability of [one's] life" in accordance with the interests of the state or empire.[33]

One of the conditions that predisposed US society to accept the military service of Japanese Americans (but not recounted by Fujitani) was the changing concept of race.[34] By the time of the Second World War, many had begun to see race as less biological and more cultural, and hence, less immutable and more malleable. This alternative understanding became even more popular at this time because the war was against Nazis, who embraced a biological understanding of race in their pursuit of racial purity. This more cultural understanding of race enabled the dominant US society not only to make the distinction between "good Asians" and "bad Asians," but also to preach democracy as universally beneficial to all races—with, of course, a racially diverse but "harmonious" US (imperialistic) society as both the apparent model and proof.

Citizens as Macho Patriots

The gradual but equally selective inclusion of Chinese, Japanese, and other Asian Americans for the necropolitical labor of military service is just another manifestation of racism. Ruth Wilson Gilmore defines *racism* as "the state-sanctioned or extralegal production and exploitation of group-differentiated vulnerability to premature death."[35] A willingness to die *and* kill for the US through military service implies a masculinist cultural ethos. According to Kristin L. Hoganson, masculinism was already at work culturally, helping to bring about the Spanish–American and Philippine–American Wars toward the end of the nineteenth century.[36] Not only is war involving the US about masculinism, but US masculinism also leads to war. Note here the pedigree of the leading men in both *Olympus Has Fallen* and the remake of *Red Dawn*. Despite their non-US nativity noted earlier, both actors are well known for playing macho heroes on screen: the best known role for Butler is arguably that of King Leonidas in *300*, and for Hemsworth that of Thor in, well, *Thor*. Again, if the art and craft of Hollywood is any indication, US masculinity has already been a big concern before movies like *Red Dawn* and *Olympus Has Fallen*. As Brian Locke shows, the movie *Fight Club* (1999), starring Brad Pitt and Edward Norton, is about an anxiety over a crisis of masculinity supposedly caused by corporations and consumerism.[37] More significantly, like *Red Dawn*'s Corporal Smith, there is also a character with an Asian face but a non-Asian family name in *Fight Club*. Just like *Red Dawn*'s Corporal Smith, the choice to cast an Asian actor for the role of Raymond K. Hessel (Joon B. Kim) in *Fight Club* is an intentional change from the original novel of the same name and on which the Hollywood movie is based. In the novel, Hessel, the liquor store clerk whom Pitt's hyper-masculine character bullies in a dark alley, is white. For Locke, the movie's casting choice is tellingly understandable for two reasons. First, by the time of the movie's production, Asian clerks and cashiers have become a constant and pervasive presence in the corner convenient stores of many US cities. Second, because the Civil Rights movement made it more difficult to emasculate African American men, Asian men have become the epitome of a deficient or feminized masculinity.[38]

Locke's point about males of Asian ancestry being racialized as feminized is on target and well supported,[39] but it has a much longer history than Locke suggests. His reference to Norman Mailer's 1957 essay on the "white negro" and the "hipster" shows that white men's anxiety over their own masculinity started way before the making of *Fight Club* and the end of the twentieth century. After all, Mailer's "white negroes" are white urbanites who mimic black men in order to come across as more masculine.[40]

Given the attention to militarism and war in this chapter, let me point to Karen Kuo's work on a Hollywood movie made between the two World Wars: Frank Capra's *Lost Horizon* (1937).[41] According to Kuo, in that movie, *Asia* represents an alternative to a militarized masculinity for four white men and a white woman. These five white people try to leave China in a small plane because of a violent revolution there, but they end up finding themselves in Shangri-La. Led by a soldier-turned-diplomat, this group of white people encounters and is served by a utopian community of Asians who are characterized by "pacifism, nonaggression, cooperation, and even, at times, nurtur[e]."[42] Not only did the representation of a non-militarized or deficient masculinity as Asian start earlier than Locke suggests, but the dominant US society's representations of Asian masculinity through Hollywood are also more nuanced than Locke's analysis implies. The title of Locke's own article—"The White Man's Bruce Lee," a phrase used by the film's stunt coordinator to describe Pitt's performance in *Fight Club*—shows that Hollywood is not necessarily one-dimensional in its understanding and rendering of Asian masculinity.

Again, men of Asian ancestry with a hyper- or even militarized masculinity can already be seen on the silver screen in anti-Japanese Second World War movies like *God Is My Co-Pilot* (1945). The difference between twentieth and twenty-first century Hollywood is less the nature and more the level of threat that Asian bodies pose to the US national body. In addition to a deficient masculinity, which might corrupt and soften US masculinity, Asians (particularly Koreans) now might also embody a hyper-militarized masculinity to declare war on not only the outlying harbors but also the continental US (*Red Dawn*) and even the heart of the US government (*Olympus Has Fallen*). Yet what has been consistent over the decades and across the centuries is the dominant US society's concern with masculinity in general and its emphasis on a macho or militarized masculinity in particular. Also consistent has been the need for Asian American men to develop a masculinity that is *not* deficient but devoted to the US, despite the danger of death, if they are to become legitimate members of the citizenry.[43]

Christian Martyrdom and the Role of Religion

The movie *God Is My Co-Pilot*, made during and about the Second World War, provides me with a perfect transition to talk about the connections between religion and conditional citizenship for Asians through US military service. This movie is based on the autobiography of a fighter pilot. While flying with a Christian priest, the protagonist fighter pilot is taught a prayer, which the priest had heard from another fighter pilot. The prayer goes:

> They who hath scorned the thought of any strength,
> Except their own to lean on, learned at length,
> How fear can sabotage the bravest heart.

> When human weakness answers to the prod of terror…calls,
> "Help us Oh, God!"
> Then silence lets the Silent Voice be heard,
> Bringing its message like a spoken word:
> "Believe, believe in me."
> "Cast out your fear."
> "Oh, I'm not up there in the sky,
> But here, right here in your heart.
> I am the strength you seek."
> Believe!
> And they believed!

The function of the prayer is pedagogical. It is meant to teach the protagonist not to put his faith in only himself or in luck. However, it assumes that the Christian God is on the side of the US military. President Dwight Eisenhower, while serving as a five-star general during the Second World War, famously and tellingly compared the war to a "crusade."[44] In her work on the "Cold War" era, Angela M. Lahr argues that US national identity became more and more closely connected with Christianity during this time to "combat perceived and real threats" and to laud "patriotism and cultural bias."[45] Not only was the phrase "under God" added to the pledge of allegiance in 1954, but a proposal to build a "memorial to God" in Washington, D.C. was also made by President Lyndon Johnson a decade later. In the words of one supporter, this memorial would show that "The God of our American heritage is the Judeo-Christian God of the Bible."[46]

The coming together of Christianity, militarism, and US national identity during threats of war helps explain US support for the Chinese nationalist leader, Jiang Jieshi, before the Second World War and all through the "Cold War." Jiang was not an immigrant to or a resident of the US. He was, however, not only a military general fighting against Chinese communists and the Japanese, but also a Christian convert; not to mention the fact that he married Soong Mei-ling, a Chinese Christian woman who was educated in the US. In fact, the Women's Army Corps recruited a unit of Asian American women to serve in the Air Forces during the Second World War, known as the Madame Jiang Jieshi unit.[47] Jiang was so popular that he appeared on the cover of Luce's *Time* magazine ten times between the 1920s and the 1950s. His experience basically shows what it takes for an Asian man to find acceptance in the US, especially during times of war.

Within the dominant and popular cultural ethos of the US, there are connections between (1) militarism and masculinity, (2) militarism and Christianity, and (3) masculinity and Christianity. It has been reported that *Fight Club* is the favorite movie for members of one of the largest Christian churches in the US.[48] More importantly, for my purposes here, risking one's life to prove one's love and loyalty defines a martyr within the Christian tradition. Martyrdom—dying like a *man*—is the way to show or prove one's loyalty to the Christian God, and thus also to a so-called Christian nation. Daniel Boyarin contrasts a Jewish cultural system, which emphasizes a "feminized" trickster figure like Jacob to characterize, among others, "antiphallic modes of resistance," with "Romanized Christianity." Romanized Christianity has produced "the predilections of our own culture toward 'manly' *virtus* and *honestas*" with its (mostly? almost?) univocal glorification of martyrdom as "a centrally valorized practice."[49] Since Boyarin is a Jewish scholar working and living in the US, I take his emphatic use of the first-person plural pronoun in this quote—"our own"—as a reference to US culture. Attitudes and discourses concerning martyrdom become, for Boyarin, "the greatest cultural difference between rabbinic Judaism and the [Christian] church," as it differentiates a faith or religion as something to "love by" *or* "die for," despite the shared culture, twin births, and sibling rivalries of Judaism and Christianity.[50]

In addition, Boyarin suggests that the Christian emphasis on martyrdom itself underwent a change during late antiquity: from being the undesirable result of refusing to do something negative or unacceptable (e.g., bowing down to an idol), giving one's life as a martyr—what Boyarin calls "dying for God"—became not only a consummation of love but also a sign of divine grace and favor.[51] This kind of martyrdom, one that becomes "the highest of spiritual experiences" as well as a "spiritual requirement," has in many ways become a Christian ideal.[52] Christians are supposed to love God more than life itself, and martyrdom is the proof. After all, as *Actes and Monuments* (also known as *The Book of Martyrs*) by the sixteenth-century English hagiographer John Foxe betrays, martyrdom—in a way that is reminiscent of classicist Page duBois's argument about torture—is often taken to be a means to authenticate "truth," and thus "a test, a trial to determine whether something [or someone] is genuine or real."[53]

Martyrdom as an exemplary and eroticized Christian fulfillment of a need or a test requirement, I argue, contributes to the cultural ethos and practice that establish military service as proof of patriotism and hence condition of citizenship for Asian Americans, especially in the context of US militarism. According to Candida Moss, Christianity in late antiquity had already developed a tradition of military martyrs on how soldiers might be related to Christian martyrdom.[54] As non-Christians, soldiers were first witnesses to and then converted by martyrdom of Christians (such as the centurion who witnesses Jesus' crucifixion in Mark 15:39, Matthew 27:54, and Luke 23:47). As (Christian) soldiers, they were still within the chains of command of the Roman and Byzantine military, which required soldiers to perform acts such as swearing allegiance to the emperor or offering sacrifice for the emperor. As Christians, however, these same soldiers found themselves within a church that forbade them to perform such acts. Thus, Christian soldiers were more likely to find themselves in conflict with such orders, and as a result martyred for their Christian faith. As Boyarin suggests, these martyrdom stories "have enormous impact on social practice and the molding of subjectivities."[55] We can see, for example, in Elizabeth Castelli's *Martydom and Memory* that these cultural stories—of how Jesus and his early followers died—and the memories of them have led to particular readings of the Columbine High School shooting years ago, even though that tragedy had absolutely nothing to do with early Christian martyrdom.[56]

Moreover, this "molding of subjectivities" actually involves the shaping of "social, physical, and political bodies."[57] In other words, ideologies of martyrdom work to construct identity, community (including the national community), and race.[58] Let us not forget that these constructions of identity, community, and race are not only boundaries to differentiate between who belongs and who does not belong, but also reality about who is right and who is wrong. Martyrs are often assumed to be victims who lost their lives for a noble cause, and martyrdom is assumed to be the Christian ideal. By embracing or claiming Christianity as its cultural ethos—including martyrdom in the form of a Christian ideal—the dominant US society within a context of US militarism is able to justify US aggression in Asia, as well as against Asian raced bodies both inside and outside the US. Going back to Pratt's "anti-conquest strategy" in my discussion of *Olympus Has Fallen* and *Red Dawn*, one way of justifying US aggression is by depicting other people as perpetrators and persecutors.[59] Martyrdom in US society, like militarism and masculinism, is a path for seizing and securing cultural and political power.

René Girard has, of course, famously proposed that Jesus and his gospel are meant to put an end to the system of sacrifice and violence, and that a "sacrificial reading" of Jesus' death is a misreading to be rejected.[60] Misreading is, however, still a reading, and this reading is already found within the New Testament, as Girard's own work admits. Mel Gibson's *The Passion of the Christ* (2004), which grossed over 370 million at the US box office alone, demonstrates the prevalence and popularity of this reading. This very violent and bloody movie by a traditionalist Catholic with allegedly racist views about Jesus' heroic—that is, masculinist—suffering and sacrifice as a loyal and faithful martyr of and for God was nominated for three Oscars and won that year's People's Choice award for Favorite Dramatic Motion Picture.

Be-Longing and In-Gesting

Gus Lee's two autobiographical fictions *China Boy* (1991) and *Honor and Duty* (1994) are also popular cultural works. These two novels, set in the context of a post–Second World War US, illustrate well the dynamics that I am trying to explore and expose, despite their lack of cultural power vis-à-vis Hollywood movies. Although they have not been turned into movies, Lee has his Chinese American protagonist, Kai Ting, articulate that "movies are like truth."[61] He then links Kai's knowing of US history with his watching of US movies through Kai's father: Kai's father, "to introduce [his children] to American culture, got the family hooked on the cinema."[62] As a result, Kai often compares people he meets with actors he has seen in movies. Kai talks about how US movies "emasculated Chinese" and create a world "where good guys carried guns and won every ninety minutes."[63] In other words, the truth found in US cinemas is partly the masculinism and militarism of US society. In *China Boy*, Kai, a sensitive and frail seven-year-old, learns boxing to finally stand up to his oppressive white stepmother, who torments and forces him to give up everything Chinese. In fact, this novel ends with a simple but telling dialogue in the final confrontation between these two characters:

> "You—you would raise your fist—to—to your *mother*?" she cried.
> I kept my guard up. "You not my Mah-mee!" I said. "*I ain't fo' yo' pickin-on, no mo'!*"[64]

The intentional use of black vernacular is significant here, of course, in light of our earlier discussion of African American (hyper-)masculinity by way of Locke and Mailer.[65] In fact, Kai's transformation is facilitated not only by African American men but also through boxing lessons at a local YMCA (Young Men's Christian Association), which is, however directly or indirectly, linked to Christianity.

In Lee's sequel, *Honor and Duty*, the representation of Kai's assimilation challenge as an "American" has shifted from his white stepmother to West Point. A grown-up Kai enrolls as a cadet to fulfill his parents' wishes and finds "uniforms that made everyone look alike."[66] Kai's father, Lee writes, "had given [Kai] to Edna [i.e., Kai's white stepmother] to make [Kai] American…[and] had pointed [Kai] to [West Point] to give [Kai] true American citizenship."[67] While West Point is somewhat like Edna,[68] it is also different. For example, the boxing skills that Kai has learned back home are not necessarily transferrable to or helpful for his new challenge. As his new boxing coach at West Point tells him, "Skills ain't the ticket here. The Point just wants a guy who'll wade in for blood";[69] as a result, anytime someone in the boxing ring "back[s] up at the Point, ya lose."[70] West Point, in other words, is even more masculine than the (assumed) hyper-masculinity of the (African American) "hood."

Just as in *China Boy*, Lee's Kai makes a point to connect Christianity with masculinity and the military. At West Point, all meals are "preceded by prayer," but religion there is restricted to "Protestant, Catholic, or Jewish."[71] In addition, most cadets are Protestants.[72] West Point is "the unattainable dream" for Kai's father because of his foreign nativity.[73] Still, Kai's father substantiates his view about the gallantry of US soldiers by how they would "[e]at last, sleep last, up hill first, die first."[74] Major Schwarzhedd, Kai's lone sympathetic white male mentor and model figure in the novel, presents the ministry and the military as "two noble professions" that "require leadership."[75] Despite the macho demands at West Point and the dissuasion of his Chinese uncle and sister—even with the traditional saying about "good boys not becoming soldiers"[76]—Kai soon becomes enamored by the culture. He thinks that at West Point, "suffering had a purpose and hunger made [him] feel noble…proving [his] patriotism as a measure of self," and he entertains the idea that a soldier's life is "the price" for "the highest value"; it is "a sacrifice" for honor "at all costs."[77]

However, Kai fails to complete his studies at West Point because of his deficient performance in electrical engineering. Having to leave this "place of honor and of belonging," Kai becomes a drill sergeant in the army but feels "orphaned by West Point, the parent [he] would always love, and always miss."[78] Just as he feels orphaned by his birth parents and his white stepmother, Kai seems destined to continue longing to belong, even at the end of the novel. Could his desire to be "all-American" be fulfilled only by graduating and being sent out to Vietnam to risk his life alongside his West Point classmates?[79]

In addition to showing how conditional citizenship for Asian American men is based on a less-than-holy trinity of masculinism, militarism, and martyrdom, Lee's novel also opens a window for us to see why a minoritized population might continue to support or even promote the US military. Although Lee's comment refers to African Americans, it applies to Asian Americans as well: "[I]ts members had offered too many sons and fathers to the [US military], for patriotism and in the hope of equality, to decry it."[80] Perhaps that is also why Lee makes the point that most cadets are not only Protestants but also "children of World War II veterans."[81]

Setsu Shigematsu and Keith L. Camacho have amply demonstrated that the developments of militarism (and masculinism) in "Asia and the Pacific" are inextricably linked to the region's imperial history involving the US.[82] Jin-Kyung Lee makes a similar but more elaborated argument regarding South Korea.[83] I would venture to add that the same might be said of many North Koreans and likely a good portion of the Asian American population. For example, to imitate and cultivate the white masculinism and militarism of the US, both North and South Korea have had mandatory military service required of all men, with such military service serving, in turn, as a basis and justification for giving men even more advantages and privileges in Korean societies.[84] There is hence a third meaning of conditional citizenship for Asian Americans. Besides the willingness to kill and be killed by joining the US military when the conditions of the US need and desire such selective inclusion, Asian Americans might also be *conditioned* or colonized to incorporate the militaristic/masculinist ethos and internalize the martyr complex of the dominant US culture.[85]

Similarly Conditioned, Dissimilar Consequences

From Okada's *No-No Boy* and Lee's *China Boy* to the teenage Wolverines and Corporal Smith of *Red Dawn*, I see a conditional citizenship for Asian Americans that has been consistently at work for at least the last 70 to 80 years. This constancy exists despite ethnic shifts from Chinese to Japanese to Korean, and the geographical shift between warfare on "foreign" and US soil. This longer view enables us to see how this conditional citizenship relates to not only race but also generation and gender. The use of the noun *boy* in both Okada's and Lee's novel, as well as the ability of a make-shift band of teenagers to wreck havoc on the North Korean soldiers in *Red Dawn*, indicates that US citizenship represents maturity and adulthood. Most Asians cannot attain this maturity and adulthood until or unless they literally transform themselves through the donning of a US military uniform and participation in "patriotic" warfare to protect and expand the interests of the US, as Choi/Corporal Smith does in *Red Dawn*.

As noted earlier, the Wolverines in *Red Dawn* include "kids" from different races (except Asian), several of whom lost their lives in their "resistance" effort. As a Japanese American Vietnam veteran writes, "We send our teenagers to kill…kids, too young to comprehend the political forces that have sacrificed their lives and too fully indoctrinated to turn back, wounded and dead before they can finish growing up."[86] These young Wolverines are of both genders, and gender, as the movie shows, is not a discriminating factor when it comes to death in combat. The ideas or ideals of masculinism, militarism, and martyrdom are, in states of exception, applicable to and needed for women as well as for teens, thus once again proving that the exception shows the rule. While we do not see Asian or Asian American women joining and dying in military combat in this movie, the portrayal and hence ideology of Asian raced women sacrificing and dying out of love for a white male is pervasive and thus readily transferrable to incorporate women into the cultural logics of patriotic martyrdom for the US.[87] Women's need to submit to male authority and sacrifice their lives for the country is more explicitly affirmed in *Olympus Has Fallen*. Lim (Malana Lea), the female technological expert who works for and under the terrorist villain, ends up losing her life deservedly but not heroically because she fights for the wrong cause and wrong country.[88] The US Secretary of Defense, who is played by a white female actor (Melissa Leo), has to be brave and strong enough to endure some severe kicks and blows from the North Korean terrorist like a manly military man.[89] Even though she is willing to die to protect her part of the nuclear launch code, she has to obey the white male President's order and give her code to Kang. When she is subsequently dragged out by the enemies to face what is likely an execution, she does not cite the Lord's Prayer or, as Jesus does on the cross in Mark's Gospel, cry out to God (Mark 15:34); instead, she tellingly recites the US Pledge of Allegiance. As far as the movie's portrayal is concerned, there is no question regarding her patriotism, her fitness to be a citizen, and her obedience to her male superior.

The condition of necropolitical labor through military engagement that is created for Asian Americans might, therefore, be applicable to different age groups and genders of the nation's white population, especially in "exceptional" conditions. We see plenty of white males killing *and* dying for the US in both *Olympus Has Fallen* and *Red Dawn* (including the protagonist played by Hemsworth), as well as in Gus Lee's story when West Point graduates are deployed to Vietnam. In other words, those of the dominant culture can be both promoters and victims of conditional citizenship. However, there is one more revealing message in *Olympus Has Fallen* that confirms Jin-Kyung Lee's suggestion that necropolitical labor, like military service and engagement, is often also "surrogate/prosthetic labor," which "enables someone else to live" on the basis of a "hierarchy of race, class, and gender."[90] The white female Secretary of Defense lives despite what looks like her certain demise, but the Latino Vice President of the US is killed. Death also becomes inevitable for an unnamed white female White House staff, as well as numerous males—both white and black—who attempt in their roles as Secret Service agents or military men to protect or take back the White House. *Olympus Has Fallen* betrays how race, class, and gender are negotiated for minoritized subjects through its decision on who lives and who dies. Race/ethnicity often trumps gender and class for minoritized subjects and makes their lives disposable. In addition, lower-class white males—like racially/ethnically minoritized subjects—are more vulnerable to becoming "necropolitical" and "surrogate" laborers. As such, they must risk or give their lives so that people like the white female Secretary, the white male President, and the President's young son may live.

One of the white males who dies in this movie is the former Secret Service agent who had become a private security contractor. He became a turncoat for the North Koreans by offering them details about the White House security setup to facilitate the terrorist takeover. When the US President chides him for betraying his country for money, he becomes enraged. He countercharges the President for selling out to Wall Street to get elected, and wants to fight or hit the President but is restrained by the North Koreans. In another scene, the President is horrified and expresses disbelief when the North Koreans shot the anonymous white female White House staff in the head. In response, the turncoat agent says to the President, "There is a reason I did not vote for you."

These scenes seem to suggest that this agent sees the President as lacking in principle and being soft. In other words, the President is not strong and masculine enough. As John F. Kennedy's assassination reminds us, there are US citizens who do not believe the US can ever appear weak by compromising or making deals with "enemies"; militarism is for them the way to show its muscles and strength.[91] While the turncoat agent's mention of his vote (and hence the democratic system of public election) may imply that this hired gun (so literally a surrogate and necropolitical laborer) sees himself in some way as equal to the President, he is not. In the end, the one he fights is not the President but another necropolitical and surrogate laborer: Butler's super agent. The turncoat agent loses the fight and his life, but the President is saved and resumes his office.

Conclusion

When Kang, the chief North Korean villain, says to the US President in *Olympus Has Fallen*, "I have read *your* Bible…" (emphasis mine), he underscores two things. First, Christianity as a religion provides "the cultural preconditions of the public" in US society.[92] Second, people of Asian ancestry are racialized as non-Christian "pagans" or "heathens" (even though neither white people nor US society can monopolize the Bible). The Christian idea(l) of martyrdom, US masculinism, and militarism works in ways that inform and reinforce each other, but its appeal no longer needs to be explicitly "Christian"; it also does not only appeal to Christians. With this trinity of US culture and the facilitation of all kinds of cultural work, a US military uniform can signify Americanization and military service eligibility for citizenship for those of Asian ancestry. When it fits the state's goals and interests, however, this cultural ethos also demands a subset of the nation's population—not only people of color but also lower-class whites of both genders and various ages—to serve as necropolitical and surrogate laborers whose potentially premature deaths work to ensure the life and privileges of others. Through various novels and movies, conditional citizenship as a form of US imperialistic interpellation calls out to condition its subjects; depending on the conditions of the US society and one's condition within the US society; however, conditional citizenship may also have different meanings and contrasting consequences for different persons.

Notes

1. Keith Hopkins, "Novel Evidence for Roman Slavery," *Past and Present* 138 (1993): 3–27 (6).
2. George Lipsitz has also argued that modern US popular culture after the Second World War contains and creates a collective social memory; see *Time Passages: Collective Memory and American Popular Culture* (Minneapolis: University of Minnesota Press, 1990). We must not forget, of course, the late Edward Said's point that imperial power depends on cultural work, and that cultural work is always-already embedded in political and imperial relations; see *Culture and Imperialism* (New York: Alfred A. Knopf, 1993).
3. Antoine Fuqua, interviewed by Caitlin Hughes, "Why Antoine Fuqua Played with Action Figures for 'Olympus Has Fallen'?" *Film School Rejects*, March 21, 2013, http://filmschoolrejects.com/features/why-antoine-fuqua-played-with-action-figures-for-olympus-has-fallen.php.
4. Quoted in Mireille Rosello, *Postcolonial Hospitality: The Immigrant as Guest* (Stanford: Stanford University Press, 2001), 165.
5. This is similar and indebted to Eve Kosofsky Sedgwick's suggestion that differentiating a population into two binary groups by sexuality (heterosexuals against homosexuals) might have effects on not only gays and lesbians but also "people across the spectrum of sexualities"; see *Epistemology of the Closet* (Berkeley: University of California Press, 1990), 1.
6. Henry R. Luce, "The American Century," in *The Ambiguous Legacy: US Foreign Relations in the "American Century,"* ed. Michael J. Hogan, (New York: Cambridge University Press, 1999), 11–29 [original, 1941].
7. Christina Klein, *Cold War Orientalism: Asia in the Middlebrow Imagination, 1945–1961* (Berkeley: University of California Press, 2003), 3–9.
8. Heonik Kwon, *The Other Cold War* (New York: Columbia University Press, 2010).
9. See George Orwell, "You and the Atom Bomb," *Tribune*, October 19, 1945.
10. Kwon, *The Other Cold War*, 16. Similarly, Jin-Kyung Lee uses a different adjective and a plural noun—the "hot wars"—to refer to the "anti-Communist" warfare of the US in East and Southeast Asia and how these wars led to the economic domination that the US continues to enjoy and exploit in these regions of the world; see *Service Economies: Militarism, Sex Work, and Migrant Labor in South Korea* (Minneapolis: University of Minnesota Press, 2010, 1). The rest of Lee's book is then devoted to detailing numerous linkages between militarism and globalized capitalism in the so-called development of South Korea. The story of how its involvement in the Second World War helped move the US out of an economic depression is well known, so one should never lose sight of the military–industrial complex and its long

history for the last 70 years. See, for example, Gregory Hooks, *Forging the Military-Industrial Complex: World War II's Battle of the Potomac* (Urbana: University of Illinois Press, 1991); Christina D. Romer, "What Ended the Great Depression?" *The Journal of Economic History* 52 (1992): 757–784; and Paul A. C. Koistinen, *Arsenal of World War II: The Political Economy of American Warfare, 1940–1945* (Lawrence: University Press of Kansas, 2004).

11. Mary Louise Pratt, *Imperial Eyes: Travel Writing and Transculturation* (New York: Routledge, 1992), 7. One might arguably use *anti-Communist* as a synonym or parallel term for Pratt's *anti-conquest* strategies in discussing the role of the US in the "Cold War." That is to say, since the 1940s, communism has been the culprit or cover which legitimizes US policies of expansion.
12. See Russell C. Leong and Don T. Nakanishi, eds., *Asian Americans on War and Peace* (Los Angeles: UCLA Asian American Studies Center, 2002), 53–104.
13. Lisa Sun-Hee Park, *Consuming Citizenship: Children of Asian Immigrant Entrepreneurs* (Stanford: Stanford University Press, 2005).
14. Christine So, *Economic Citizens: A Narrative of Asian American Visibility* (Philadelphia: Temple University Press, 2007).
15. John S. W. Park, *Elusive Citizenship: Immigration, Asian Americans, and the Paradox of Civil Rights* (New York: New York University Press, 2004).
16. Nadia Y. Kim, *Imperial Citizens: Koreans and Race from Seoul to LA* (Stanford: Stanford University Press, 2008).
17. Juliana Chang, *Inhuman Citizenship: Traumatic Enjoyment and Asian American Literature* (Minneapolis: University of Minnesota Press, 2012).
18. This operation by (selective) inclusion is the premise for a politics of recognition; together, they work to keep racialized Others within the trap of trying to appropriate and assimilate into a self-sufficient, transparent, and European subjectivity. See Denise Ferreira de Silva, *Toward a Global Idea of Race* (Minneapolis: University of Minnesota Press, 2007). I am indebted to Andrea (Andy) Smith for introducing and recommending this book to me. Note that de Silva's exploration of racialization emphasizes both historical and global—that is, a temporal and a spatial—dimensions, as my chapter is also attempting to highlight.
19. For racial dynamics focusing on African Americans during the Second World War, see Daniel Kryder, *Divided Arsenal: Race and the American State During World War II* (New York: Cambridge University Press, 2001); and Kevin M. Kruse and Stephen Tuck, eds., *Fog of War: The Second World War and the Civil Rights Movement* (New York: Oxford University Press, 2012).
20. K. Scott Wong, *Americans First: Chinese Americans and the Second World War* (Philadelphia: Temple University Press, 2005), 175.
21. Wong, *Americans First*, 58.

22. See Judith Bellafaire, "Asian-Pacific-American Servicewomen in Defense of a Nation," http://www.womensmemorial.org/Education/APA.html.
23. Donald L. Chu, personal communication quoted in Wong, *Americans First*, 123.
24. Mae Ngai, *Impossible Subjects: Illegal Aliens and the Making of Modern America* (Princeton: Princeton University Press, 2003). Ngai shows that laws, even or especially immigration laws, often work to racialize bodies. Ngai also affirms the importance of taking a long view of things, as her book covers roughly three decades of immigration history (1924–1965).
25. See, for example, Wong, *Americans First*, 112–118.
26. See, for example, Angelo N. Ancheta, "Filipino Americans, Foreigner Discrimination, and the Lines of Racial Sovereignty," in Antonio T. Tiongson, Jr., Edgardo V. Gutierrez, and Ricardo V. Gutierrez, eds., *Positively No Filipinos Allowed: Building Communities and Discourse* (Philadelphia: Temple University Press, 2006), 97–99.
27. John Okada, *No-No Boy* (Seattle: University of Washington Press, 1976).
28. Takashi Fujitani, "Right to Kill, Right to Make Live: Koreans as Japanese as Americans During WWII," *Representations* 99 (2007): 13–39 (22, 34, 23, 13–14). Provocatively, Fujitani's article parallels US treatment of Japanese Americans with Japan's treatment of Koreans as "targets of bio-power and governmentality" during this same historical period of war (28).
29. Fujitani, "Right to Kill," 30.
30. Ibid.
31. Quoted in Fujitani, "Right to Kill," 33.
32. War and militarism have a different connection with another group of Asian Americans. Many persons of Southeast Asian—especially Vietnamese and Hmong—ancestry were granted immigrant status in the US as refugees of the "Cold War," partly or even largely because many had also fought in "secret" armies alongside the US military during the seemingly never-ending Vietnam War. Mimi Thi Nguyen focuses on those of Vietnamese ancestry and suggests (with Foucault's ideas of bio-power and governmentality and alongside Jacques Derrida's work on the gift and hospitality) that the so-called salvation, freedom, and opportunities, which the US provides for these refugees, are part of an exchange economy. This exchange comes with a condition attached: they are supposed to repay their "debt" and prove themselves to be "gift-worthy" by being politically conservative; see *The Gift of Freedom: War, Debt, and Other Refugee Passages* (Durham: Duke University Press, 2012). See also Yen Le Espiritu, *Body Counts: The Vietnam War and Militarized Refugees* (Berkeley: University of California Press, 2014). In other words, US citizenship for these Asian Americans is no less conditional than for Chinese Americans and Japanese Americans. Of course, ideas of gift and salvation are deeply religious, or even theological, but that is another topic for another time and another article.

Note that South Asian Americans are also not exempted from the realities and legacies of war and militarism. According to Susan Koshy, the South Asian diaspora is "embedded" in "three major world-historical forces that have shaped global modernity: capitalism, colonialism, and nationalism"; see "Introduction," in Susan Koshy and R. Radhakrishnan, eds., *Transnational South Asians: The Making of a Neodiaspora* (New York: Oxford University Press, 2008, 3). The connection between militarism and colonialism, as well as nationalism, should need no explanation; the same is true of capitalism, if one remembers the military–industrial complex I mentioned earlier.

Although my paragraph on and through Fujitani's work emphasizes what has been done to Japanese Americans, it should not be read as a denial or dismissal of Japanese American agency and resistance. For examples of Japanese American working and struggling for justice during and after the war years, see Roger Daniels, *The Japanese American Cases: The Rule of Law in Time of War* (Lawrence: University of Kansas Press, 2013).

33. Lee, *Service Economies*, 5–6.
34. Klein, *Cold War Orientalism*, 11.
35. Ruth Wilson Gilmore, *Golden Gulag: Prisons, Surplus, Crisis, and Opposition in Globalizing California* (Berkeley: University of California Press, 2007), 28.
36. Kristin L. Hoganson, *Fighting for American Manhood: How Gender Politics Provoked the Spanish-American and Philippine-American Wars* (New Haven: Yale University Press, 1998).
37. Brian Locke, "'The White Man's Bruce Lee': Race and the Construction of White Masculinity in David Fincher's *Fight Club* (1999)," *Journal of Asian American Studies* 17 (2014): 61–89. This understanding that corporations and consumerism—in sum, capitalism—weaken US masculinity is rather interesting to pursue in light of the arguments by Jin-Kyung Lee that I mentioned previously about militarism/masculinity and capitalism as twin developments in both the US and South Korea. What we have here ideologically speaking, I suggest, is a circular dynamic, which turns out to be mutually reinforcing and perpetuating: if militarism facilitates capitalist developments and capitalist developments weaken masculinity, then society needs to emphasize and reinforce masculinity/militarism, which will in turn weaken masculinity and demand the reemphasis of masculinity/militarism, and on and on it goes and continues.
38. Locke, "'The White Man's Bruce Lee,'" 63–64, 82–84.
39. See, for example, David L. Eng, *Racial Castration: Managing Masculinity in Asian America* (Durham: Duke University Press, 2001); and Daniel Y. Kim, *Writing Manhood in Black and Yellow: Ralph Ellison, Frank Chin, and the Literary Politics of Identity* (Stanford: Stanford University Press, 2005).
40. Locke, "'The White Man's Bruce Lee,'" 74. See Norman Mailer, *The White Negro* (San Francisco: City Lights Books, 1957).

41. Karen Kuo, *East Is West and West Is East: Gender, Culture, and Interwar Encounters Between Asia and America* (Philadelphia: Temple University Press, 2013), 97–137.
42. Kuo, *East Is West and West Is East*, 99.
43. My statement about the twentieth century and my admittedly quick movements between the Second World War and the "Cold War" years are not meant to suggest that changes, especially how and how much masculinity and militarism were being emphasized, did not take place over the decades. Nevertheless, it is telling that the Chinese American protagonist—Wang Ben Loy—in Louis Chu's *Eat a Bowl of Tea* (New York: Carol Publishing Group, 1961; movie version, 1989) is a military veteran from the Second World War. In spite or perhaps because of developing a habit of visiting (white) prostitutes with his fellow soldiers, Wang suddenly finds himself struggling with sexual impotence in his marriage to a Chinese woman after the war. Given the context of Chu's writing and that of the story he wrote, this change in Wang might be read as implying the need for Chinese or Asian American men to find a new way to demonstrate and establish their masculinity with the ending of the Second World War and the beginning of the "Cold War." For a helpful reading of another novel, which was made into a musical, as well as a movie, in the same time period—C. Y. Lee's *Flower Drum Song* (New York: Penguin, 2002 [original, 1957]; musical, 1958; movie, 1961)—with particular emphases on the beginning of the "Cold War" as a context and the very beginning of the model minority construction for Asian Americans, see David Palumbo-Liu, *Asian/American: Historical Crossings of a Racial Frontier* (Stanford: Stanford University Press, 1999), 156–170.
44. Dwight D. Eisenhower, *Crusade in Europe: Personal Account of World War II* (New York: Doubleday & Company, 1948).
45. Angela M. Lahr, *Millennial Dreams and Apocalyptic Nightmares: The Cold War Origins of Political Evangelicalism* (New York: Oxford University Press, 2007), 65, 81.
46. Cited in Lahr, *Millennial Dreams and Apocalyptic Nightmares*, 66.
47. See Bellafaire, "Asian-Pacific-American Servicewomen."
48. Molly Worthen, "Who Would Jesus Smack Down?" *The New York Times*, January 6, 2009, http://www.nytimes.com/2009/01/11/magazine/11punk-t.html?pagewanted=all.
49. Daniel Boyarin, *Dying for God: Martyrdom and the Making of Christianity and Judaism* (Stanford: Stanford University Press, 1999), 49, 57, 101. Other scholars have also emphasized a diversity of views about martyrdom among early Christians in the first two centuries. See, for example, Elaine Pagels and Karen L. King, *Reading Judas: The Gospel of Judas and the Shaping of Christianity* (New York: Viking, 2007), 59–98; and Candida R. Moss, *Ancient Christian Martyrdom: Diverse Practices, Theologies, and Traditions* (New Haven: Yale University Press, 2012).

50. Boyarin, *Dying for God*, 65, 73.
51. Ibid., 95–96, 107.
52. Ibid., 107, 114.
53. Page duBois, *Torture and Truth* (New York: Routledge, 1991), 11. For a discussion of Foxe's book, see Moss, *Ancient Christian Martyrdom*, 163; though Moss does not make the connection between martyrdom and torture as I do here.
54. Candida R. Moss, *The Other Christs: Imitating Jesus in Ancient Christian Ideologies of Martyrdom* (New York: Oxford University Press), 69–73.
55. Boyarin, *Dying for God*, 116.
56. Elizabeth A. Castelli, *Martyrdom and Memory: Early Christian Culture Making* (New York: Columbia University Press, 2004).
57. Moss, *Ancient Christian Martyrdom*, 167.
58. While Moss's "physical body" refers only to "bodily experiences such as pain, hunger, fasting, grief, and joy" (*Ancient Christian Martyrdom*, 166), I would feature race as the common and thus constructed understanding and practice to categorize humans by physical—that is, bodily—traits, such as skin color and facial features.
59. See Candida R. Moss, *The Myth of Persecution: How Early Christians Invented a Story of Martyrdom* (New York: HarperOne, 2013), 249–255.
60. René Girard, *Things Hidden Since the Foundation of the World*, trans. Stephen Bann and Michael Metteer (Stanford: Stanford University Press, 1987).
61. Gus Lee, *Honor and Duty* (New York: Ivy Books, 1994), 56.
62. Gus Lee, *China Boy: A Novel* (New York: Dutton, 1991), 26. See also Lee, *Honor and Duty*, 106.
63. Lee, *Honor and Duty*, 21, 56.
64. Lee, *China Boy*, 322.
65. Focusing on the writings of two post–Second World War writers—Ralph Ellison and Frank Chin—Daniel Y. Kim argues that to combat a racist "castration," both Ellison and Chin "share…a highly masculinist conception of literature," which becomes (1) homophobic; (2) agonistic to a degree that hinders rather than promotes solidarity between African American and Asian Americans; (3) cannibalistic to appropriate, imitate, or swallow any languages, discourses, or models that they encounter; and (4) ironic with their homosocial desires for white men (*Writing Manhood in Black and Yellow*, xvii). I cannot help but think that Kim's arguments are helpful to think about Lee's work, given (1) Kai's insatiable appetite for food throughout his growth and development (e.g., Lee, *China Boy*, 2, 242; Lee, *Honor and Duty*, 13, 180, 209, 211, 365), (2) Kai's less than satisfactory relationship with two female romantic interests (Lee, *Honor and Duty*, 179–186, 402–403, 422), and (3) Kai's shift from forming a kind of brotherhood with and learning from African Americans in a black neighborhood in *China Men* to losing contact with his African American buddies and attending West

Point with a mainly white cadet population in *Honor and Duty*. I am, however, less sure if Lee ever, as Chin does, makes male homosexuality *the* signifier for racial inauthenticity or betrayal.

66. Lee, *Honor and Duty*, 31.
67. Ibid., 215.
68. Ibid., 78.
69. Ibid., 112.
70. Ibid., 111.
71. Ibid., 212, 12.
72. Ibid., 54.
73. Ibid., 363.
74. Ibid., 45.
75. Ibid., 365.
76. Ibid., 29–30, 106.
77. Ibid., 87, 281.
78. Ibid., 6, 383.
79. Ibid., 382.
80. Ibid., 391.
81. Ibid., 54–55.
82. Setsu Shigematsu and Keith L. Camacho, eds., *Militarized Currents: Toward a Decolonized Future in Asia and the Pacific* (Minneapolis: University of Minnesota Press, 2010).
83. Lee, *Service Economies*, 21–30, 37–77.
84. I am indebted to Anne Joh and Nami Kim for bringing this to my attention. Because of continuing gender discrimination in terms of employment possibility and pay scale, more and more women in South Korea are seeing military service as an avenue for social and economic mobility; see http://www.koreabang.com/2013/stories/korean-women-flock-to-military-careers.html. Regarding women in North Korean military, see, for example, http://www.dailymail.co.uk/news/article-2381052/Kim-Jong-Uns-mini-skirted-robot-army-North-Koreas-female-soldiers.html.
85. See Palumbo-Liu's argument that Maxine Hong Kingston's *Tripmaster Monkey: His Fake Book* (New York: Knopf, 1989), given its plot setting in the "Cold War" era of the 1960s, involves Hong Kingston's own reconsideration of Asian American subjectivity in light of nuclear militarism (*Asian/American*, 400–407).
86. Michael F. Yamamoto, "Stop the Bombing, Stop the War," in Russell C. Leong and Don T. Nakanishi, eds., *Asian Americans On War and Peace* (Los Angeles: UCLA Asian American Studies Center Press, 2002), 189–191 (191).
87. Yen Le Espiritu gives *Madame Butterfly* and its contemporary version, *Miss Saigon*, as examples of this popular and pervasive narrative and cultural logic; see "Ideological Racism and Cultural Resistance: Constructing Our Own Images," in Alma M. Garcia, ed., *Contested Images: Women of Color in*

Popular Culture (Lanham: AltaMira, 2012), 2–26 (12–13). While the opera *Madame Butterfly* has been adapted into a movie more than once, the musical *Miss Saigon* has not yet appeared on the silver screen, despite a long-running rumor that this is about to take place. Gina Marchetti looks at two movies, *China Gate* and *The Lady from Yesterday*, as conflated and updated versions of both the Pocahontas and Butterfly narratives, and proposes that these interracial heterosexual romance narratives about an Asian woman and a white man also function to metaphorize and legitimize a masculinized white ruling over a feminized Asian as well as a strong (militarized?) US having and deserving the allegiance of an Asian raced person both within and beyond US soil; see *Romance and the "Yellow Peril": Race, Sex, and Discursive Strategies in Hollywood Fiction* (Berkeley: University of California Press, 1993), 78–108.

Portrayals of women "dying like a man" are understandably tricky for the desire to construct, reinforce, and maintain the superiority of male over female, because they may communicate a kind of "sameness" and "equality" between men and women. Instead, portrayals of women "dying for a man"—with "man" representing not only a white male but also the imperial US—may arguably facilitate the same insidious purposes of empire-building with less risk of compromising any patriarchal principles.

88. Lim's death is not actually portrayed on screen, but can simply be assumed, as all the North Korean terrorists involved in the White House takeover are supposedly killed when the super-agent played by Butler and the US military are able to take back the White House and save the white male President.
89. Many of the early Christian martyrs are women. For example, we have extant writings about the martyrdom of "Perpetua, Felicitas, Blandina, and Thecla but also, if to a lesser extent, Agathonike, Agape, Irene, and Chione" (Moss, *Ancient Christian Martyrdom*, 22).
90. Lee, *Service Economies*, 9, 13–14.
91. Another movie about a terrorist attack on the White House, *White House Down* (2013), was released three months after *Olympus Has Fallen.* While people of Asian ancestry do not play a role in the plot of this movie, the attack is engineered and facilitated by government insiders who disagree with the peace-seeking foreign policies of an African American President (Jamie Foxx). Like *Olympus Has Fallen*, the attack is eventually thwarted and the African American President saved by the bravery and military skills of a white man who used to serve in the US army (Channing Tatum). Both *Olympus Has Fallen* and *White House Down*, like Gus Lee's *Honor and Duty*, seem to affirm the superiority of white masculinity over the (assumed) hyper-masculinity of African Americans.
92. Judith Butler, *Parting Ways: Jewishness and the Critique of Zionism* (New York: Columbia University Press, 2012), 115.

CHAPTER 3

Demilitarizing Haunted Genealogies as Transgenerational Affective Work of the Holy Ghost

Amy R. Barbour

Christian justice and love cannot be imagined apart from exhumation and reparation of hurt bodies and hurt memories. The Christian Bible is itself a vehicle carrying forward the story of a traumatized community's *response-ability* to transfigure a hurt body and to transform the shame and horror of hurt memories into a proclamation of good news.[1] In this regard, Christian sources and theologies are re/sources valuable to the productive work of mourning the proliferating losses associated with the ongoing Korean War and US militarization of South Korea. By re-reading the genealogical recitation in Matthew 1 to see how this pericope works to relate Mary, Joseph, and Jesus to each other within a militarized context, I offer a pneumatological lens for the Korean diaspora[2] to relate to the hurt bodies and hurt memories attached to the militarized figures of the *yanggongju*, US soldier, and Korean War orphan. In so doing I argue that the Holy Ghost configures the *yanggongju*, the US soldier, and the

A.R. Barbour (✉)

N. Kim, W.A. Joh (eds.), *Critical Theology against US Militarism in Asia*,
DOI 10.1057/978-1-137-48013-2_3

Korean War orphan (cum adoptee) into another familial (or kinship) relation within a hypersexualized context of ongoing militarization. In both familial configurations, militarization is simultaneously both the predicate of possibility and barrier to recognition. Christian traditioning deifies[3] the (once) shameful relations connecting Mary, Joseph, and Jesus; while appearing impotent to attribute anything but shameful exclusion to the web of militarized relations constituting the *yanggongju*, the US soldier, and the Korean War orphan as a haunting figural family. However, a close reading of Matthew 1 suggests otherwise by being a material example of how a traumatized community transformed their experiences of shame and secrecy into a narrative of redemption.[4]

Of the genealogies found in the Christian Bible, one of the more complex genealogical recitations occurs in the opening chapter of Matthew. The genealogy in Matthew 1 is not an historical genealogy in the sense that it traces flesh-and-blood genetic lineage. Yet, "even objects that are understood as illusions or fancies have a story to tell, a story that is not independent of the story of those for whom such illusions and fancies are tantalizingly real. A ghostly history may be no more or less real than any other."[5] However real, Matthew 1 introduces an odd type of story. As Anne McClintock observes, "[g]enealogies are presented less as accurate records of family relations than they are records of political power."[6] The political dimension of Matthew 1 is in its not ostensibly previewing gospel as a narrative of triumphant overcoming but as a scandal. The genealogy's surface carries Jesus' pure blood lineage back to Abraham, but its depth harbors Mary's and Joseph's non-normative kinship ties.

Mary is the progeny of four intentionally selected ancestral mothers. The genealogy names Tamar (Genesis 38), Rahab (Joshua 2, 6), Ruth (the Book of Ruth), and "the wife of Uriah" (aka Bathsheba; II Sam 11–12) before naming Mary. A relationship exists among these women; one that connects Mary as *in relation to* and as *a relation of* these other biblical women. As appearing in Matthew, these women figure a genealogy of sexually compromised women[7] within Jesus' bloodline. This overlooked (haunting) genealogy suggests that even while the hetero-patriarchal structure of the patrilineal genealogy purports a kind of genealogical and moral purity, it is much more heterogeneous and complex. As heir, Mary is not only the consummation of her foremothers but, perhaps more powerfully, also their vindication.

A feminist recovery of these female figures involves not only honoring their creativity but also remembering the grave personal losses that triggered their situations of social rupture, which function as the background to their stories.[8] God kills two of Tamar's husbands, and then her father-in-law marginalizes her. War with the Israelites ends in the total liquidation of Rahab's city and people. Ruth's husband dies (causes unknown). David kills Bathsheba's husband, functionally coerces[9] her into sex, and then God kills *their* child as retribution for *David's* infidelity.

These losses function as conversion points (i.e., moments when "potential is converted into threat"[10]). Each of these women's biblical stories includes a moment when she is (further) compromised because of an unauthorized, non-normative relation to sex triggered by a tragic loss, which initially destabilizes her claim to social belonging. The unauthorized, non-normative sexual behavior functions as the means by which these women re-secure their communal belonging. They are doubly compromised by both death and deviation from established norms for gendered behavior.

The women are judged as compromised according to a constitutive pillar of the stories' moral universe—patriarchy (i.e., a social distribution system that confers unwarranted symbolic and material privileges according to a hierarchal logic structured through the binary of man/woman).[11] Each moment of compromise destabilizes communal belonging as some right that can be taken for granted; it is exposed as a privilege mediated and conferred onto and revoked from women *by* men.[12] These women are "threatening [because they are] not related (or not properly related) to a man." "This is the moment in which woman is not sanctified, her position not secured either in heaven or on earth, when the anomaly of woman [within a patriarchal structure] is most anomalous."[13] Each story records how the woman draws on her powers of creativity (an attribute also traditionally associated with the Holy Ghost) to negotiate a life-threatening situation through to a life-affirming resolution. However, each story equally records the resolutions as ultimately the re-establishment of patriarchal kinship ties,[14] which releases the tension triggered by the women's losses.

The cruelty in their stories lies in the fact that compounding their grave personal losses is their communities' responses.[15] Instead of gathering around these women, the community moves against them, framing them as a social problem. One notes that none of the communities had to respond this way. Patriarchy is not an inevitable dimension of being but a social practice reproduced through situations such as these; it is historically contingent on such reproduction.[16]

Instead of interpreting the women as a problem, community members could have assessed the new vulnerability of the women as evidence that something was wrong with the system of relationality *because* it framed them as a problem. Instead, because the community invests itself—knows itself to be itself—in the righteousness of its normalized cultural practices, members become captive to the hetero-patriarchal logic undergirding them. The logic is fixed, if accommodating. I note this to denaturalize the patriarchy within these stories and to highlight how its power as a social organizing principle is not simply an abstract category for analysis but a force shaping material realities and policing imaginaries. To imagine a comprehensive and self-reflexive revision of relational structures might have been beyond the pale of communal imagination surrounding these women, but not later, as Matthew 1 demonstrates.

Of the women named in Matthew 1, I lift up Rahab's story because it shares pointed affinities with both Mary and the figure of the *yang-gongju*.[17] Rahab's appearance in Matthew 1's genealogy is, from the first, confusing. Although Matthew 1:5 invites a recalling of her story, one has to figure out who this Rahab is. Biblical scholar Jane Schaberg observes that the "statement that Boaz was her child by Salmon and that she was an ancestress of David (cf. Ruth 4:21; 1 Chr 2:11) has no support in the Christian Old Testament or elsewhere."[18] Yet Rahab's inclusion marks a kind of insistent claiming of her: the author knows she belongs to this genealogy, needs to belong, but does not know exactly how or where. Regardless of genetic accuracy, the author appears compelled to include her. If the genealogy is taken as a strategy for transmitting a people's history, then the author recognizes that the history of Jesus' people would be incomplete without her and exercises authorial authority to ensure her inclusion.

The genealogy simultaneously dis/places Rahab. Even if the author of Matthew cannot definitively root Rahab, biblical scholars have (tried). The most likely Rahab is the Rahab spoken of in Joshua 2 and 6.[19] This Rahab protects two scouts (i.e., spies), whom Joshua has sent on a reconnaissance mission. Their objective is to gather intelligence about the city of Jericho, which Joshua imminently plans to conquer (Josh 2:1). Unfortunately for the spies, the king of Jericho receives counter-intelligence about the spies' presence and location in the "house of a prostitute," Rahab's house (Josh 2:2–3).

Rahab's home in Jericho is located *in* the city's outer wall, which suggests that she literally lives as far away from the center of Jericho as possible.

Her professional status as a prostitute might have contributed to her placement at the city's edge, but her location on the edge facilitates her encounter with the spies. Had she lived more centrally, would the spies have avoided her house? Her spatial and cultural abjection are what provide her the opportunity to betray: they become the conditions of possibility for survival.

When the king's soldiers come to her house that night to interrogate her, Rahab lies. She admits to the spies having been there but lies about not knowing that they were spies, and she lies about their departure. Rahab has hidden the spies on her roof. She provides misinformation to the soldiers, which sends them out of the city on a dead-end search (Josh 2:4–7). Then, Rahab strikes a bargain with the spies.[20] In exchange for facilitating their escape from the city and evasion of the soldiers hunting them, Rahab exacts an oath to ensure her family will be spared during Joshua's siege.[21] She becomes a traitor to her people: she trades their lives for hers, her family, and "everyone who belongs to them" (Josh 2:13). Rahab and her family are the only people of Jericho to survive. The bargain positions Rahab as a co-conspirator—a collaborator—in the conquering of Jericho and the extermination of her people.[22]

After the siege, Joshua has space *outside* of the camp of Israel set up for Rahab and her family. The placement outside the camp of Israel seems to re-inscribe her outsider status, but eventually she does move into the camp.[23] One could reasonably infer from her story that no such movement inward was possible in Jericho; so her choice to align herself with the Israelites saves her life and gives her new opportunities, but there is a deep moral ambivalence. On the one hand, her complicity with the enemy (Israel) facilitated the annihilation of her people. On the other hand, it saved her family. The ending does not indicate (exactly) that she and her family ever assimilated into the Israelites, but it does say that she "lived in Israel ever since" (Josh 6:25). Schaberg reads her as "a survivor in the world of men at war, unfaithful to her own people but faithful to her own household and to Israel and its God."[24] Perhaps she is less dramatically a survivor, but Jesus' genealogy remembers her as more.

Her treasonous act is the basis for her memorialization in Matthew's genealogy, as well as in two other biblical passages. Hebrews 11:30 praises "Rahab the prostitute" for her "faith," which led her to "receive the spies in peace."[25] James 2:25 uses Rahab as evidence that justification involves both faith and works: "was not Rahab the prostitute also justified by works when she welcomed the messengers and sent them out by another road?"

James is interesting because the translation changed *spies* into the more innocuous *messengers*, but kept Rahab as "the prostitute." *Spies* needs revision but "Rahab the prostitute" does not. It could be that the author uses this revision to intensify the contrast between social attachments to *messengers* and *prostitute* as moral categories of people. However, that tactic also serves to emphasize that being a prostitute is no barrier to Rahab's story becoming an honored memory. Her act of treason can become an act of faith, of peaceful hospitality, yet her memorialization as an ancestor seems to require remembering that she was a prostitute. This genealogical memory of her as a prostitute carries forward no secrecy or shame; somehow these social (affective) attachments have been transformed in the process of memorializing her. One deduces that sexual compromise, to the point of collaboration with an enemy and conspiracy to commit genocide, is not sufficient grounds for forgetting or hiding her story.

I would like to pause over the fact that Mary's ancestral foremothers' stories close not with an unmitigated (feminist) triumph but ambivalence. On the one hand, these women actively shape the trajectories of their lives. They respond to or use their sexual compromise in strategic ways to open up new relational potentials. Had it not been for their creativity and willfulness, their stories would have ended much differently, and perhaps not been worthy of inclusion. On the other hand, in the moral universe of the stories, sexual compromise is not morally ambiguous; it is bad. Further, although they take initiative, their stories find resolution because patriarchal figures arbitrate and judge the women to be righteous; the male word makes it so. Those male figures resolve the tension in ways that re-incorporate the women and their revised relations as an elaboration of the patriarchal structure—not a breakdown of it. In this way, patriarchy becomes localized, with multiple patriarchies existing (i.e., there is not one patriarchy but multiple patriarchies, which cannot be understood as transcending social cultural conditions). Patriarchal structures tolerate these women and their novel ways of relating because they represent outliers, which do not challenge patriarchy as such. The revised patriarchal logics normalize the women's relational innovations by absorbing them as exceptions.

Something happens between the Christian Old Testament accounts of these women's stories and Matthew 1's genealogical recitation. I cannot give a definitive account of how or what solidified subsequent generations' commitment to remember them, but in their doing, something is set right-er or healed (or anticipated as going to be healed). Matthew 1's memorialization affirms them as important to the *communal* (divine) history that the genealogy recalls. Their being sexually compromised, either by the actions they take or suspicions circulating around them, does not make their names unspeakable or remembering them *as* sexually compromised anathema. Internal to the pericopes, loss marks points of conversion into threat, but response to sexual compromise provides points for counter-conversion. Sexual compromise becomes their opportunity to make relationship in situations in which the possibility for communal belonging seems foreclosed. Matthew 1's memorialization signals that they are not simply tolerated or remembered, but that a community as its practice continually claims and honors them. In this process of transmitting these stories, the community effectively transfigures them into sacred ancestors.[26] Matthew 1's genealogy records not only that their lives mattered and continue to matter, but also that they should matter.

Immediately, their lives matter to Mary, who is the last woman named in Matthew's genealogy. The unambiguously negative cultural response to Mary's pregnancy reflects a continuity with that of her ancestral mothers' stories and conversion into threat. The pregnancy threatens her place in the social order because being pregnant without a husband is bad and impugns her righteousness. She's framed as a moral problem and becomes a communal threat. Again, as with the other women, her community did not have to respond in the way that it did. It could have been a moment when the prevailing systems and customs, which intensify Mary's vulnerability and precarity, were interrogated, challenged, and deconstructed. On the horizontal level, Mary's community responds in predictable ways, given the community's hetero-patriarchal familial norms. Mary's precarity is flooded with shame; a shame demanding concealment for survival.

Shame and secrecy are the social attachments to Mary's pregnancy, Joseph's parenthood, and Jesus' birth. Like her female ancestors, Mary's story needs a patriarchal figure to (help) manage the situation.[27] She needs Joseph, and Joseph in particular because he represents a certain kind of patriarch. Compared with Mary, Joseph needs no justification. Joseph is righteous from the start. The text says so explicitly: "Joseph, being a righteous man" (Mat 1:19). However the author works hard to demonstrate Joseph's righteousness in terms of genealogy, call, faith, *and* action (Mat 1:20). Also, Joseph is justified (i.e., righteous) regardless of whether he chooses to marry Mary. He has the (patriarchal) right to refuse to marry her, and, if he so desires, he is no less justified in marrying her.

The story then further emphasizes his righteousness by recounting his decision-making process in terms consonant with a prophet's call story. Common to Christian Old Testament prophets, God calls Joseph in a dream bearing all the marks of a typical call story. An angel of the Lord (i.e., God) appears to Joseph (Mat 1:20). The appearance of the Lord (even mediated by a dream) incites fear in Joseph, which is a common response of the faithful to an appearance of the Lord (Mat 1:20). The Lord reassures Joseph with the typical, do not be afraid, and then assigns him tasks (i.e., marry Mary and name the to-be-born baby Jesus). What it lacks is any dialogical interaction: Joseph is a passive recipient of the Lord's message during the dream. Upon awaking, Joseph demonstrates his receptivity to the message by complying, which again affirms the righteousness of his faith. Then, he takes an additional action by refraining from sex with Mary until after she gives birth to Jesus (Mat 1:25). The call story presents Joseph as almost excessively righteous; he's righteous not only by the legitimacy afforded him by his Davidic bloodline but also by calling, faith, and action. The first chapter of Matthew builds up his character into, well, biblical proportions.

The author gives Joseph a superlatively righteous character and a strategic part to play in the narrative—but not a direct genealogy. By connecting Jesus primarily to Mary (i.e., not directly to Joseph), and then Joseph to Mary, the genealogy dislocates, even devalues, Joseph's patriarchal position. He is present only in direct relation to Mary, as Mary's husband (i.e., Mary is not there as Joseph's wife); therefore, his relation is mediated through and conferred by relationality with Mary. Unlike the patriarchal figures of the other women's stories, he does not maintain a position over Mary, even though it is his excessive righteousness and patriarchal privilege that protects them (i.e., Joseph's righteousness extends to protect Mary by securing her communal belonging). Joseph does not dis-identify with patriarchal privilege but uses it in strategic ways.

Still, the genealogy suggests that the relationship between Joseph and Mary is not quite right; something is off. Although they do not completely transcend or escape reproducing the hetero-patriarchal family form, the way in which Joseph and Mary come to belong to each other through marriage and the end toward which they put it does not fit the normative understanding of this type of union. By marrying Mary, Joseph does not become her patriarch but her collaborator (or even her supporter). Their marriage becomes an alibi concealing the (perceived) illegitimacy of her pregnancy. Instead of socially confirming their respectability, the marriage becomes the institution concealing their shame. Joseph leverages his access to patriarchal privilege, and he does so by using it in a way that socially destabilizes him. Just as Joseph's righteousness extends protection to Mary, Mary's shame and need for secrecy extend and stick to Joseph.[28]

The marriage of Joseph and Mary puts pressure on traditional patriarchal logic, but if its scope is widened, one can see that the inclusion of the child (i.e., Jesus) breaks it. Matthew 1's genealogy records what Schaberg calls a "shattered pattern."[29] As indicated above, instead of recording Jesus as begotten by a male, the genealogy suggests Jesus is closer to Mary (than Joseph). In relation to Mary, the New Revised Standard Version of the Bible (NRSV) translates the Greek verb *gennan* as "of whom was born," but every other time (i.e., 38 times) this verb appears in the genealogy, the NRSV translates it as "the father of." Schaberg indicates that the irregular formulation "Joseph, the husband of Mary, begot Jesus"[30] (Mat 1:16) registers something other than who begot Jesus. In what follows, I argue that the shattered pattern points to a shattering of patriarchal genetic bloodline as the exclusive or even privileged genealogical logic.

In fact, Joseph does not beget Jesus. Matthew 1 tells us that the Holy Ghost begot Jesus. Inclusion of Jesus into the family of Mary (and Joseph) creates confusion by disordering the patriarchal structure, which dictates a male gendered head of household. The pattern shatters because the Holy Ghost's begetting Jesus breaks the patriarchal line by transforming it into a genealogy of the Spirit. The child's inclusion changes the genealogical flow, and henceforth, what it means and the means to constitute family. Instead of a parent—either father *or* mother—it is a child who is "the bearer of hope and the beginning of the future." The Holy Ghost's genealogy incarnates into a "*messianism of the Child*,"[31] which finds root not in blood filiation but in intentional affiliation.[32]

Just by virtue of being the Messiah, Jesus affirms this change in genealogical logic as righteous. Relationship by affiliation opens the way for individuals and groups to constitute family in unpredictable and novel ways (i.e., the Holy Ghost queers the political category of family). The women named in Mary's genealogy figure as prefiguring this change. Jesus enfolds his parents into a messianic genealogy, but in a way that unshapes the exclusivity of patrilineal genealogical logic into a proliferating mass of knotty irregular relations. Kinship no longer runs along a fixed, predictable, and exclusive axis.

An investigation of Mary, Joseph, or Jesus as individual characters or a focus on any of the dyadic relationships fails to register this revision because to see how the three together constitute a revised genealogical logic through the child's inclusion requires a wider pneumatological lens. Unlike in the previous women's stories, patriarchy by definition cannot so easily absorb the logic of the Holy Ghost's genealogy because the Holy Ghost's begetting Jesus displaces the role of a male gendered patriarch.[33] The Holy Ghost does not simply replace a human patriarch, leaving the same relational and power distribution undisturbed. The Holy Ghost's power is associated with being directive (i.e., orienting)—perhaps even deeply compelling—but not ordering[34]; it does not concretize into a specific material form but is available for channeling into a multiplicity. The Holy Ghost's generative power makes family possible where no family seems possible (i.e., where no patriarch exists). The power of the Holy Ghost as a force for proliferating relational logics becomes clearer when set against another (even more obscure) genealogy in Matthew 1.

In addition to the more textually present genealogies of Jesus, Mary, Joseph, and (even) the Holy Ghost, Matthew 1 registers the seething presence of another force, whose threat is sensed by its virtual textual absence. Matthew 1 gives no direct mention of it, providing only oblique references. That presence is the presence of war and empire thread through the entire genealogical landscape. Matthew 1:11, 12, and 17 record the first Babylonian deportation (587–539).[35] This is the deportation graphically prophesied and witnessed to by multiple biblical books, including Jeremiah and Lamentations. Matthew 1 makes a direct genealogical connection between the gospel story it previews and this historical experience. Although the genealogy specifically names the mass dislocation produced by Israelites' deportation to Babylon, this also names the first Temple's brick-by-brick destruction.

To recall this story of destruction, death, and exile (diaspora) is to recall the affects attached to that experience and/or to learn what they were and should be. Along with words, those affects are carried forward through intergenerational transmission and compose a critical dimension of narrative meaning. To pass on those affects is an integral part of passing on the story's meaning and value; sharing those affects becomes a way of affectively belonging to the community. To experience the affects attached to those stories is to experience them in the present; the past comes to permeate the present, to affect how one perceives, makes sense of, and responds to the present because those affects come to inhabit the space and time of living bodies. By Matthew 1, the first deportation might seem temporally far away, but to Matthew's contemporary audience, who lives under similar threatening conditions, its felt proximity is immediate. The passed memory of the one into their current situation effects a touching of two temporally and spatially separated traumas.

Matthew's time frame names the Babylonian exile and first destruction of the Temple, but not the second destruction of the Temple, which followed Rome's catastrophic destruction of Jerusalem (70 C.E.) after a multi-year Jewish revolt.[36] During that revolt, "to demoralize the enemy, five hundred Jewish fugitives were crucified per day in front of besieged Jerusalem under Titus in 70 C.E."[37] In addition to mass crucifixions, these memories would also include the actual defiling of the Temple, 1.1 million causalities (in addition to the causalities during the revolt), and the taking of (just under) 100 thousand people as prisoners; prisoners who were sent to work in mines, sold on slave markets, and forced to fight to the death in arenas across the empire's provinces. Just as devastating as the physical destruction was the theological loss of certainty that Israel's God would intervene to save the Jews from Roman rule; that God could and would defeat a caesar augustus through combat.[38] To name the more temporally distant first destruction of the Temple and Babylonian exile is to name simultaneously the other. With that naming comes a flood of negative affects. These shared social memories figure war and empire not as triumphant and glorious, but as horrific and wounding. Matthew 1 figures the genealogy of war and empire from the position of the vanquished—as a *genealogy of horror*.

In both cases, dislocation functions as an horrific way of disciplining and punishing rebel groups and not incidentally because of how it works to destroy relational ties. Subject to Rome's imperial disposition, subjugated peoples could be uprooted and forcibly re-located. They were not re-located en mass but broken up and dispersed across Roman-occupied areas. Mass dislocation functioned as an imperial strategy of forced assimilation. Conquered cities would be emptied of all but perhaps the poorest people, who were left behind to tend farming. Once cities were liquidated, others would move in to re-settle the cities; taking over whatever was left, leaving the scattered diaspora no home to which to return. The goal of this conquer-and-divide strategy is to break down (or at least make it very difficult to sustain) any identification (cultural or otherwise) that might compete with Rome or diminish the desire to be a Roman citizen; one desire is frustrated to create a new desire. In the midst of this lived experience, the Holy Ghost's genealogical logic of affiliation in situations in which communities and families could be broken apart begins to clarify the import of the Holy Ghost's genealogy in Matthew 1.

This imperial control manifests not only as extraordinary violence, but also through systems structuring everyday living. As the reference to the first Babylonian exile indicates, the threat of domination is an ongoing one, and as ongoing, the threat manages to seep into the landscape of the ordinary. Directly relevant to the birth narrative is the backstory Luke 2 provides. Luke 2's account of the (first) Roman census provides a glimpse into how the Roman empire overwhelms and violently rearranges bodies; not only on the macro level of entire communities but also on the micro level of individuals and their families. In its hubris, this census presumes "all the world" as its scope (Luke 2:1–4) and requires people to return to their hometowns to be counted and registered. This mandate to return compels Joseph and Mary to travel, despite her advanced pregnancy.

The place Mary gives birth registers that even though the imperial order forces people to return to their so-called hometowns, they may in fact have no home to which to return. Perhaps Joseph's family had had a home and land in Bethlehem, but when Joseph and Mary return, they find themselves marginally sheltered in a stable because they have no house, and there are no available rooms to rent (Luke 2:6–7).[39]

A linking of memories of Temple destruction, exile, and census begins to flesh out the personality of war and empire. As a genealogy, Matthew 1 traces war and empire as a force that terrorizes by gripping bodies and forcing them to move in certain ways and under varying intensities of threat, whether through the spectacular events of war or the (seemingly) less violent census.

The most insidious way that war and empire grips lives is the way in which the violence it enacts against particular populations becomes unevenly distributed across a given population such that the violence comes to appear as if members of the community are the source, which works to fracture and undermine the ties that bind communities together. As Matthew 2 shows, Mary and Joseph's becoming a family to enable this child to be born is not only their intimate social re-figuring, but it also leads to a tragedy, which ravages their wider (albeit numerically relatively small) community and neighbors.

Rome did not only stress communities by dislocating them. It also did so by making its terrorizing power felt in communities. Matthew 2 includes a specific manifestation contemporaneous with Matthew 1. Joseph and Mary flee with Jesus in a nighttime flight to Egypt. A dream warns them that Herod Antipas is coming for Jesus and tells them to leave *immediately*. Herod, a client king of Rome with jurisdiction over Bethlehem, fears (Jewish) revolt. When he hears of Jesus' birth and his prophesied destiny, Herod attempts to trick three men searching for Jesus to give up Jesus' exact location (Mat 2:5). His deception fails after a dream warns the three men to avoid returning to Herod (Mat 2:12). When Herod realizes he will not receive the information he wants from the three men, he abandons the finely targeted approach for a more general one—mass killing. He orders the killing of all male babies two years old and younger within a specified geographic area: Bethlehem and its districts (Mat 2:16).

This massacre of male children in Matthew 2 points toward the larger yet unnamed context and character of Roman imperial rule by what it implies. It implies Rome has an organized and standing professional military. Given the age stipulation and the urgency of Joseph and Mary's fleeing, this military force would need to be strategically located within close enough proximity to the targeted populations that they could respond within a timely manner, if not immediately. Further, this geographic proximity to the small town of Bethlehem itself suggests two things. First, it suggests that the interests of Rome include a type of comprehensive military infrastructure designed to keep communities under direct military control. Second, it implies a certain character of soldier formation,[40] which enables soldiers to comply with an order to kill small children up close and possibly belonging to people with whom they might have had previous encounters.[41] Joseph, Mary, and Jesus live under heavily militarized imperial surveillance and control.

Joseph, Mary, and Jesus reside in Egypt until Herod dies. Then the text indicates that they return. Bethlehem is not a large cosmopolitan city into which they could melt; it is a small town. One wonders how they faced their neighbors, and what kind of reception they received. To create and protect one shameful family, other families are ripped apart, and a community's heart is broken. In addition to the trauma of those families whose children were murdered are the often unimagined and unaccounted for effects that ripple through the families of soldiers who executed Herod's order, who killed those children. How do the soldiers live with the memories of killing those children? How does carrying the weight of those memories affect how they are able to be partner or parent within their own families? To secure the birth of one child, others died and countless more are (morally) wounded.[42] The many are *not* saved for the one.[43]

Even as the biblical text already works to figure Jesus as the one sacrificed for the many, many are sacrificed for Jesus.

To imagine the massacre from the perspective of those targeted involves recovering a sense for the affective character of Roman Empire, which Matthew 1's reference to the exile does. In the words of philosopher Adriana Cavarero, "If we observe the scene of massacre from the point of view of the helpless victims rather than that of the warriors…the end melts away, and the means become substance. More than terror, what stands is horror."[44] From Herod's perspective, killing those children made sense as a way to thwart rebellion through an act of state terror. However, Cavarero's point is that terror is terror from the perspective of the one who terrorizes. The ones terrorized, however, experience senseless horror. By conjuring the first Babylonian exile, the author of Matthew 1's genealogy figures the genealogy of war and terror from the perspective of the ones terrorized—as a genealogy of horror.

This genealogy of horror connects Rahab and Mary in a very concrete way. War and empire push them into situations with no morally "good" choices. Their experiences are incommensurate, but both point toward how war and empire affectively texture lives in the midst of traumatic situations and after they end. Rahab has to choose between death and treason—her family over all her people's families. Mary and Joseph have to choose between the death of their baby and the deaths of other babies—their family over their neighbors' families.[45] These are horrific choices, and what compounds them is that often there is no time, no space recorded in the stories given to passing on how to mourn these particular losses; except on the meta-level of the gospel.

As these stories pass on, missing are explicit stories of how the community mourned, grieved. Matthew 2 provides one of the only acknowledgments: "A voice was heard in Ramah, wailing and loud lamentation, Rachel was weeping for her children; she refused to be consoled, because they were no more" (Mat 2:18). One verse, but it remains one of the most powerful and affectively crushing biblical passages. There is no mourning; only a defiant choice for melancholia. The refusal of (even the possibility of) consolation suggests that the affect of grief here is intimately mixed with other affects, such as rage.

These experiences and their affective attachments become folded into the fabric of what the ordinary everyday feels like for Rome's subjugated peoples; it begins to feel like having to make these life-or-death decisions, which have no "right" answers. The everyday begins to feel like living wounded with an unspeakable, let alone unhealable, moral or spiritual injury, but this condition of being wounded becomes normalized to the point of fading out of focus—except for the affective remains, which surface in strange ways. These are ways that the genealogy of war and empire insinuates itself into family and community genealogies, becoming part of the texture of their stories, the broader background; a background which needs hardly any reference to evoke. Affective connections thread through sociality, shaping how it feels to be a neighbor, to be a parent, to be a part of a community, or to be a part of a community with no part.

Although the genealogy of horror might feel abstract and distant, it is in fact insidiously intimate because of how it conditions people to relate to themselves and others. It positions people according to "the hierarchical oppositions of Self versus Other."[46] To face your neighbor (or a stranger) is to face an enemy. This imperial conquest-based "combat"[47] logic dictates that peace is only through a dominant Self conquering an inferior Other: Self versus Other; me versus you; us versus them; Caesar versus God.

New Testament scholar Brigitte Kahl explains that this imperial logic figures a caesar as embodying "the superior self, claiming to be the sole force entitled to unite and capable of uniting and ruling...Such unity in 'Caesar' is achieved solely within the confines of the imperial logic of combat, an order that turns Self against Other in endless spirals of violence, competition, and oppression."[48] This logic is the logic that the stories evoked in Matthew 1's genealogy breaks. The point that the Holy Ghost does not simply move into the position of patriarch by begetting Jesus, leaving the genealogical logic undisturbed, becomes critical here. The personality of the Holy Ghost that emerges through its work is one that does not engage through combat logic but through a logic that re-structures teleoaffectivity in ways that enable production of novel relational forms to emerge.[49]

These rearrangements do not register as spectacular victories or unmitigated liberations. They are tense, negotiated, and not morally pure. Nonetheless, they enable Mary's ancestral mothers in Matthew 1 to re/inhabit (dangerous) spaces, times, and memories; with life-preserving (albeit ambiguous) results. For example, the overarching system of hetero-patriarchy is not dismantled, but the women find ways to re-inhabit it, to live within it. With this in mind, Matthew 1's genealogy frames the narrative as a narrative of rearranged relationality, which will come through the Holy Ghost—in the midst of terror and horror. By witnessing to war and empire as a genealogy of horror, Matthew 1 creates a polemical contrast with the personality of the Holy Ghost's genealogy.

My literary reading of Matthew 1 leads me to several biblically grounded conclusions. A sexually compromised woman can become an adored ancestor (e.g., Rahab). The beneficiary of unearned privileges can leverage those privileges to bend systems of gross inequity toward life-saving ends (e.g., Joseph). Individuals can constitute families according to a variety of genealogical logics, whose fluidity keeps them continually open to rearrangement. A shamed family, living on the run and hiding themselves and the circumstances of their belonging to each other, can become theologically transfigured into a revered holy family (e.g., Mary, Joseph, and Jesus).

The theological question raised by this narrative arc is whether the transformation of this shamed family into a revered holy family has anything to say to how the Korean diaspora could transfigure the *yanggongju* from shamed ghostly figure into honored ancestor. Could a communal claiming similar to Rahab lead to such transfiguration? My claim here is affirmative and my theological response organized around a pneumatological axis.

Grace M. Cho makes the case that the figure of the *yanggongju* (Western princess) haunts the Korean diaspora. She is incoherent, unrooted from belonging in any one time, and spatially dismembered. As a figure, Cho says, she "is the embodiment of the accumulation of often unacknowledged grief from events…there are storie*s* to be told."[50] She comes to re-present a particular dimension of the ongoing traumatic experience of the never-ending Korean War and the presence of the US military in Korea as a material figure.

The category *yanggongju* absorbs all Koreans who have sex with US Americans. Stereo/typically, these sex workers are females whose primary cliental comprises male US soldiers (both enlisted and officer) stationed in South Korea. However, it is more than a simple category. Cho clusters this word with other Korean words and meanings:

> *yanggalbo*. Yankee whore. Western princess. GI Bride. *Yangssaekshi*. GI's plaything. UN lady. Bar girl. Entertainment hostess. *Wianbu*. Fallen woman. Formerly a comfort woman. Formerly called a comfort woman. Daughter of a comfort woman. Camptown prostitute. Military bride.[51]

Yanggongju and all these relative words stick together, and each bears the negative social attachments of shame and secrecy. The ongoing Korean

War and US militarization of South Korea make particular contributions to the shame and secrecy associated with the Korean diaspora and thereby enable Cho's focused account of why claiming the figure of the *yanggongju* as an honored ancestor remains difficult, perhaps unthinkable: the shame and consequent compulsion toward secrecy themselves mitigate against doing so. No one wants to remember or honor the figure of the *yanggongju* for the lives and living she makes possible; perhaps resentment sticks to the shame and secrecy. Given Katherine H.S. Moon's observation that "statistically 15 relatives follow one former prostitute to the United States,"[52] the *yanggongju* is a very real, flesh-and-blood relative to transnational immigrants from Korea to the US. Still, whether an actual blood relative, her relatedness to the Korean diaspora exceeds bloodlines.

Cho describes the *yanggongju* as a threatening presence, a ghostly figure floating through Korean diasporic genealogies. Not claiming her as an ancestral figure does not dissolve this tense relation but rather affectively preserves it as shame and secrecy; the denial and disavowal become the affirmation. Unclaimed, she does not threaten some but all members of the Korean diaspora, however unevenly. She could be anyone's ancestor because she is no one's ancestor. She is just there, somewhere, but not anywhere. She is one of the *abject peoples*, and she lives in *abject zones*, whether that zone is imagined as the geopolitical space of the camptown, a region of the Korean diaspora's imagination, or social (affective) memories occupying living bodies.[53]

Eng and Han observe that "in Asian American cultural politics, the numerous political, economic, and social conflicts arising from difficulties of immigration, assimilation, and racialization processes are often configured as *intergenerational* and *intersubjective* struggles."[54] Cho follows this practice: part of what is at stake in Cho's understanding of haunting is her argument for its transgenerational character. The haunting is not *a* generation's experience but an experience across time and space, which is transmitted among generations. (Chung) Hyun Kyung notes that in Korean society, the shaming of women who give birth out of wedlock "does not stop in their generation. It passes on to their children. In the Yi dynasty, which lasted until the dawn of the twentieth century in Korea, children of a surrogate mother could not take exams to hold government offices," and that such practices continue to exist, "although in a subtle way."[55] Cho obliquely points to this dimension of the *yanggongju*'s haunting with the translation, "daughter of a comfort woman." I take both Chung and Cho to mean that the experiences and social attachments attributed to the *yanggongju* exceed the boundaries of particular bodies, and carry meaning for and to her descendants, her female gendered children in particular. But who are they, her children?

The figure of the Korean War orphan is perhaps the most available to being figured as the *yanggongju*'s relation, as her child, and frequently is. In Korea, the history of coerced and voluntary sex workers and abandoned children pre-dates the more recent Korean War experiences. For example, during Japan's colonization of Korea, Japanese imperial forces conscripted female Koreans to be their coerced sex workers (*wianbu*); *sex worker* is a bit of a misnomer because they were systematically raped. As social categories, the *yanggongju* and the Korean War orphan become figured in specific ways because of the Korean War and US militarization of Korea. Signs of the mother–child relationship between the *yanggongju* and the Korean War orphan appear in a variety of places and spaces; for example, in memoirs such as Jane Jeong Trenka's *Fugitive Visions*[56]; Korean American literature, such as Marie Myung-Ok Lee's novel, *Somebody's Daughter*[57] and Hei Kyong Kim's collection of poetry and prose, *The Translation of Han*[58]; and academic investigations, such as SooJin Pate's *From Orphan to Adoptee*,[59] Arissa H. Oh's *To Save the Children of Korea*,[60] and David Vine's *Base Nation*.[61]

Just as the *wianbu* has an historical context, which gives her particular meaning, the *yanggongju* and the Korean War orphan are also historically particular. Instead of Japanese military, the *yanggongju* are the un/coerced sex workers for US military personnel working by US bases in Korea. In fact, many former *wianbu* became *yanggongju* in the process of the US military's self-narrated liberation of Korea from Japanese colonial rule (e.g., US military literally moved into Japan's former comfort stations when instituting its infrastructure). The category *yanggongju* cannot exist apart from the US military personnel who incarnate US militarization.

In relation to the Korean War orphan, Pate provides an in-depth reading of how and toward what end the figuring together of the US soldier and the Korean War orphan occurred. Parallel with Moon's argument that the *yanggongju*'s body becomes the material condition of possibility for managing and maintaining friendly diplomatic relations between the US and South Korea, Pate argues that the disciplining of the Korean War orphan's body (into the Korean adoptee) becomes the material condition for brokering and maintaining the neocolonial relationship of Korean dependency on the US, which began with the US military's occupation of Korea in 1945.[62] The categories of *yanggongju*, Korean War orphan, *and* US soldier (in South Korea) transition from being social categories appropriate for a discrete temporal period to being normalized into regular, ongoing social categories.[63] As the Korean War and US militarization of Korea are ongoing realities, so too is the ongoing production of the *yanggongju*, Korean War orphan, and US soldier; they are figured together as a militarized family, which is ensconced spectrally in the imaginaries of both US Americans and Koreans. Imperial power pushed these figures together, but the Holy Ghost can rearrange these militarized relations into flows of living attention (or loving relation).

As Cho notes, shame and secrecy might be transgenerational inheritances, but every generation has the opportunity to metabolize that shame and secrecy into other social attachments. The transgenerational work of the Holy Ghost becomes a succession of receiving the unfinished work of ancestors as a responsibility to which each generation is called upon to respond. The figuring of the *yanggongju* is a projective consequence of the Korean diaspora's attempt to externalize and distance itself from the horrific losses associated with the Korean War and US militarization of Korea. Through the violent opening of her body, she has paid for and opened doors to alternate futures, which becomes a kind of guilty accumulated privilege for the Korean diaspora. If open and willing to join unending hymns not only of praise but also of lamentation, ways of transforming affects of shame and secrecy at being a torn open, wounded body can be discerned—just as Matthew 1's genealogy does, and more widely, as the Christian gospel does. The Korean diaspora can transfigure the militarized family of the *yanggongju*, US soldier, and Korean War orphan from its spectral status.

The author of Matthew 1 who claims Rahab and all those who belonged to her and Christians who continue to claim Mary and all those who belong to her demonstrate the possibility of such transfigurative work. It might take generations on generations to tend to the wounds passed on and accumulated transgenerationally. However, the stories of the Korean diaspora cannot be told without her, and there need not be any secrecy or shame because of that. Chung notes that "Mary, a Jewish woman, also became another symbol of new humanity for Asian women through her words and deeds,"[64] and that this reclaiming of Mary is possible because of the communal work they do to interpret her through their own "experiences of survival in the midst of oppression and on their efforts to liberate themselves."[65] In other words, this transfiguring of Mary did not simply happen, but was the product of Asian women's intentional work of re-appropriation. Such work must be seen as an act of resistance because it happens within theo-cultural contexts in which both the Protestant churches' "oppressing of women by eliminating Mary" and the Roman Catholic Church's "exercis[ing] control over women by domesticating Mary" mitigate against such creative theological imagination.[66]

The Korean War and the US militarization of Korea are ongoing realities, which continue to produce *yanggongju*, and thus continue to affect Korean and US practices of imagining and socially disposing of Korean orphans. Instead of taking the *yanggongju* and orphans to be the problem, we can assess the vulnerability of these women and children as evidence that something remains wrong with the logic undergirding the cultural practices of militarized relationality. At different times and in different places, different things are imaginable. To imagine a comprehensive and self-reflexive revision of relational structures might have seemed beyond imagination in prior generations, but not now. The failure of love is often the failure of the human imagination. The failure of Christians to love is often the failure of theological imagination. Instead of telescoping down to a narrow, rigid account, this chapter is an effort to use the sense of a billowing Spirit toward demilitarizing an abject zone beyond the pale of theological imagination: the zone of relationality among the figures of the US soldier, the Korean *yanggongju*, and the Korean War orphan, which structures the camptowns bordering US military bases in Korea.

The failure of imagination is never an individual but communal one. This chapter reflects an effort to contribute to a communal response-ability, which claims and transfigures the abandoned relationality of the *yanggongju*, the US soldier, and the Korean War orphan toward revitalizing the Christian theological imagination in a way that emerges out of the experiences of some of the least considered but most vulnerable populations. Abject zones and peoples abandoned by theological imagination do not disappear but haunt. They demand an account and an incorporation into our collective narrative that transfigures them, resurrects them as ancestors whose bodies and lives paved the way for generations of Koreans and US Americans to have alternate futures. A Christian refiguring of these figures' relationality requires claiming to be one among the generations of the Holy Ghost, whose redemptive work includes the affective reparation of the hurt bodies and memories that ongoing US militarization produces.

When Jesus exhaled his last breath while dying on the cross, he breathed out affects for circulation into the environment: affects of suffering, pain, torture, and despair. Those affects became implicit memories carried in the blood of those sharing that environment. These affects are re-presented with the presence of the Holy Ghost, the breath of God. In that way, the trauma of the Christ event continually haunts Christian imagination and communal liturgies. And Christians are called to breathe it in, to find ways of remembering, transforming, and circulating negative affects as living attention. The Holy Ghost is not simply a breath that washes over, but one that enters and re-arranges how bodies are and relate. It is there in the breaths shared that it becomes possible to begin to feel differently and to make alternate affective attachments.

Notes

1. Kelly Oliver, *Witnessing: Beyond Recognition* (Minneapolis: University of Minneapolis, 2001), 206–208. I appropriate *response-ability* out of Oliver's analysis of Emmanuel Lévinas's understanding of the subject's responsibility to be open to the other. For Oliver, the process of narrativizing one's self becomes an act of bearing witness "by not [only] listening to the other but also telling oneself to the other. It is not the content of its testimony that solidifies the ego; rather it is the bearing witness itself, the relationship of telling one's self to the other, that solidifies the ego" (206). Here, I use it to signify that the early Jesus followers came to constitute themselves through the practice of narrativizing the experiences of remaining after the traumatic experience of the historical Jesus' torture and Roman execution; in a situation in which the terror of the cross was intended to sufficiently horrify and therefore subjugate them to the point of breaking their capacity to respond in ways other than to submit to Roman authority.
2. Crystal Mun-hye Baik, "Unfaithful Returns: Reiterations of Dissent, U.S.–Korean Militarized Debt, & the Architecture of Violent Freedom," in *Journal of Asian American Studies* 18 (February 2015): 66 (7ff).
3. Deification (theosis) is a work of the Holy Ghost, who enables creation to fully participate in the nature and life of the Trinitarian God by uniting creation through grace.
4. On methodology: although the chapter's structure implies linear and discrete movement *from* biblical text *to* historical experience (in a unidirectional way), methodologically, I positioned each toward the other to function as both reader and critic of each other. In other words, on the one hand, my reading the biblical texts with the historical experiences of the Korean War and US militarization of South Korea opened up and enabled a contextual recovery of the texts; on the other hand, my interpreting the historical experiences of the *yanggongju*, US soldier, and Korean War orphan through the biblical texts exposed the potential for a theological project of reparation.

5. Sara Ahmed, *Willful Subjects* (Durham: Duke University, 2014), 5.
6. Anne McClintock, *Imperial Leather: Race, Gender and Sexuality in the Colonial Contest* (New York: Routledge, 1995), 320.
7. The decision to name this a genealogy of sexually compromised women is over against categorizing them as erotic tricksters, which would be the more in line with a Hebrew Bible reading of Tamar, Rahab, Ruth, and Bathsheba. The main reason being that Mary's character (Bathsheba's, too) is not that of an erotic trickster. Sexual compromise emerges as more consonant across the stories. For the phrase *erotic trickster*, see Eugene Rogers, Jr., *After the Spirit: A Constructive Pneumatology from Resources Outside the Modern West* (Grand Rapids: William B. Eerdmans, 2005), 105.
8. The phrase *creative response-ability* is the product of combining my reflections on the work of theologian Victor Anderson and theorist Kelly Oliver. See Victor Anderson, *Creative Exchange: A Constructive Theology of African American Religious Experience* (Minneapolis: Fortress, 2008); Kelly Oliver, *Witnessing: Beyond Recognition* (Minneapolis: University of Minnesota, 2001).
9. The category of command rape emerged within the context of the US wars in Afghanistan and Iraq, and has since come to be used to describe the particular type of soldier-against-soldier sexual violence. The opportunity for command rape involves an asymmetric power dynamic institutionalized by rank such that the superior (i.e., person with higher rank up the chain of command) mobilizes his/her command power to order a subordinate soldier into life-threatening situations as the potential consequence for refusal to consent to sexual actions. See *rape* entry in *Encyclopedia of Military Science* edited by G. Kurt Piehler, (Thousand Oaks, CA: Sage Publications, 2013), 1181; for an example of usage, see David Swanson, "Command Rape: The Ordeal of Suzanne Swift," *counterpunch* (online newsletter), Weekend Edition July 8–10, 2006, http://www.counterpunch.org/2006/07/08/command-rape/.
10. Sara Ahmed, *Willful Subjects* (Durham: Duke University, 2014), 20.
11. Despite the problematic categorical assumptions inherent in the category of patriarchy, as a lens for interpretative analysis, it names a way of constituting dominative relations that might easily be naturalized to the point of melting into the stories' landscapes. However, to leave this dimension of the stories unnamed (in any way) must trivialize the life-threatening conditions contextualizing these women's actions to the point of the absurd.
12. To say that patriarchy limits their agency does not evacuate them of any agency. The women find ways of normalizing their social position by manipulating the constraints of cultural systems, which do not assume their survival or flourishing independent of men. Yet, however they negotiate novel ways of re-inhabiting their everyday lives, the everyday continues to be an everyday life structured and delimited by patriarchy. I read them and feel ambivalence.

13. Jane Schaberg, *The Illegitimacy of Jesus: A Feminist Theological Interpretation of the Infancy Narratives* (Sheffield: Sheffield Phoenix, 2006), 43.
14. Deniz Kandiyoti, "Bargaining with Patriarchy," *Gender & Society* 2, no. 3 (Sept., 1988): 274–290. For Kandiyoti's revision of her bargaining argument, see also "Gender, Power, & Contestation: Rethinking Bargaining with Patriarchy," in *Feminist Visions of Development: Gender, Analysis & Policy*, eds. Cecile Jackson & Ruth Pearson (Abington, Oxon: Routledge, 1998; 2000 reprint), 135–152.
15. See Gina Messina-Dysert, *Rape Culture & Spiritual Violence: Religion, Testimony, & Visions of Healing* (London/New York: Routledge, 2015); 26, 54, 63, 65–67, 76, 80, 83, 86, 89–93, 96–97, 101–104, 111–114. Messina-Dysert addresses the structural issues implicated in how rape cultures generate social practices that "twice damn" or constitute a metaphorical "second rape" of rape victims. I include this reference because Messina-Dysert's analysis addresses how cultural practices (e.g., communal rejection, blaming, and shaming) elaborate already physically violent traumatic experiences into deeply spiritually wounding experiences, which she argues can result in *han* and spiritual death.
16. Gi-Wook Shin, *Ethnic Nationalism in Korea: Genealogy, Politics, & Legacy* (Stanford: Stanford University, 2006), 9–10. See Shin's work for a definition and explanation of historical contingency in relation to the rise of the Korean nation-state, which I use here.
17. Kwok Pui-lan, *Postcolonial Imagination & Feminist Theology* (Louisville: Westminster John Knox, 2005), 33–34. Following Kwok Pui-lan's acknowledgment of Delores William's accomplished use of the "figure of Hagar as a heuristic key to recover the struggle for survival and quality of life for African American women," in *Sisters in the Wilderness*, I use the figure of Rahab here in a similar way (i.e., heuristically, and not strategically to construct an essentialized subject).
18. Jane Schaberg, *The Illegitimacy of Jesus: A Feminist Theological Interpretation of the Infancy Narratives* (Sheffield: Sheffield Phoenix, 2006), 35–36.
19. Ibid., 36; 28n.
20. After the soldiers leave, Rahab goes to the roof to bargain with the spies (Josh 2:8). Rahab is not an Israelite, but she has heard the fantastic stories of their god drying up the Red Sea and liberating them from bondage in Egypt. The stories scare her and convince her that the Israelites will conquer Jericho by the power of their god. She knows that their conquest includes the total destruction of Jericho and a complete slaughtering of all its inhabitants. She does not want to be murdered. She does not want her family to be murdered.
21. Rahab then lowers a crimson rope down from her window, which is outside the city wall, and gives the spies instructions on which direction to go and how long to lie low before returning to the Israelite camp. Before descending down the rope, the spies tell her to tie the same crimson rope outside the

same window when their siege begins. This crimson rope is the sign for the Israelite soldiers to pass over her house. The spies follow Rahab's instructions and safely return to their camp. Her help becomes a divine sign to them that they are meant to conquer Jericho. They share their information with Joshua, and the attack proceeds.

22. Just before the infamous last shout that levels Jericho's city walls, Joshua gives his soldiers orders. They are to destroy everything, but, for God's treasury (i.e., bank), they should take all silver, gold, and bronze and iron vessels (Josh 6:17–20, 22–25). He also gives two prohibitions: they are not to take anything "devoted to destruction" (i.e., people and livestock), and they are to leave untouched Rahab and everyone gathered in her house. The walls fall; the siege begins. (One wonders how her house—inside the outer wall—survived the collapse.)
While Joshua oversees the killing of "both men and women, young and old, oxen, sheep, and donkeys" (Josh 6:21), he gives more explicit instructions to the two spies. They are to go to Rahab's house for her and all her kindred gathered there, remove them from the city, and make camp for them "outside" the camp of Israel (Josh 6:23).
23. I can note only in passing that Rahab easily figures as a refugee of war and transnational immigrant, who lives in diaspora.
24. Jane Schaberg, *The Illegitimacy of Jesus: A Feminist Theological Interpretation of the Infancy Narratives* (Sheffield: Sheffield Phoenix, 2006), 36.
25. One notes that the pericope in Joshua does not specify whether she had faith in the Israelite god; only that her hearing of their stories scared her.
26. I am indebted to the trailblazing work of womanist theologian Delores S. Williams, who in her seminal work, *Sisters in the Wilderness*, recovers the material and theological value of African American women's lived experiences within a system of non/coerced surrogacy during the US practice of chattel slavery and its ongoing legacies.
27. Arguments have been made that Mary is the patriarchal figure, in a kind of gender reversal (which would, from this perspective, open Mary up to the question of the extent to which she re-inscribes patriarchy). For example, Eugene Rogers, Jr., argues through equivalence that Mary is less a prophetic figure (although still a prophetic figure) and more a patriarchal figure because in narratively thematic ways she is the New Testament analog to Abraham: "The very thing that distinguishes Mary from most prophets—that she accepts her call with alacrity—puts her in correspondence with a figure usually regarded as less a prophet and more a *patriarch*...she represents the Abraham of erotic consummation. Mary like Abraham follows God without complaint and offers senseless erotic sacrifice." See *After the Spirit: A Constructive Pneumatology from Resources Outside the Modern West* (Grand Rapids, MI: William B. Eerdmans, 2005), 108–109,

emphasis in the original. However, here the study is not on figures who can be seen as analogically relating to each other as much as a reflection on how relationality constitutes the figures. The emphasis then is not on individual choices as reflecting personal moral character, which then leads to the conclusion that the person functions as a patriarch; such analysis avoids the power analysis *patriarchy* names. The emphasis is on how systems like patriarchy exert social pressure on and through people to position themselves in certain relational arrangements to be recognizable to one's self and others, with the attendant theological claim that alternate constellations are possible by the Spirit as an embodied social power with a different *telos*.

28. Even when their dislocation to Egypt (Mat 2) seems to offer the perfect opportunity to leave the secrecy and shame behind (by leaving the social situation) in a distant geographic location and sealed past, Mary and Joseph cannot. They continue to conceal the circumstances of their marriage, and with that concealment comes secrecy and shame. The secrecy and shame stick to them, move with them. Even if they do not actively conceal their origins by simply saying nothing, their silence itself constitutes concealment. For them, to say nothing is (to attempt) to pass as normal (i.e., a reproduction of the patriarchal family form).
29. Jane Schaberg, *The Illegitimacy of Jesus: A Feminist Theological Interpretation of the Infancy Narratives* (Sheffield: Sheffield Phoenix, 2006), 43.
30. Ibid.
31. Jürgen Moltmann, *The Spirit of Life: A Universal Meaning* (Minneapolis: Fortress, 1993 [second impress of English edition]), 160.
32. Edward W. Said, *The World the Text & the Critic* (Cambridge: Harvard University, 1983), 19: I am primarily appropriating Said's phrasing and less the entire methodological apparatus. In addition, the shift to affiliation does not claim that adoption did not happen in the ancient world; it did; or that parenting a child who was not a biological relation did not happen. For example, adoption in the ancient world happened when the father of a (typically) male child died and left the child an inheritance, which then meant he needed a guardian to guard and administer the inheritance. However, to say it is a cultural practice and to say that this is how God constitutes family are two very different things and carry very different theological as well as material consequences.
33. Although it is true that a chain of equivalence can re-inscribe a patriarchal logic that codes the Spirit as both male and masculine, of the three persons of the Christian Trinity, the Spirit is the least traditioned in this way. To say *Spirit* does not conjure a male figure in the same way as *God* is dominantly imagined as God-the-Father or even Christ as incarnated in the male body of Jesus. Comparatively, the Spirit's body is not over-determined.

34. Martin Heidegger, *Contributions to Philosophy (of the Event)*, Translated by Richard Rojcewicz & Daniela Vallega-Neu, (1989; Bloomington: Indiana Press [edition], 2012]), 8.
35. By naming Jechoniah, Josiah's son, the genealogy provides an historical time frame for identifying the deportation.
36. Unsure of an exact dating, composition of Matthew is dated to within the first hundred years following the Jewish Revolt against Rome, which ended in 70 C.E.
37. Brigitte Kahl, *Galatians Re-Imagined: Reading with the Eyes of the Vanquished* (Minneapolis: Fortress, 2008), 157.
38. Ibid., "Galatians," Union Theological Seminary in the City of New York, 16 February 2010.
39. I have often missed the implication that their return marks their homelessness because mention of the inn suggests that they are still en route to Bethlehem (Hebrew for house of bread), but they had arrived (Luke 2:6).
40. See John Protevi, *Political Affect: Connecting the Social and the Somatic* (Minneapolis: Regents, 2009) for an analysis of how spatial distance affects soldiers' ability to kill.
41. See CH (Maj.) Sean Wead, "Ethics, Combat, & a Soldier's Decision to Kill," *Military Review: The Professional Journal of the U.S. Army*, March–April (2015): 69–81. This article records that US military commanders—as a matter of protocol—order soldiers not to stop convoys of vehicles (delivering supplies) for any road obstruction—including children in the street—because children are viewed as potential combatants, whose strategic function is to locate US soldiers within the line of enemy fire. In particular, the author explains that the use of children is an intentional manipulation of US soldiers' morality, which works both to secure the morality of US soldiers' necessity to kill children and to figure the enemy as without any morality.
42. For a Christian discussion of moral injury as a theological and spiritual issue (as opposed to exclusively an issue of psychological pathology), see Rita Nakashima Brock & Gabriella Lettini, *Soul Repair: Recovering from Moral Injury after War* (Boston: Beacon, 2013).
43. This one for the many is, incidentally, the moral rationality most frequently deployed for defending torture. For an incisive critique of this rationality as defense for torture, see Rebecca Gordon's *Mainstreaming Torture: Ethical Approaches in the Post-9/11 United States* (Oxford: Oxford University, 2014).
44. Adriana Cavarero, *Horrorism: Naming Contemporary Violence* (New York: Columbia, 2011 [paperback ed.]), 1.
45. No one can maintain an ideal of moral purity; everyone lives with a sense of moral injury, of betraying not only their neighbors but also their own deeply held values.
46. Ibid., Brigitte Kahl, 17–25.

47. Ibid., 26.
48. Ibid., 23–24.
49. For a more detailed explanation of *teleoaffective structure* than what can be provided here, see Theodore R. Schatzki, *The Site of the Social: A Philosophical Account of the Constitution of Social Life & Change* (University Park: Pennsylvania State University, 2002). In brief, a teleoaffective structure names the dimension of social practices that is "a range of normativized and hierarchically ordered ends, projects, and tasks, to varying degrees allied with normativized emotions and even moods...coordinated with this teleological structuring are emotions and moods that participants *should* or *may* enjoy" (80, emphasis added).
50. Grace M. Cho, *Haunting the Korean Diaspora: Shame, Secrecy, & the Forgotten War* (Minneapolis: University of Minnesota, 2008).
51. Ibid., 5, emphasis added.
52. Katherine H.S. Moon, *Sex Among Allies: Military Prostitution in U.S.–Korea Relations* (New York: Columbia, 1997), 27.
53. Anne McClintock, *Imperial Leather: Race, Gender, & Sexuality in the Colonial Contest* (New York: Routledge, 1995), 72: "certain groups are expelled and obliged to inhabit the impossible edges of modernity: the slum, the ghettos, the garrett, the brothel, the convent, the colonial bantustan and so on. Abject peoples are those whom industrial imperialism rejects but cannot do without: slaves, prostitutes, the colonized, domestic workers, the insane, the unemployed, and so on. Certain threshold zones become abject zones and are policed with vigor:...the red light district, and the bedroom. Inhabiting the cusp of domesticity and market, industry and empire, the abject returns to haunt modernity as its constitutive, inner repudiation: the rejected form which one does not depart."
54. David L. Eng, & Shinhee Han, "Desegregating Love: Transnational Adoption, Racial Reparation, & Racial Transitional Objects," in *Studies in Gender & Sexuality* 7 (2006): 155.
55. Hyun Kyung Chung, *Struggle to be the Sun Again: Introducing Asian Women's Theology* (1990; Maryknoll: Orbis, 2004, eleventh printing), 4.
56. Jane Jeong Trenka, *Fugitive Visions: An Adoptee's Return to Korea* (St. Paul, MN: Graywolf, 2009), 33.
57. Marie Myung-Ok Lee, *Somebody's Daughter: A Novel* (Boston: Beacon, 2005), 108–114; 137–138.
58. Hei Kyong Kim, *The Translation of* Han (CQT Media & Publishing, 2014). This collection contains several pieces surfacing this relation, but of particular note are her works, "What You Don't Say to Your Korean Daughter," which includes references to how Korean adoptees are often told that if they had not been adopted, they would have become sex workers (27–29); and "From the Eyes of a Real Asian Man (On Korean Adopted Females)," the opening words of which are "*tramp whore slut*" (48–50).

59. SooJin Pate, *From Orphan to Adoptee: U.S. Empire & Genealogies of Korean Adoption* (Minneapolis: University of Minnesota, 2014), 15, 44–45.
60. Arissa H. Oh, *To Save the Children of Korea: The Cold War Origins of International Adoption* (Stanford: Stanford University, 2015).
61. David Vine, *Base Nation: How U.S. Military Bases Abroad Harm America & the World* (New York: Metropolitan Books, 2015).
62. SooJin Pate, *From Orphan to Adoptee: U.S. Empire & Genealogies of Korean Adoption* (Minneapolis: Regent of the University of Minnesota, 2014), 21–22.
63. Roberto J. González, *Militarizing Culture: Essays on the Warfare State* (Walnut Creek, CA: Left Coast, 2010), 57: González defines the process of routinization as "the way in which the creation of monstrous situations became routine."
64. Ibid., Hyun Kyung Chung, 74.
65. Ibid., 73.
66. Ibid., 75.

CHAPTER 4

(Un)Making Mothers, Orphans, and Transnational Adoptees: The Afterlife of the Vietnam War in Aimee Phan's *We Should Never Meet*

Mimi Khúc

It's 1975. Saigon. Bridget, a volunteer American pediatrician, walks determinedly toward the orphanage where she works, eyes and ears trying to avoid the desperate crowd at its gates. A Vietnamese woman screams a plea and presses her infant child against the bars. Bridget continues to walk. A sudden silence. She turns to see the infant on the ground. It had been pushed through the bars, its now-naked body "twisted" and covered in deep scratches. The mother was already out of sight. A page later in Aimee Phan's short story, "Bound," we learn that the baby survives. But what exactly has she survived? And what will she continue to survive in postwar life?

The unnamed mother and the injured child are but one mother–child set that populate Aimee Phan's worlds of wartime Vietnam and postwar

M. Khúc (✉)
Asian American Studies Program, University of Maryland, College Park, MD, USA

N. Kim, W.A. Joh (eds.), *Critical Theology against US Militarism in Asia*,
DOI 10.1057/978-1-137-48013-2_4

orphan life in the US in her short story collection, *We Should Never Meet* (2004).[1] When asked why she wrote this collection, Phan explicitly places these stories against the multitude of US military accounts of the war; she wanted to follow the lives of those with "absolutely no decision-making power," those who have to the deal with the consequences of decisions made by others, those who are most vulnerable to these consequences: namely, women (mothers, in particular) and children.

We do not know what becomes of that injured child, but we do know that shortly after this incident, President Ford initiated Operation Babylift, a program that would airlift 2500 children out of Vietnam to the US in the weeks before the Fall of Saigon in April 1975 and the end of what the US and most of the world would call the Vietnam War.[2] And while many would extol this program as one of the "greatest humanitarian efforts" of our time,[3] we see in Phan's stories that the lives of children of war, even those thought to be "saved," display the haunting afterlife of war and empire, an afterlife that takes on new life—new faces and forms—as it intersects with contemporary structures of violence in the US.

Making Meaning of the Vietnam War

April 1975 would mark the end of US military involvement in Vietnam supporting South Vietnam in a decade-long civil war and, before that, less official support of France's post–World War II reassertion of colonial power. April 1975 would mark the Fall of Saigon and the end of the Vietnam War, as northern communist forces overtook the southern capital. This moment would also begin the mass exodus of Vietnamese from Vietnam, the beginning of the diaspora, some by US evacuation during the Fall of Saigon, others by perilous boat escapes over the next decade, earning them the nickname of "boat people," and later, through sponsorship by various governmental programs and family members.

And it would begin the complex process of postwar reckoning by all those touched by the war. Many would grapple with this war's meanings over the decades after, continuing to today. Nguyen-Vo Thu Huong describes practices of memory and mourning from four different perspectives: the memory of victors, the memory of the American antiwar left, the memory of the US as "empire builder," and, finally, the memory of survivors—Vietnamese Americans reconciling loss, displacement, and new life in the US. For Nguyen-Vo, each of these sets of "rememberers" engages in a process that is inherently strategic, making choices on what to remember, what to forget, what stories to tell. And each set of memory has consequences, for those doing the remembering and for those around them as well. Memory as both political and ethical.[4]

Memory is also religious. This chapter approaches memory, or storytelling, as a process that engages the religious imagination, the part of human experience that makes meaning. Religion is the cultural process by which life is made sense of and given meaning, through negotiating one's relationship to the everyday and transcendent dimensions of life. This process of meaning-making is both individual and communal, tying the individual to *communities of meaning* through shared meaning-making but also through the work of defining the boundaries of community and locating an individual's place within that community. This process also is shaped and constrained by *structures of meaning*, when meaning-making systems become pervasive, or characterize a particular historical period, place, and community. Most visible are traditional religious institutions with their high levels of organization and intersections with other social structures. But structures of meaning can exist outside the traditional institutions, and this chapter is interested in the kinds of meanings made that we may normally overlook when searching for religion as traditionally understood. I am particularly interested in how meaning is made and negotiated in relation to critical historical events but also in a web of differential investment and power, in a landscape of competing meaning and context of competing resources: what I am calling the *politics of meaning*.[5] Meaning-making as a politicized act within a politicized landscape, a contested religious and cultural terrain.

For this chapter, the Vietnam War is not only a historical event that happened "in the past" but also a set of experiences that have engendered and continue to engender deep reflection and meaning-making. The labors of meaning about the Vietnam War form a complex, contested, and differential landscape, with some narratives elevated high above others. The US's postwar reckoning with military defeat, a morally questionable war, and domestic turmoil over the war and its returning veterans have led to dominating narratives of veteran loss of innocence, national mourning, and national reckoning of guilt. In other words, dominant narratives tell a story of the Vietnam War as a crisis of American morality and national unity. This can be found in official national memory projects like the Vietnam Veterans Memorial, to Hollywood's grappling on the big screen in movies such as *Apocalypse Now*, to contemporary veteran memoirs and documentaries about trauma and healing, even return to Vietnam. The last several decades have seen an explosion of Vietnamese American voices joining in these labors of meaning, pushing back against these veteran-focused and American-nationalist narratives. Vietnamese Americans have tried to center Vietnamese experiences in these tellings, in their own memoirs, war memorials, fiction, poetry, and films.[6]

Aimee Phan's short story collection represents a unique intervention, with its focus not on veterans, of any side, or even on Vietnamese refugee experiences, but on some of the most marginalized figures of this time period. My close reading of this collection here examines two things: (1) how Phan's stories renarrate the Vietnam War's legacy through the complex struggles of survival and meaning of her marginalized characters; (2) and then, what Phan suggests as a possible path toward true reckoning, and perhaps what some may call "healing."

For this chapter, a religious studies approach to war and empire traces the afterlife of war in how people engage the complex political, ethical, and ultimately religious process of meaning-making. War's legacy is in forms of violence that have an afterlife; war creates new subjects, new identities, new social locations, new intersections. Here, women become birth mothers, adoptive mothers, temporary caregivers; children become orphans, fosters, adoptees. They also become refugees, subjects in movement, displacement, of no place but always of rescue. Struggles of meaning are a part of this legacy—how to make meaning of changes, of traumas, of subjectivity. By tracing this process, we can then ask what relationship might exist between systems of meaning and "healing," or reparative work after such historical violence. "Healing" or "resolution" or "reckoning" may require new meaning-making forms that are complex and messy and unexpected.

(Un)Making Mothers

Phan's collection of eight stories features several mother-characters, providing a range of motherly subjects and experiences that are affected by and *emerge from* war.

We meet Vietnamese birth mothers who give up their children to orphanages. One mother does so after being raped by an American soldier, not wanting to face the shame of both the rape and having a child out of wedlock. And because of the stark financial realities of having to support her parents and younger siblings by working in the city alone at the age of 13.

We meet a young Vietnamese woman who forgoes her own nuclear family and the possibility of biological children, leaving her fiancé to become a Catholic nun in order to care for orphans as a way of serving her god and doing the "only thing that makes sense" in this war (81).

We meet a Vietnamese mother who must work to support her young children while her husband and oldest son are away at war, ironically leaving those children at home while she cares for orphan children at work (and for new American volunteers dealing with the emotional shock of seeing the horrible conditions and stark limitations of the orphanages); and when given the choice to flee to the US, she decides to stay to wait for her husband and son.

And we meet the American doctor mentioned at the beginning, who leaves her own young child in the US for years while she cares for orphan children in Vietnam, and ultimately wanting to adopt one of the orphans herself, with this orphan's appearance in her life finally settling her anxieties about her abandonment of her husband and daughter in the US.

While each mother-character reveals particular sets of historical and structural forces that shape their lives, together they reveal foreclosed and alternative motherhood as a major site of both violence and agency during war, and demonstrate what it looks like to survive and to make meaning from wartime gendered violence. Here, I will closely examine three: Lien, the young birth mother who gives up her child; Phuong, the Vietnamese Catholic nun who finds her place in the war by embracing Catholicism and caring for babies; and Bridget, the American doctor drawn so powerfully to Vietnam's wartime orphans.

The collection opens with Lien, a young woman from Vietnam's countryside who, after the destruction of her family's farmlands during the war, must move to the city to work. In the city, she becomes pregnant, attempts unsuccessfully to abort the pregnancy, gives birth to the baby, and then anonymously gives the baby up to an orphanage. Through this story, which moves back and forth between Lien's childhood in the countryside, her work experiences in the city, and the birth of her baby, we learn of certain effects of the war on Vietnam, particularly its women. We learn the conditions that create mothers of unwanted children during this time. Lien's experiences point to the structural conditions of agricultural destruction during war, rural–urban labor migration, changing women's labors, and gender dynamics and sexuality within the context of militarism and new labor conditions. Gender and sexuality, intersected by militarism, frame much of Lien's experiences, appearing as unwanted attention from

US soldiers and Vietnamese men with whom she works, the threat of rape (which looms darkly but is never confirmed), and the shame and despair that surround her experience of pregnancy, abortion, and single motherhood. Lien's hospital roommate is a prostitute, and through her short conversation with Lien, we learn about strategic navigation of these systems: the roommate plans on keeping her baby because it is an American soldier's and could become a way toward financial support and even escape from Vietnam. In their conversation, we also learn about orphanages in Vietnam run by Catholic nuns, hinting at the intersection of religion, colonialism, war, and the transnational adoption industrial complex. The story ends with Lien traveling by foot to one of these orphanages, leaving her baby on the doorstep, and hiding while the nuns find the baby. Through Lien's palpable relief, we learn of the conditions of despair and hope in this context. Lien thinks to herself that the child is now "safe." "This child would not have to suffer" (23). This speaks to the suffering she foresees for the child if it must stay with her, within the conditions she must live in, and to a mother's hope for even an unwanted child, hope bestowed upon a system of care that relies on nonprofit volunteers and US/first-world benevolence—and ultimately even extraction and "rescue."

Lien is not the only mother of an "orphan" that we meet. Remember the nameless mother from the opening of this chapter. In a later story, "Bound," we "meet" this mother who pushes her infant through the bars of the orphanage gate to force the orphanage to take the child. She is a minor background character; we are not really sure we even meet her. In this one act, we gain a complement to Lien's fuller story, one that displays an intensity and desperation that shows what motherhood looks like—or, how it transforms—as we get closer to the Fall of Saigon, as the war and its violence come closer geographically and temporally. This one moment points to the effects of militarized escalation, impending military loss, and impending loss of sovereignty upon motherhood, and hints at the conditions that make motherhood seem impossible, that create impossible choices, that do not support the lives of certain children. These two characters, Lien and the desperate nameless woman, give humanity and historical complexity to the mothers who bore children during the war that were given to Operation Babylift. Phan's insistence upon seeing the mothers of these children, and the conditions that form their impossible choices, works to denaturalize the "orphan" subject, placing this subject squarely within the historical and structural conditions of war, gender, and violence at that time. Phan ultimately subverts the American rescue narrative that depicts Vietnamese children as naturally parentless and naturally in need of saving while framing Americans as the natural savior.

After Lien's story, we meet one of the nuns at the orphanage (perhaps the very one that picked up Lien's baby). Phuong's story is told from her ex-fiancé's perspective, seeing her for the first time years after she broke their engagement to become a nun and work with the orphans. This is a tragic love story embedded in history, or perhaps, more accurately, a story about war, religion, Vietnamese rural life, and orphans, told through a love story. The narrative, as all of Phan's stories, moves back and forth in time and space, jumping from Phuong and Truc's childhood together in the countryside to the "present" moment of their meeting in the small city, wherein Truc helps Phuong transport some of the babies to another orphanage.

In Truc's memories and his present conversation with Phuong, we find echoes of Lien's story about rural–urban migration and changing gender dynamics during war, inflected with new themes of militarization of daily life, especially in the city, of religion and colonialism, and of the nonprofit orphanage system. But in contrast to Lien's story about the foreclosure of motherhood, here we find the possibility of a different kind of mothering for Vietnamese women: care-giving in the context of the intersection of organized religion, a transnational nonprofit system, and the US military, and outside of the nuclear family and blood kinship. Phuong is able to provide emotional and material care for these babies that Lien is unable to, but only from a particular location as a Catholic nun, working in a Catholic orphanage embedded in a network of orphanages run by international adoption agencies and staffed by mostly US volunteers. Phuong herself sees these networks. Her connection with the babies while volunteering in her hometown led her to leave her family, her fiancé, and her former life, to fully occupy the social location that would allow her to continue working with the babies. In Phuong's decision, we see what must be navigated socially and structurally in order to care for these babies.

These stories also give witness to the affective ties and relationships that grow and break in the context of war. Phuong breaks ties with her family and with her childhood love but makes a new connection with the babies, one that is intertwined with her new connection with a new god. Indeed, in her decision, we see how these new affective ties form in the context of new systems of meaning emerging out of war. During their conversation in the car ride to Saigon, Truc and Phuong argue over religion and the war:

Phuong:	You have to stop blaming the Church for everything wrong…I'm asking you to consider the other side.
Truc:	The one you joined?
Phuong:	I do not work for the South Vietnamese. I work for the Lord. I'm not on either government side.
Truc:	Our country is divided. You must take sides…Don't you want this country to be reunited?
Phuong:	If I thought that would end the suffering, I would. If I believed either of the sides was not corrupt or concerned with its own ambitions, I would take up arms. But they just want to hurt each other. Nothing good will come of this war, except for these babies. If I can help them, then that will be enough for me. (80–81)

In this exchange, Truc links Phuong's religious decisions to taking the "wrong" side in the war. When she denies taking any side, he demands that she does, because for him, that is the only way to make meaning from the war. But Phuong rejects Truc's system of meaning, offering another: only the babies that make sense in this context of suffering. Phuong's dedication to them is how she makes meaning out of seemingly meaningless violence. Indeed, this meaning comes out of choosing different forms of *love*: forgoing familial love, romantic love, and even motherly love of blood kin, for the love of a new god and a motherly love for other people's abandoned children.

In Bridget, we meet a different kind of mother. She is an American mother of a young child in the US, but chooses to temporarily leave this child and her husband because of her connection to Vietnamese babies, whom she first encounters through TV. This decision in itself points to the strength of this encounter and connection: she feels such a connection with orphans she has never met, across the world, that it supersedes her own connection with her own new child. After going to Vietnam, Bridget continues to lengthen her stay for years, only leaving at the Fall of Saigon, despite her husband's and her parents' anger and her own sense of guilt at leaving her daughter. She continues to stay because of deepening connections with the babies once she works with them. She even wants to adopt one. Bridget chooses these children over her husband and daughter, refusing to return even when her husband sends her divorce papers.

In some ways, Bridget's connections and choices resemble Phuong's: Phuong becomes a nun, forgoing any future nuclear family of her own, for a commitment to these babies. But Phuong represents meaning for a Vietnamese woman living in war in her own country and encountering Catholicism and its volunteer efforts, while Bridget represents meaning for an American woman viewing the war from across the world, with deep faith in an international system of volunteer care and adoption. This faith and the meaningful connections she makes with the babies, especially Huan, the baby she wants to adopt, form a meaning system for her within not only the context of war, but also as an American woman. While the story does not explore her life before coming to Vietnam, we are left to wonder what forces in her history would propel a woman to leave her own budding family to find meaning across the globe, in a war zone, with other people's children.

In Bridget, and her husband, whose perspective we also get to see, we access a different narrative about the experiences of Americans in the war, both those in Vietnam and those at "home" in the US. Bridget's story decenters the American veteran narrative, showing the powerful effects (and affects) on Americans during the war in different and unexpected ways. These effects and affects are rendered in a different set of connections and disconnections, with self and others. Whereas veteran narratives cite brotherly fraternity, self-alienation, combat trauma, and sometimes unexpected encounters with Vietnamese soldiers and civilians, Bridget's story highlights differently gendered relationships through transformed motherhood, affective connection with children, and alienation from family in the US. Through Bridget's connections, we also see what Jodi Kim calls the "politics of pity" in action, from the perspective of an American volunteer/rescuer.[7] While an American rescue narrative is overarching for veterans, texts are uneven in their deconstruction and criticism of this narrative. In this collection, Aimee Phan identifies a major site of this narrative's manifestation that many overlook: work with the orphans and transnational adoption. In Bridget's story, we see the complexity of an American woman wholly engaging in this discourse, providing a more complex depiction of the discourse, how it compels people, what kinds of choices people struggle with when negotiating its affective power, and ultimately the possibilities *and* limits of agency and personhood within this context.

This discourse finds expression throughout these four stories in the form of an overarching system of hope. This affective and meaning system, along with conditions of impossibility for motherhood and alternative (and fraught) forms of motherhood, ties these women together. All the women, while differentially related to the war and adoption system, believe in the power of the adoption system to provide for these children and, to a certain extent, provide meaning to large-scale violence and personal-scale sacrifice. This hope, both a structure of feeling and a structure of meaning, depends upon several related structures. Discourses of American exceptionalism, constructions of racialized victimhood and saviorhood (particularly in the figure of the refugee), and the politics of pity play pivotal roles in how these women understand their roles and the limits and possibilities for their choices and for the lives of the children. These discourses connect with other powerful structures that determine the conditions of these women's lives, such as US imperialism, militarism, and a first-world/third-world divide within globalized capitalism.

The Orphan-Refugee: Alternate Subjects of War, Diaspora, and American Citizenry

The stories that take place in the US revolve around three orphan characters whose lives reveal both the structural violence that shapes their experiences and the kinds of agency possible within those structures. Indeed, the orphan subject, or adoptee subject, has been a critical site of inquiry in the field of adoption studies. In the now-classic collection *Outsiders Within*, editors Jane Jeong Trenka, Julia Chinyere Oparah, and Sun Yung Shin describe an emergent field of study led by transnational and transracial adoptees that contextualizes the experiences of adoption within larger historical structures, especially uneven distributions of power and resources. This field redefines transnational and transracial adoption as "the intimate face of colonialism, racism, militarism, imperialism, and globalization," ultimately calling for "long-term solutions embedded in struggles for economic, racial, and global justice that address the root causes leading to children of color being removed from their families or surrendered for adoption." Trenka, Oparah, and Shin suggest that real alternatives to adoption are found in "welfare policies that support poor mothers of color rather than penalizing them, criminal justice polices that strengthen and heal communities rather than destroying them, and international policies that prioritize human security over profits."[8] Indeed, Aimee Phan's work is in direct conversation with this field, as she rejects simple narratives of rescued orphan children and happy integration, instead tracing the intimacies

Trenka, Oparah, and Shin write of, as they are embedded in histories of war, colonialism, and racism. Phan's characters struggle with their place as orphans, refugees, racial others, war's remnants struggling with belonging, their experiences butting up against and exceeding a host nation's structures of meaning. And they respond with acts of vexed survival that engage meaning through alternative community and belonging, or what Jodi Kim calls "new geographies of kinship."[9] Indeed, it is in alternative familial relationships—how they are formed, maintained, broken; and the meanings inscribed in each of these acts—that we can trace the reach and aftermath of war and empire.

The three orphans we meet represent three different trajectories for postwar orphan-refugee life. Kim is a mixed-race Babylift orphan, now 20 years old, living in Little Saigon, California, with her boyfriend, Vinh, who was an "unaccompanied minor" boat refugee and who grew up with her in foster care. Highlighted in her story are struggles with racial ambiguity and misrecognition, work and poverty, sexual abuse from foster fathers, and sexual and reproductive autonomy. The plot revolves around her attempts to disentangle herself from Vinh and his gang, through financial independence and connecting with others. However, these attempts flounder as Kim faces an unwanted pregnancy, financial trouble, and rejection. Her attempt to connect with a middle-aged Vietnamese store-owner fails when she asks the woman for money for an abortion and the woman refuses. Kim's story ends with her setting Vinh's gang on the store-owner in retaliation.

Vinh's story revolves around his connection with an old Vietnamese man who he chats up while scouting that man's home as a possible mark for a home invasion. Because of their conversation, Vinh becomes reluctant to go through with the home invasion. But he is pressured by his gang, and the story ends with the gang's violent attack upon the old man and his family. From Vinh's perspective, we see a variety of emotions and relationships: his love for Kim, which rivals his loyalties to his gang; his anger at the US nation-state, which he blames for the war, his migration, and the state violence of the foster care system; and his unexpected intimacy with the old man—and then violent response when the man recognizes him during the home invasion.

Mai, we actually meet briefly in Kim's story, as the long-time foster friend who Kim both admires and disdains for her stable foster home and high academic achievement. Mai is poised to leave the community of fosters permanently. Her story representing an upward climb toward what most would deem success: she is about to go to college; she is about to "get out." But she struggles with feelings of inadequacy because her fosters never adopted her. She has survivor's guilt with respect to Kim's experiences of sexual violence. And she feels a deep ambivalence for "abandoning" Kim.

Each of the orphans has vexed ties to the alternative family of foster children, ties that compete with other relationships in their lives. Each faces multiple belongings, loyalties, and accusations of betrayal. Kim's and Vinh's stories revolve around their connections with older Vietnamese parent figures and then the violent destruction of that connection in moments of emotional turmoil. Both pull back, at least momentarily, into the relative "safety" of their alternative kin. But this safety is unstable: they choose the violence and poverty of the gang, financial instability, sexual exploitation, and lack of reproductive options (for Kim) as tradeoffs for a safety built to protect them from the failures of the state and of adults in their lives. Mai, on the other hand, chooses differently. She leaves this alternative network behind for a more stable economic future. But Mai faces self-alienation as she must perform both a fetishized version of herself for her college essay and a kind of model minority subjectivity for upward mobility. In these characters, Phan shows that survival is not a single act but a continuous negotiation and that, indeed, "rescue" itself is sometimes what one must survive. For these orphan-refugees, it is through navigating structures of community, loyalty, and betrayal that they find ways of vexed survival and meaning.

Much more can be said about the ways these characters navigate their identities, communities, and the forces that violently shape their lives. What I want to emphasize here is how Phan intricately traces the continuing life of war and empire through the orphan-refugee subject. War creates these subjects, and then this historical violence intersects with contemporary structures of race, sexism, and capitalism as these orphan-refugees navigate life in the US. Phan demonstrates what scholars of adoption studies argue: that adoption and orphans need to be understood in the larger contexts of colonialism, racism, militarism, imperialism, and globalization. Orphans are not simply naturally existing. Adoption is not simply the dehistoricized and depoliticized process of matching babies with parents and "completing families." And complex transnational, transracial dynamics are not simply disappeared by colorblind love and assimilation.[10]

Return and Reckoning

Wartime motherhood (as foreclosed or alternatively routed) and postwar orphan children's identities and relationships act as Aimee Phan's sites of excavation. She finds that war reroutes motherhood and creates orphan-refugees within a transnational adoption industrial complex. We see the path of violence that war wreaks, but also, because of this, the sites of struggle for agency and personhood—and meaning. In this section, I trace what Phan suggests might be "resolution" coming out of war, in order to better understand the afterlife of violence, the life of trauma, and the complexities of anything we want to call "healing."

Healing is ambivalent throughout Phan's collection. After the first seven stories, healing seems entirely beyond reach, the violence and trauma seemingly unredressable. But Phan's final story ends much more hopefully, with two of the orphans' return to Vietnam. Here we see Phan's imagining of what postwar "healing" or "closure" might look like. This return trip, written from the perspective of Huan, a black-Vietnamese Operation Babylift adoptee, is marked by deep anxiety and resentment around issues of anti-mixed-race (and anti-black) racism and ethnic rejection/abandonment. The plot revolves around several negative encounters—one with local police and another with a child hawker—as Huan travels through Vietnam, ostensibly to get in touch with "his past," particularly through visiting the two orphanages he lived in as a child. Mai, a long-time friend, accompanies Huan on this trip, and Huan works through many of his feelings in conversations with her throughout the story, but Mai herself is reserved about her own responses to being in Vietnam, until the last scene.

> I was afraid of hating everyone here, Mai says.
>
> Huan looks at her.
>
> They sent us to America because of you. Mai shrugs her shoulders. Our parents saw pictures of you full of food and in rich people's arms. They thought we'd get that, too. But we came too late. We weren't babies anymore, so nobody wanted us. It was no different from Vietnam (242).
>
> How do you feel now? Huan asks.
>
> I know better. It's not our parents' faults. Or anyone else's here. How could I be angry with them, expect them to do right when there was no such thing? When everything here was wrong?
>
> Huan nods, understanding. It was a war.
>
> It was. (243)

In this conversation, the statement "it was a war" is imbued with so much meaning, between Mai and Huan and for the entire collection. It is a condensed form of what the collection tries to illustrate, theorized throughout but finally articulated here. War is not simply a military action between nations occurring in a distant past. War is also the profound upheaval and restructuring of lives; affecting societies, communities, and individuals at multiple levels. Its violences reach through time and space. War creates impossible choices and dehumanized people who try to find and express their humanity in those choices. War makes "everything…wrong." And it is almost impossible to create "right" out of this wrong, even in (or especially in) the attempt to "save" orphan children, or refugees more generally.

In this moment of shared understanding, Mai and Huan demonstrate a reckoning that does not erase trauma or require reconciliation, but instead connects the personal to the structural, the individual to the social, and recognizes violence and trauma at these interconnected levels. Phan argues that true reckoning with war requires fuller understanding of violence and what it takes to survive and find one's (and a community's) humanity. It also requires recognizing that violence is continual, that the legacies of war join other structural forces in the present, and that survival is thus also a continual, evolving act. Phan's version of what we might call "healing" looks quite different from healing narratives that center family reunion, personal "forgiveness," or even returning to or visiting sites of trauma. She offers something perhaps akin to memory practices suggested by Vietnamese American scholars, such as Viet Thanh Nguyen's "ethical memory" or Nguyen-Vo Thu-Huong's "complex remembrance."[11]

Viet Thanh Nguyen distinguishes between "minority memory" and "national memory," with minority memory often working as "counter-memory" in response to dominant forms of memory. In relation to the Vietnam War, Nguyen identifies three major players in the contest over the memory of the war's ghosts: "American nationalism, Asian American and minority discourse, and Vietnamese nationalism fight over these ghosts, seeking to reclaim them for their own brands of justice." For Nguyen, Vietnamese Americans are caught in this three-way tug of war: "Vietnamese refugees find themselves at the crossroads of these competing versions of memory. Absent or misrepresented in all three, refugees are just as likely to stage their own competing memory." What worries Nguyen the most are the ethical implications for the ways in which rememberers invoke the war's ghostly figures. While forms of counter-memory indeed respond to dominant memory, they are not necessarily resistant or inherently ethical.[12]

Nguyen-Vo Thu-Huong echoes Nguyen, presuming memory as a terrain of struggle. She highlights agency in the act of remembering and insists this agency has political and ethical implications, that "remembering is a political and ethical act involving choice." Indeed, for her, ethics are the ultimate stakes of memory, and she asks us to imagine what "ethical mourning" might look like in relation to the Vietnam War:

> How shall we remember?...How shall we remember rather than just appropriate the dead for our own agendas, precluding what the dead can tell us? Thus we must ask: Whom among the dead shall we mourn? How do we retrieve our histories containing events that had passed, with the dead, into accomplished fates? Finally, how shall we speak to those who survived, who now remember various histories amongst us? How we remember will either open or foreclose our paths to our various presents and futures.[13]

Here, I read Phan's rendering as both complex and ethical in its efforts to capture the multivalence of violence and personhood, trauma, and agency. In her closing story in particular, we can appreciate the ways in which it differs from other, more expected, return narratives. The story does not center veterans and their desires to assuage guilt; it does not even center adoptee searches for birth parents. Indeed, Huan finds meaning in unexpected places: not in visiting the orphanages of his past but in interacting with locals in difficult ways, in seeing contemporary youth culture in Vietnam, in bonding with Mai, who is also an orphan but differentially related to structures of displacement, adoption, and race. But despite this complexity, return in this story is still a one-time experience and not a continuous relationship with contemporary Vietnam. Not even taking into account that return is not possible or even desirable for all Vietnamese abroad, I worry about the use of Vietnam as a place for diasporic grappling with trauma, arguably almost as appropriative as veteran practices of return. Vietnam becomes a place to tell us things about ourselves, instead of its own place with living people still there making life, making meaning—in relation to war, to the diaspora returning, to their own state apparatus, to their own social and cultural structures, to a globalized world.

And what about mothers? What is healing for women? We have a glimpse of Huan's adoptive mother and her well-meaning but cringeworthy attempts at being supportive of Huan's experience and journey. But no other "mothers" appear in the present-day, in contemporary Vietnam or in the diaspora. If we follow the path Phan begins to trace, then we are left to ask what motherhood looks like, in contemporary Vietnam, in the diaspora, and how the Vietnamese family has transformed because of the ways motherhood was so violently reshaped during war—and what kinds of meanings are being made as women, and their families, reckon with these changes.

Phan provides us a beginning step, opening a much-needed door to the complex life of war and trauma, and the tricky paths of survival. Indeed, this chapter ultimately suggests an expansive understanding of both religion and violence in order to trace how these two engage one another, and to expand how we might think of healing in the aftermath of violence. But as Phan beautifully and tragically illustrates, violence is ongoing, especially in marginalized lives. So, I offer another suggestion: if injury is a condition of living in the afterlife of war and empire; if, as Ann Cvetkovich suggests, depression is a condition of living in contemporary capitalism; if, as Jim Lee suggests, "woundedness" is inherent in the human condition; then what we think of as healing must shift away from notions of personal or collective redress or even "repair." We must ask: if the world is full of violence, if life is the negotiation of wounds, then how do we make meaning from these experiences, *and* how do the meanings we make actually address our wounds and the wounds of those around us? In other words, are the ways we make meaning sufficient for the kinds of injury we experience—and cause—on a daily basis? Perhaps we need to explore what Cvetkovich suggests: "new ways [or practices] of living,"[14] or Lee's "pedagogy of suffering," which he hopes will create new ways of acknowledging and living in "inherent" woundedness, allowing us to "make social meaning in that woundedness."[15] Indeed, what might it look like then to approach "healing" as a relentless life practice? Here, religious studies might offer a framework. If religion is life practices of meaning-making, then healing might be a process whose goal is perhaps not restoration or wholeness per se, but continual meaning-making of that wounding, through it, and sometimes in spite of it. A reckoning through labors of the religious imagination, throughout one's life, a community's life. Relentless, political, ethical.

For Aimee Phan, it takes looking in forgotten corners to reveal this complex world that layers directly over the worlds remembered and made meaningful by other cultural works. Thus, the work of memory and meaning here is not only a rejection of dominant Vietnam War memory as "what happened" or even "what was important," but also a rejection of those worlds, those meanings, those ways of defining community, those ways of understanding how life (and death) happen. For dominant US memory, this is an intervention, a rejection and subversion. But it is also an offering, of new knowledge and meaning, of new ways to truly reckon with the Vietnam War and with postwar, racialized, gendered life and death in the US. For Vietnamese America, this is an offering that is also a plea, asking the community to remember and *see* the "dust of life" in our community, to count membership and who matters, differently.[16] In thinking about the war, it asks Vietnamese America to define loss differently and thus mourn differently—and even draw on alternative affective responses outside of conventional modes of mourning and healing. Ultimately, it asks the community to *be* differently in our lives as Americans, Vietnamese Americans, and *Viet kieu* in diaspora. For second-generation Vietnamese Americans, Phan's call is particularly poignant and challenging, raising questions of how this generation is to remember the war and experience its legacies in "postmemory."[17] Phan does not depict a nostalgia for a lost motherland as their "inheritance" for the second generation, as many other Vietnamese American productions have. Instead, she asks the second generation, of which she is a part, to attempt their own complex remembrance. For Phan, this critical engagement requires the second and future generations to take on different lenses in viewing the war, the Vietnamese American community and its practices, their place within American society, and their relationship to the larger diaspora and Vietnam. It is in this complex remembrance and radical shift in lens that Phan's hope for the future lies, for all of us.

Notes

1. Aimee Phan, *We Should Never Meet: Stories* (New York: Picador Press, 2004).
2. Vietnamese would call it by other names too, including the American War. Some Vietnamese and Vietnamese American scholars choose to write "Viet Nam," as it would be written in Vietnamese. This chapter uses the conventional name and spelling, Vietnam War, for ease of reading, recognizing that this name and spelling have politicized histories and presents.
3. "Operation Babylift: 40 Years After Bay Area Opened Arms To Vietnam's Orphans, Historic Sites Hidden In Plain Sight." http://sanfrancisco.cbslocal.com/2015/04/15/operation-air-drop-40-years-after-bay-area-opened-arms-to-vietnams-orphans/, 15 April 2015.
4. Nguyen-Vo Thu Huong, "Forking Paths: How Shall We Mourn the Dead?" *Amerasia Journal* 31, no. 2 (2005).

5. The term "politics of meaning" has been used in other fields to discuss discourse and contested social and cultural meanings, but not usually used in a religious sense. Most notable use in religion would be Micheal Lerner's book, *A Politics of Meaning: Restoring Hope and Possibility in an Age of Cynicism* (New York: Basic Books, 1997), which argues that contemporary American life is marked by a spiritual poverty, meaninglessness, and lack of deep connection with others, that both the political and the religious left and right do not fulfill, and Lerner's solution is a "politics of meaning" that shifts a materialism-oriented culture to a "meaning-oriented" one, from "a focus on profit or other material values to a focus on ethical, spiritual, social, and ecological values" (216). So, Lerner is using meaning in its religious sense, and proposes a particular formation of politics of meaning. This chapter uses the term politics of meaning to highlight the political nature of meaning, which resonates somewhat with Lerner's use, though I am not proposing an adoption of a particular kind of meaning system. I am interested in investigating and evaluating the politics of the kinds of meaning-making that occurs in these cultural sites.
6. For religious readings of the Vietnam War's legacy, see Walter H. Capps, *The Unfinished War: Vietnam and the American Conscience*, 2nd ed. (Boston: Beacon Press, 1990) and John Hellmann, *American Myth and the Legacy of Vietnam* (New York: Columbia University Press, 1986). Major scholarly works on memory and memorialization include Marita Sturken, *Tangled Memories: The Vietnam War, the AIDS Epidemic, and the Politics of Remembering* (Berkeley: University of California Press, 1997); Julia Bleakney, *Revisiting Vietnam: Memoirs, Memorials, Museums* (New York: Routledge, 2006); Kristin Ann Hass, *Carried to the Wall: American Memory and the Vietnam Veterans Memorial* (Berkeley: University of California Press, 1998); Patrick Hagopian, *The Vietnam War in American Memory: Veterans, Memorials, and the Politics of Healing* (Amherst: University of Massachusetts Press, 2009). Notable works of fiction and memoir include Tim O'Brien's memoir *If I Die in a Combat Zone, Box Me Up and Ship Me Home* (1969), novel *Going After Cacciato* (1978), and short story collection *The Things They Carried* (1990); Frances Fitzgerald's journalistic account and analysis of Vietnamese culture *Fire in the Lake* (1972); Philip Caputo's memoir *A Rumor of War* (1977), novel *DelCorso's Gallery* (1983), and novel *Indian Country* (1987); Larry Heinemann's novels *Close Quarters* (1977) and *Paco's Story* (1986) and memoir *Black Virgin Mountain* (2005); Michael Herr's journalistic account of wartime Vietnam *Dispatches* (1978); James Webb's novels *Fields of Fire* (1978) and *Lost Soldiers* (2001); and John Del Vecchio's novels *The 13th Valley* (1982) and *Carry Me Home* (1995). The most famous and oft-cited films within the Vietnam War film genre are Michael Cimino's *Deer Hunter* (1978), Francis Ford Coppola's *Apocalypse Now* (1979), Oliver Stone's *Platoon* (1986) and *Born on the Fourth of July*

(1989), Stanley Kubrick's *Full Metal Jacket* (1987), and perhaps the *Rambo* action series (beginning in 1982).

For Vietnamese American interventions, see scholarly works of Yen Le Espiritu, "The We-Win-Even-When-We-Lose Syndrome: U.S. Press Coverage of the Twenty-Fifth Anniversary of the 'Fall of Saigon,'" *American Quarterly* 58, no. 2 (2006); Viet Thanh Nguyen, "Remembering War, Dreaming Peace: On Cosmopolitanism, Compassion, and Literature," *The Japanese Journal of American Studies* 20 (2009); Viet Thanh Nguyen, "Speak of the Dead, Speak of Viet Nam: The Ethics and Aesthetics of Minority Discourse," *CR: The New Centennial Review* 6, no. 2 (Fall 2006); and Viet Thanh Nguyen's forthcoming monograph, *Nothing Ever Dies: Vietnam and the Memory of War* (Harvard University Press, 2016). Major works of Vietnamese American literature include Le Ly Hayslip and James Wurts, *When Heaven and Earth Changed Places* (New York: Doubleday, 1989); Jade Ngoc Quang Huynh, *South Wind Changing* (Saint Paul: Graywolf Press, 1994); Nguyen Qui Duc, *Where the Ashes Are: The Odyssey of a Vietnamese Family* (Reading, Mass.: Addison-Wesley, 1994); the anthologies *Watermark: Vietnamese American Poetry and Prose* (New York: Asian American Writer's Workshop, 1998) and *Once Upon a Dream* (Kansas City: Andrews and McMeel, 1995); Andrew X. Pham's popular memoir *Catfish and Mandala: A Two-Wheeled Voyage through the Landscape and Memory of Vietnam* (New York: Farrar, Strause, & Giroux, 1999); Truong Tran's poetry collection *Dust and Conscience* (Berkeley: Apogee Press, 2002); Andrew Lam's collection of personal essays *Perfume Dreams: Reflections on the Vietnamese Diaspora* (Berkeley: Heydey Books, 2005); and a series of fiction, the most well-known being Lan Cao's *Monkey Bridge* (New York: Viking, 1997); le thi diem thuy's *The Gangster We're All Looking For* (New York: Knopf, 2003); Linh Dinh's short story collection *Fake House* (Seven Stories Press, 1998) and novel *Love Like Hate* (Seven Stories Press, 2010); Monique Truong's *Book of Salt* (Houghton Mifflin, 2003) and *Bitter in the Mouth* (Random House, 2010); G.B Tran's graphic novel *Vietnamerica* (Villard, 2011); and most recently, Lan Cao's *The Lotus and the Storm* (Penguin, 2015), Vu Tran's *Dragonfish* (W.W. Norton & Co, 2015), and Viet Thanh Nguyen's *The Sympathizer* (Grove Atlantic, 2015).

7. Jodi Kim, *Ends of Empire: Asian American Critique and the Cold War* (Minneapolis: University of Minnesota Press, 2010).
8. Julia Chinyere Oparah, Sun Ying Shin, and Jane Jeong Trenka, "Introduction," in *Outsiders Within: Writing on Transracial Adoption* (Cambridge: South End Press, 2006), 7. Adoption studies has grown, especially in the last five years, with most studies focusing on Korean transnational adoption. Major titles include Eleana Kim, *Adopted Territory* (2010), Kristi Brian, *Reframing Transracial Adoption* (2012), and SooJin Pate, *From Orphan to Adoptee* (2014). For a historical investigation of the

organizational and institutional structures of the adoption industry, see Cathy Choy, *Global Families* (2013).

9. Kim, *Ends of Empire*, 203. Here, Kim draws on Toby Alice Folkman from *Cultures of Transnational Adoption* (Durham: Duke University Press, 2005).
10. Phan's intervention differs as well from other Operation Babylift narratives. The documentary *Operation Babylift* (2009), for instance, focuses on adoption/orphanage workers (aside from adoptees) and does not include Vietnamese mothers. It also does not examine wartime forces and changes in Vietnam, and explores adoptee experiences of racialization and alienation mostly through the lens of interpersonal racist violence instead of structural violence. While the documentary does emphasize the kind of community that adoptees yearn for and build with each other, its analysis of both these desires and meaning-making is not located contextually within histories of racialized violence. Alternative community for Phan, however, is layered and shot through with these histories and structures.
11. Nguyen-Vo Thu-Huong, "Forking Paths"; Viet Thanh Nguyen, "Just Memory: War and the Ethics of Remembrance," *American Literary History* 25, no. 1 (2013): 144–163; Viet Thanh Nguyen, "Speak of the Dead, Speak of Viet Nam: The Ethics and Aesthetics of Minority Discourse," *CR: The New Centennial Review* 6, no. 2 (Fall 2006): 13, 31.
12. Viet Thanh Nguyen, "Just Memory: War and the Ethics of Remembrance," *American Literary History* 25, no. 1 (2013): 144–163; Viet Thanh Nguyen, "Speak of the Dead, Speak of Viet Nam: The Ethics and Aesthetics of Minority Discourse," *CR: The New Centennial Review* 6, no. 2 (Fall 2006): 13, 31.
13. Nguyen-Vo, "Forking Paths," 159.
14. Ann Cvetkovich, *Depression: A Public Feeling* (Durham: Duke University Press, 2012), 26.
15. James Kyung-Jin Lee, "Elegies of Social Life: The Wounded Asian American," *Journal of Race, Ethnicity, and Religion* 3, no. 2.7 (January 2012), 21.
16. "Dust of life" is a translation of *bui doi*, what Vietnamese colloquially, and pejoratively, called the mixed-race children of US soldiers and Vietnamese women during the war.
17. Marianne Hirsh coins the term "postmemory" to describe the generational transmission of trauma. Hirsh writes: "Postmemory is a powerful form of memory precisely because its connection to its object or source is mediated not through recollection but through an imaginative investment and creation." Marianne Hirsh, "Past Lives: Postmemories in Exile," *Poetics Today* 17, no. 4 (Winter 1996): 659.

CHAPTER 5

A Mission of Biopower: The United States Colonizes the Philippines

Jeremy Posadas

The US project in the Philippines, with its multiple prongs, was a mission to transform the islands into a *biopolitical* archipelago: a chain of practices designed to regularize the behavior of an entire body politic in order to inculcate the capacities desired by the US in its "little brown brothers" (and sisters). The efforts of US Protestant missionaries, particularly in the first few decades after the 1898 invasion, must therefore be understood as part of this archipelago, joined with the administrative, geographic, public health, educational, and other practices of US military and civilian forces. Across nearly all the Protestant denominations active in the Philippines during this period, missionaries did *not* have a program of

This piece is dedicated to the memory of my late brother, Filipino-American writer and Iraq war veteran Adam Cajiuat Posadas (1985–2016): the brutalities he experienced and witnessed in the war, which contributed to his suicide, have made the political achingly personal in this essay; and his brilliant reflections on war, love, and justice will inspire me always. I wish also to express special gratitude to Profs. Anne Joh and Nami Kim for their encouragement all along the way.

J. Posadas (✉)
Austin College, Sherman, TX, USA

N. Kim, W.A. Joh (eds.), *Critical Theology against US Militarism in Asia*,
DOI 10.1057/978-1-137-48013-2_5

goals and methods that was fundamentally distinct from the program pursued by military and civilian leaders; missionary activities were mobilized by the same mindset as military and civilian ones and often took similar (or highly compatible) forms. This mindset is most insightfully understood as the mindset of what social analyst Michel Foucault conceptualized as *biopower*, which I will explicate in the first section below. Biopower provided a common framework within which US military personnel, missionaries, bureaucrats, educators, public health officers, and their co-imperialists made sense of what they were doing in the Philippines and why they were doing it; biopower made their various activities comprehensible to one another. Indeed, one does not find a plethora of instances where US missionaries opposed military and civilian approaches, and when they did so, it was often in order to further promote biopolitical projects, rather than to diminish them.

By analyzing US Protestant missionaries as fundamentally operating within a common framework with military and civilian personnel, one can more fully understand how seamlessly integrated religious practices were within US imperial strategy and technique. Protestant leaders and workers were not simply swept up in the tide of colonial adventure, nor was missionary participation in imperialism simply a deal with the devil to reach millions of Asians deemed in need of salvation. Rather, biopower provided a strategic paradigm shared among military personnel, missionaries, bureaucrats, educators, public health officers, and others, which they used to identify their place in the Philippines and to pursue their program of "uplifting" the Filipino body politic.

This chapter primarily considers how US personnel (military, civilian, and religious) organized the occupation and colonization of the Philippines, especially in the first two decades after the US Navy landed in Manila Bay. In the first section, I give an overview of Foucault's concept of biopower, including both its disciplinary and its regulatory modes. Following that, I discuss the racialized and race-exterminist context of the US occupation, which provided the basis for overarching strategies of biopower as the US extended its dominance over the archipelago. I then consider some of the basic contours of the biopolitical project shared by US military personnel and missionaries, before turning to instantiations of biopower in educational and public health practices; what becomes evident is the extent to which Protestant missionaries partnered fully with their US military and civilian authorities. I intentionally focus on the colonizers rather than the colonized because my goal here is to explicate commonalities between how US colonizers understood their project and certain technical forms deployed to accomplish it. Thus, the myriad ways Filipinos resisted (and sometimes adopted) US biopower, which deserves its own detailed consideration, fall outside the scope of this chapter.

Biopower as a Mindset for Governing Populations and Bodies[1]

Methodologically, Foucault sought to conceptualize power outside the paradigms of liberal and Marxian political theories. Power for Foucault was not a commodity possessed in a zero-sum fashion, where one can only gain power by decreasing the power of others. Instead, Foucault conceptualized power in terms of a relationship in which individuals and groups seek to lead each other to act in specific ways: to "con*duct* the *con*duct" of one another, to use a Foucaultian phrase.[2] Thus, power is not solely a matter of endless violence or oppression, but rather all the different techniques through which people seek to get other people to act in specific ways. By implication, then, power (i.e., not oppression, but attempting to con*duct* one another's *con*duct) infuses every interpersonal and intergroup interaction, because in every interaction, people are trying to lead one another to act in particular ways. Power is about individuals and/or groups shaping the fields of action available to one another, constantly in reaction and relation to another, in order to make some actions more likely than others—but always liable to the other's attempts to counter-conduct the situation.

By using this overall conception of power, Foucault then offered an account of the operations of power in the context of Western European societies (along with the lands and societies colonized by or governed in the manner of them), roughly from the sixteenth century onward. Within this setting, Foucault identifies a "general economy" of power, which he names in at least three different ways: *biopower* (in volume 1 of *The History of Sexuality* and the lecture series *Society Must Be Defended*), *security* (at the start of the lecture series *Security, Territory, Population*), and *governmentality* (at the end of that same lecture series, as well as in several later essays). For clarity, I have chosen here to consistently use the term *biopower* (and the adjectival *biopolitical*) to refer to the overall phenomenon of this general economy of power, without meaning to deny the distinctions among Foucault's different formulations.

Biopower congealed as a general economy of power over several centuries, with initial rumblings as early as the Protestant Reformation and beginning to assume its present form in the eighteenth century: concurrent, that is, with waves of European colonization of Latin America, Asia, and Africa. Two major shifts in Western societies prompted its emergence. The first was the shift from two "totalizing institutions"—the Church and the Empire (Roman, then Holy Roman alongside other sovereignties)—to one, the modern nation-state. A different form of power operated through each of the totalizing institutions, "pastoral power" for the Church and "political power" for the Empire. Pastoral power works through a concern for "all and each," for the total well-being of a group of people (the "flock" cared for by the "shepherd" [Latin: *pastor*]) and for the individual welfare of each member of the group. Pastoral power's techniques of ascertaining truth (primarily through forms of confession and autobiography) allow it to individualize each sheep in the flock. At the same time, pastoral power must maintain the total health of the flock overall. Thus, in Foucault's oft-repeated phrase, pastoral power is simultaneously "individualizing and totalizing."

The shift from Church-and-Empire to modern nation-state is its own story (the details of which do not bear centrally upon my argument here). What is important to note here is that by the sixteenth century, the modern nation-state had begun to incorporate pastoral power's two modes to accomplish its own projects for its own uses. This appropriation was rapidly advanced by the emergence of an entirely new domain of knowledge: the study of humans as systems comparable to the system of natural, physical forces that modern physics was beginning to comprehend around the same time. In this domain of knowledge, human individuals were organisms whose birth, vitality, development, decay, and death were all knowable by rationalist science. And human collectivities, from families to tribes to towns to whole societies, could be determinately understood in the same way. This domain of knowledge has come to comprise, in the present day, the immense range of biomedical as well as social and behavioral sciences. The latter are sometimes referred to in Europe as the human sciences. These sciences all focus on understanding humans as living systems, along with all the forms and structures of intervention, therapeutics, services, and policy generated by the application of these sciences.

The biomedical, human, and social and behavioral sciences have enmeshed themselves within the structures of the modern nation-state to the extent that these sciences have become the basis for the state's program of governing all of society.[3] These sciences provide the state (and other networks of agency) with new ways to analyze the overall field of societal life, as well as new techniques for managing it. Indeed, Foucaultian biopower could be most concisely defined as *the rational management of human life, on the basis of the human sciences, toward the optimal functioning of human society*. The state, in turn, has adapted the two modes of pastoral power—individualizing and totalizing—that it appropriated from the church. Foucault and other analysts of biopower use several different pairs to name the joint operation of individualizing and totalizing power: anatomo-politics and bio-politics, discipline and bio-politics, or discipline and security. Here I consistently use *disciplinary biopower* and *regulatory biopower* to name, respectively, the individualizing and totalizing modes of power derived from pastoral power. Biopower is the general situation of modern Western (and West-governed) societies in which discipline and regulation—on the basis of contemporary biomedical, human, and social and behavioral sciences—are the pervasive, predominant techniques for con*duct*ing the *con*duct of individuals, populations (groups of bodies), and whole societies.

Biopower functions more as a mindset than as an instruction manual. It provides a lens through which patterns of conduct by individuals, populations, and whole societies can be perceived, interpreted, and evaluated. In other words, biopower operates as a basic paradigm within which individual and group behavior becomes meaningful and significant at all. All human activity is understood by reference to its alignment with or deviation from whatever is categorized as "normal" behavior. And the task of defining *normal* is especially the purview of experts in the biomedical, human, and social and behavioral sciences. However, the mindset of biopower links such judgments to particular genres of intervention by various authorities within society.

A distinguishing feature of biopower is that its interventions are much more finely calibrated than a blanket threat of death and rule by intimidation on the basis of it. Foucault contrasts biopower with sovereign power, which, in his reading, was much more characteristic of pre-modern European societies. Sovereign power works primarily by raising the threat of being killed: the monarch's power arises from his prerogative to decide whether to execute someone who has offended his honor or committed a similar violation. A nation-state's biopower, by contrast, derives from its ability to make subjects live—and motivates individuals and populations to live—in manners established by governing authorities. Sovereign power seeks to eliminate threats by killing or expelling bodies, while biopower seeks to prevent threats from emerging in the first place by training out of bodies behavior that is perceived as threatening and placing bodies that falter in re-training environments. Governing authorities design biopolitical interventions to continuously modify behavior so that it more closely aligns with their definitions of normalcy, ideally in a self-correcting way. Such interventions are both totalizing and individualizing by targeting whole populations (*regulatory biopower*) and the individual bodies that constitute them (*disciplinary biopower*).

In its regulatory mode, biopower enables governing authorities to manage the life outcomes of the populations (groups of bodies) that constitute a society so as to reach whatever is considered an "optimal" level of the overall vitality, productivity, health of a society. These life outcomes include such demographic basics as birth rate, fertility, life expectancy, and conditions of healthiness and disease. In addition to these basics, life outcomes include all aspects of human "development," such as educational success, non-adequate yearly performance, patterns of residential separateness, and the growth or decline of sectors of the economy and the "labor forces" associated with them. Regulatory biopower seeks to coordinate the activities of populations within a society as an aggregate, in order to maintain alignment with established norms of collective functioning. The key is understanding that reaching a goal of collective functioning does not require equal development of all populations. Often, strategies of biopower (intentionally or implicitly) enhance the vitality and health of particular populations within a given society, while exposing the health or social productivity of other populations to greater risks. Each population's life outcomes need to be managed only so that they do not pose a threat to the health of society overall. For example, the logic of biopower allows for decreasing the death rate of this population and increasing the income accrual rate of that population to the degree that is necessary to maintain what is thought of as a "Healthy Economy in a Healthy Society"—however governing authorities define *healthy*. Biopower understands each population as contributing to achieving and maintaining the overall societal health by performing a specific role that is governed by biopower's own programs and initiatives. These performances also become accepted as the *normal* behavior appropriate for each individual within that population. This is the point where biopower's disciplinary mechanism kicks in.

Disciplinary biopower consists of those processes that train bodies to act, speak, and feel in particular ways that have been defined as normal and align with the overall goals set through regulatory mechanisms. It works continuously through biomedical, human, social and behavioral sciences, and governmental policy to define and authorize certain ideas of what constitutes normal and appropriate behavior for a worker, soldier, native, and so on. On the basis of these sciences and policies, biopolitical regimes then secure multiple systems of techniques needed to train all the capacities of each individual body (from physical movement to verbal and non-verbal expression) toward repeatedly performing these particular behaviors. In the domestic context of the US, for example, biopower conditions the behavior of low-wage workers and affluent rentiers toward the norms set by governing authorities. Similarly, in the Philippine colonial context, US disciplinary biopower trained the behaviors of US soldiers, Filipino urban elites, and rural villagers toward advancing the goals of the US occupation and colonization.

The ecology of an archipelago becomes a metaphor Foucault uses to describe how a chain of institutions work toward achieving a common goal by using biopower to discipline bodies, whether individual or group, into consistently and self-correctingly acting, speaking, and feeling in particular ways congruent with the norms required by regulatory biopower.[4] Foucault is clear, however, that biopower does not simply replace sovereign power *in toto*. Rather, mechanisms of sovereign power and biopower can cooperate in varying configurations.[5] Over time, biopower may supplant the primacy of sovereign power, but sovereign power remains as a reserve structure, ready to assert itself if biopower's efficacy should fail. The US military occupation of the Philippines can be understood as proceeding in both modes. The US occupation was propelled initially by a sovereign-power strategy, which continued to offer ever-present threats even as strategies of biopower were activated across multiple practices of the occupation. When US forces first arrived, their task was to take possession of Manila (and eventually all of the Philippines). This they accomplished through the holding of territory and persons on the threat of destruction and death. The Filipino populations who did not resist were contained or forcibly moved (through the US policy of "re-concentration"), but not primarily though biopolitical techniques of discipline and regulation because the goal was simply to remove threats to the expansion of US military force.[6] The portion who did resist were imprisoned, killed, or both. Yet once the US occupied a critical mass of territory and contained a critical mass of the population, US military and civilian personnel shifted toward using biopolitical strategies and tactics to pursue goals across a variety of areas, including health care, education, and missionary work.

The Racialization of the US Occupation

Although the Philippine-American War (the first phase of the US occupation) was highly racialized from the outset, and despite concepts of "race war" being central to Foucault's account of the emergence of biopower, the Philippine-American War was a race war that operated through sovereign power rather than biopower. The key distinction is that the US caused the death of or simply killed hundreds of thousands of Filipinos to establish US sovereignty over Philippine territory, including the people in it—but not with the overarching goal of purifying either US or Philippine societies. US political and military elites, as well as everyday soldiers and civilian personnel, understood themselves as racially superior to the Filipinos. For them, the war was a conflict in which a "civilized" people sought to contain and subdue a "savage" one. Political and military leaders rationalized American efforts with the racialist notion of "Anglo-Saxon" heritage, which they used to justify imperialism and colonization. In their view, these projects would inculcate the republican virtues necessary for inhabitants of the Philippines to eventually establish their own self-government, which would protect liberty (as well as property).[7]

A dimension of this mindset was the common characterization of the inhabitants of the Philippines as unclean, immoral, immature, unmanly, and otherwise lacking the basic capacities for civilized living. In the early weeks of the US invasion, military troops came to articulate their general perceptions of Filipinos with a racist specificity typical of US racism as white supremacy. By tracing usage of the category "nigger" in letters home, historian Paul Kramer documents how US troops adapted domestic US racist discourse to the Philippine context within a very short time frame. During the first few weeks of the war, a soldier from Oregon writes letters to his family of "natives" and "Philippinos" [*sic*], but after several more weeks, his language changes. Instead of "natives" and "Philippinos" [*sic*], he explains how one Army unit "chased out the niggers [and] run them across the swamps…" Similarly, a soldier from Nebraska wrote upon his arrival that "the natives are bright and intelligent as the average run of people," but two weeks later, he describes the place as "swarmed with the indians" [*sic*]; and another two weeks after that letter, he also tells of how his unit has "commenced to chase niggers."[8] This translation of US racism into the Philippine context was not lost on a number of black US soldiers. In letters home, some black US soldiers noted the similarities between how white soldiers mistreated Filipinos and how black people were mistreated in the US. One black US soldier decried how white soldiers were "establish[ing] their diabolical race hatred in all its home rancor in Manila..."[9] The paradigm of racial subordination that governed domestic affairs in the US provided a basic framework for relations between white US personnel and Filipinos.

Alongside the application of the category "nigger" to Filipinos, white US military personnel constructed the novel racial category of "goo-goo" (or "gu-gu"). Although its etymology is not definitively known, one main account is that it was at first meant to mark the shape of Filipino eyes as racially other. US soldiers used "gu-gu" both to express their possessive desire for Filipino women and to mock Filipino men's masculinity.[10] Its status as a term unfamiliar to US domestic audiences is marked by the common practice of soldiers explaining the meaning of the term in their letters home. According to Kramer, it "formed part of a distinctive Philippine-American colonial vocabulary that focused hatred around a novel enemy and lent American troops a sense of manly, insider camaraderie."[11] The categories "nigger" and "goo-goo" constituted the initial racial formation by which white US military personnel homogenized the many ethnic groups living in the Philippines into a single monolithic population composed of a racially other enemy upon whom they were justified in unleashing mass violence. The conclusion that this racial formation was animated by sovereign power (and not biopower) is supported by the frequent prideful references to chasing, hunting, and killing "goo-goos" and "niggers": "Killed 22 niggers ... [W]e shot the niggers like a hunter would rabbits," wrote one enlisted soldier; another soldier, this one an officer, described that his men entertained themselves by going out on nighttime "nigger hunts," which were "great fun."[12] "We would kill all in sight if we could only receive the necessary orders," wrote one soldier.[13] Kramer characterizes this strategic mindset of the early phases of the war as the pursuit of *racial exterminism*.

A program of racial exterminism (similar to the annihilation of Native Americans in the Americas, Kramer observers) led to widespread violence against and killing of Filipinos. For instance, racial exterminism became "the means by which earlier distinctions between combatants and noncombatants—already fragile—eroded or collapsed."[14] If all Filipinos were lumped into one racialized category, it became much easier to then categorize all Filipinos as the enemy. Once this equivalence is accomplished, then *any* Filipino is a fair target for killing.[15] Thus, for example, one general ordered that "all persons [be] killed who are capable of bearing arms in actual hostilities against the United States," and then clarified that any Filipino over age ten was "capable of bearing arms."[16] Over the entire war, US soldiers killed Filipinos outside the norms for war officially espoused in US military regulations. US soldiers killed not only prisoners of war and Filipinos who had collaborated with the US, but also whole groups of non-combatants. US soldiers themselves attested to these numerous incidents, which were often officially denied until years after the fact.[17] One of the war's most notorious exterminist practices—the so-called "water cure"—horrifically captures the sovereign power driving all this wanton violence. This torture practice, in which a Filipino victim was forced to rapidly swallow extreme amounts of water (often dirty) and then his or her engorged stomach was painfully beaten or kicked, was ostensibly done to extract intelligence. But in fact its primary purpose was to terrorize Filipinos into giving up their resistance. Rather than seeking to transform or channel bodily capacities—a hallmark of biopower—the water cure sought to destroy bodily capacities, often to the point of death.[18] Surveying the many aspects of exterminist military strategy, Kramer finds that the "estimate of 250,000 Filipino war deaths appears conservative."[19]

US military leaders justified this racial-exterminist approach as the necessary response to Filipino forces' fighting tactics. In the latter part of 1899, the Philippine Army was dispersed throughout the archipelago into smaller units to pursue guerilla warfare rather than traditional large-scale battlefield warfare. Guerilla warfare was outside the conventions of Euro-American military doctrine. US military leaders dealt with their disorientation by claiming, in essence, that because Filipinos were breaking (Western) rules of engagement, the US was not morally bound to adhere to its own standards: "guerilla war, as 'savage' war, was entirely outside the moral and legal standards and strictures of 'civilized war.' Those who adopted guerilla war…surrendered all claims to bounded violence and mercy from their opponent."[20] (Filipinos pushed back using hallowed Western ideals of the right to defend one's liberty.)

One upshot of the shift to guerilla warfare was that it created a military context in which tactics of biopower could be useful for the US. If the enemy was dispersed throughout the territory, then it would be necessary to establish finer-grain knowledge grids by which the enemy could be more efficiently identified and targeted. To deal with the dispersal of the enemy throughout the population, it might be necessary for the US to re-construct the body politic wholesale—an eminently biopolitical project.

When the US initially entered into the conflict between Spain and the Philippines, it did so on the side of Filipino independence. At that point, the US simply wanted to gain leverage over Spain within the context of its broader rivalry with Spain. However, when the Treaty of Paris included Spain's transfer of the Philippines (along with Guam and Puerto Rico), the US moved to impose its sovereignty over not only the land but also all the peoples living in the Philippines. The only clear US military objective during this first phase of the US occupation was to secure control of the Philippines as a strategic Pacific port; toward that end, its use of sovereign-power tactics (i.e., racial exterminism) made sense. However, in deciding whether to "annex" (colonize) the Philippines, US leaders and the US public debated what, if anything, they might wish to enforce upon the Philippines beyond sovereignty. The terms in which this debate was resolved marked the emergence of biopower-oriented strategies in the occupation.

The Emergence of Biopower

At first, US military imperialists favored a strategically minimalist policy. With US businesses looking for new markets, they imagined the Philippines serving as a "'stepping stone' to Asia and the fabled 'China' market."[21] The Philippines would serve as a strategic location for refueling and a military base to protect their trade. Even in this less expansive policy, military and missionary aims were already linked because the Philippines was to "provide communication links and logistic support for commercial and missionary enterprises."[22] To the minds of many Protestant US missionaries, the Philippines would open the door to converting all of Asia's peoples to (Protestant) Christianity: "Victory for Protestantism and Americanism in the Philippines meant a better chance to succeed in the Orient as a whole." Gradually, the imperial vision expanded to include all of Luzon and then the whole archipelago. The US president, William McKinley, followed a similar trajectory, albeit lagging behind the strongest proponents of annexation by several months.[23]

Although possessing all of the Philippines was justified on military grounds—one port embedded in a territory held by competing imperial power would hardly provide an effective "stepping stone"—US imperialists buttressed this with what they thought was a higher, moral justification for their colonial project, based on their view that Filipinos were incapable of governing themselves or developing, on their own, to the point of civilization. Because the Philippines was the first colony outside its national borders, US political and military leaders needed to provide their domestic audience with some justification for denying Filipinos the right to self-governance, a right long enshrined in the American political imagination. They used their negative racialist views of Filipinos to argue that they were incapable of governing themselves or developing to the point of civilization without US intervention. Filipinos became characterized as too immature to take on the responsibility of self-governance; so immature, in fact, that they were incapable of giving their consent to be (self-)governed.

If, in the project of racial exterminism, Filipinos were imagined as savages who could be hunted for sport, during the annexation, the dominant image of Filipinos—individually and as a whole people—was that of a child. Major US newspapers characterized the resisting Filipino as a misbehaving child. A colonel leading an invasion of towns in Luzon called for the US to "say to the nations Europe hands off, this is our foster-child."[24] And Albert Beveridge, who would become one of the most rabidly imperialist members of the US Senate, extolled fellow US citizens on the campaign trail in 1898 that just as "[w]e govern the Indians without their consent...[and] we govern our children without our consent," so the US was justified in governing the Philippine people without their consent, because "[t]he rule of liberty that all just government derives its authority from the rule of the governed applies only to those who are capable of self-government."[25]

This discourse of Filipinos as children was based on perceptions of their mental, moral, and political immaturity. Foundational to this perception of immaturity was a theological understanding that because they had not been exposed to the Protestant virtues (e.g., self-possession, self-control, and productivity), they lacked the capacities necessary for self-government. At the most extreme, they were seen as "an illiterate, semi-savage people, who are waging war, not against tyranny, but against Anglo-Saxon order and decency."[26]

The most that US imperialists would acknowledge is that Filipinos, while "void of that finer feeling and sense of fitness which makes for a high conception of life and its possibilities," were nonetheless mentally "plastic as wax...malleable to the tools of the spirit, and almost as tractable and docile as they were easily influenced and attracted."[27] This malleability and docility, in fact, opened the door to a project of biopower: "While there is to-day a palpable unfitness for self-government among

[Filipinos], there is in them a capacity for future development, for future preparation for self-government," opined future US President (and Chief Justice) William Taft as he began his term as the head of the commission that was establishing civilian US government over the archipelago.[28] Given this developmental opening, the project envisioned by US leaders bore all the distinctive features of biopower, in both its disciplinary mode and its regulatory mode. Indeed, the development of living human material from immaturity toward a desired end-state of maturity is the primary goal of biopower. The US sought to foster life for the Filipinos—but only on its own terms.

The disciplinary edge of the project can be seen in the repeated emphases on training and education. The task was "to educate Filipinos" so that they would be "made to understand that they must recognize our authority and obey"; to "reduce them to obedience to law and order by the gentlest and most conciliatory methods."[29] US imperialists conceded that sometimes Filipinos might have "to be whipped into respectful submission," but were confident that "the Filipinos will love us later, for the fullness of the lesson we taught them."[30] Of course, Filipinos themselves were unlikely to regard the widespread killing, disease, dislocation, and resource expropriation as gentle or conciliatory, and therefore even less likely to be grateful.

The disciplinary impulse in the US strategy of biopower was conveyed in what Kramer calls a "tutelary" metaphor, which became one of the main ways US personnel understood their relationship to Filipinos. This metaphor casts "the colonial state in its entirety as a school and made its task the active transformation of Filipinos in an unsteady and necessarily indefinite movement toward 'Americanism.'"[31] The logic undergirding this developmental metaphor is that of "evolution," which instantiated biopower's regulatory mode in the US occupation: "US colonialists...[cast] Philippine history on the whole as a series of racial invasions by progressively more civilized elements," from the Spanish to the US. Eventually, Filipinos would "progress still further...[and] they would 'evolve' from ignorant peasants to English-speaking students; from filthy urban denizens to sanitary subjects; from recalcitrant to disciplined workers."[32]

All these new individuals would constitute a wholly re-constructed society, one that conformed to ideals of the modern West and white Protestant America.[33] This forced "evolution" of the body politic would be driven by "elaborate rituals of data-gathering" and large-scale "capacity to produce and authorize knowledge about the Philippines and its people," thereby enabling "rule by 'expertise.'"[34] Such a comprehensive biopolitical apparatus would act not to exterminate the Filipino race, but to re-create it, as the "little brown brother of the US."[35] Thus, the long-term project of the US occupation, beyond the initial military invasion, was conceived of in biopower's terms from the outset: biopower would be the engine driving the US occupation, with the hope (in imperialists' minds) of bringing the Philippine population to a state resembling the US.

Protestant US missionary impulses provided even more power for that engine. Pervasive in the debate over whether to colonize the Philippines was a sense that the US had a special mission in the world; whether the US ought to annex the Philippines hinged on whether that would be proper to that special mission or violate it. Nineteenth-century US Americans, writes literary scholar Susan Harris, "held a profound belief in the superiority of U.S. political and social institutions and a conviction that the U.S. had a…mandate to help other countries follow its example."[36] This mandate was regularly framed in religious terms (often specifically Protestant ones, such as Manifest Destiny) even in the discourses of formally non-religious institutions. An editorial from the Burlington, Iowa, *Hawk-Eye* was typical: "Unexpectedly and through the unseen hand of divine destiny, we have the Philippine Islands," and anti-colonial traditions should not "stand in the way [of the] compelling moral, military, religious, and commercial reasons for keeping them."[37] Framed in this way, one sees how religious, economic, and political aims become co-constituted and mutually reinforcing.

The US Christian mission was proclaimed in the halls of government and on the campaign trail. While stumping for candidates in the Midwest, President McKinley argued that the US gained possession of the Philippines because it was willing to "go to war in a holy cause."[38] "Providence has given the United States the duty of extending Christian civilization, we propose to execute it," declared pro-annexation US Senator Knute Nelson (from Minnesota) in a floor speech.[39] Albert Beveridge, having reached the Senate, asserted that the "divine mission of America" is to "lead in the regeneration of the world"; and this divine mandate "is also a racial mandate; references to what Beveridge calls 'our expanding race' occur throughout the [Congressional] debates."[40] As Harris demonstrates, the assumption that the US had a Christian mission was not confined to those who favored annexation. Anti-annexationist (and long-outspoken white supremacist) Senator Ben Tillman, from South Carolina, affirmed that the US was "a Christian people, and…those imbued with the missionary spirit, clamor for the annexation of these islands..."[41] What was not up for debate was the validity of this claim that the US had a special mission as a Christian nation under divine mandate. This idea was constructed in a way that made biopower a natural, effective tool for the task: "the story of the U.S. special mission became a means of creating a community and specifying who belonged to it. The insiders were those who either were white Protestants or who had fully assimilated to white Protestant culture. The outsiders were everyone in need of uplift..."[42]

A comment by President McKinley conveys well the linkage of a broadly missionary impetus to a strategy of biopower. As reported by a member of a group of fellow Methodists with whom he was meeting, McKinley stated: "there was nothing left for us to do but take them all, and to educate the Filipinos, and uplift them and civilize them and Christianize them."[43] The foundational purpose of the US special mission (to "Christianize") is wholly integrated with biopower in both its disciplinary mode (to "educate") and its regulatory mode (to "uplift and civilize"). McKinley "sees 'civilization' as 'Protestant' and 'education' as inculcation into a national culture based in Protestant ideas,"[44] and the Protestant US missionary establishment was, for the most part, eager to take up this work. Just two weeks after Dewey's invasion of Manila Bay, the Presbyterian General Assembly declared that "God has given...into the hands of American Christians, the Philippine Islands...By the very guns of our battleships, [God] summoned us to go up and possess the land."[45] Miller documents missionary publications across the Protestant denominational landscape endorsing the colonial project: from casting Dewey as a present-day Joshua (and his guns as "God's own trumpet-tones") to asking what God had intended "by laying these naked foundlings at our door," and simultaneously castigating anti-imperialism as "the invention of the devil to oppose foreign missions" while qualifying that "only in carrying out divine purpose can we advocate the adoption of a colonial purpose."[46]

There were some protestations against such craven imperialism on the part of the church and its missionaries. One Protestant leader chided that the kingdom of heaven was to come "as a mustard seed and not as a thirteen-inch shell"; another asked "how grand larceny and 'criminal aggression' could become high Christian civilization in the Philippines?"[47] (Catholic leaders, of course, took great offense at any suggestion that the Philippines, with its large numbers of baptized Catholics, needed to be "Christianized" at all.) Nonetheless, "on the whole the Protestant establishment supported annexation, and when it became accomplished fact clerics and laity prepared to do their part in the service of gospel and flag."[48]

Moreover, the part Protestant missionaries were prepared to do was highly conducive to biopower, in the form of re-making the peoples of the world in the image of the US. Missionary leader Josiah Strong wrote that it looked "as if God were…preparing in our Anglo-Saxon civilization the die with which to stamp the peoples of the earth…"[49] Miller finds that, "[l] ike secular imperialists, missionaries bristled with an aggressive and highly romantic Anglo-Saxonism…American expansion into the Pacific marked the beginning of the 'Anglo-American Mission of the Holy Trinity.'"[50] "The peal of the trumpet rings out over the Pacific," echoed a minister writing to supporters of foreign missions in the newspaper of one of the largest US denominations, adding, "I believe in imperialism because I believe in foreign missions." The biopolitical edge emerges more definitively when the same minister lauds how imperialism is "not for domination but for civilization; not for absolutism but for self[-]government": in other words, training populations to govern themselves in conformity to Western norms of what it means to be civilized.[51] The 1902 annual lecture of a major missionary organization, the American Board of Commissioners for Foreign Missions, pushes this even further by characterizing the power of Christianity at work in missions as one that "makes states strong, it develops institutions for society without, by transforming the individual within."[52] This is a perfect summary of biopower's aim and its target.

In most cases, missionaries understood themselves as agents of the same biopolitical enterprise as were military, civil-administrative, public health, educational, and other US personnel. For example, within one week of the occupation of Manila, officers of the YMCA (Young Men's Christian Association) were holding services for US troops.[53] Most missionaries adopted the US military view that Filipino forces were pursuing an "insurrection" against the lawful sovereign rather than a "war" against an unlawful invasion. Even as violent atrocities were publicly exposed, missionaries persisted in holding "the more common view was that isolated acts of cruelty were unfortunate but inevitable, and should not distract attention from the generally praiseworthy conduct of the military."[54] The Protestant and missionary press, moreover, "continued faithfully to defend the army and the policy of imperialism."[55] The US military persisted in a sovereign project of racialized violence, but missionaries were supportive of this project, at least up to a point, because such violence formed a constant background to terrorize Filipinos into cooperation with apparatuses of disciplinary and regulatory apparatuses. Although the missionaries' activities largely took the form of biopower, their activities were enabled by the US military's continuing undercurrent of sovereign violence. Thus, no major Protestant mission in the Philippines articulated a program that broke away from the logic of biopower as the organizing principle of US colonization.

As US activities transitioned from sovereign power to biopower, Protestant missions in the Philippines largely signed on to the project wholesale. Most of them agreed with assessments that Filipinos, collectively and individually, lacked the mental and moral capacities necessary for independence and self-government. As Kenton Clymer documents, perceptions of Filipinos as children "was an extremely common motif, present in the correspondence of virtually all Protestant groups."[56] This was reflected in the missions' internal organization. A matter of intense dispute between US and Filipino mission workers was the degree to which—if any—Filipinos should lead missions. The typical practice was for all managerial roles to be held by American men.[57] Clymer sees the missionaries as "allies of the government in what both perceived as a 'civilizing' mission"; a provincial governor went so far as to call the missions "one of the strongest governmental agents we have."[58] Despite a fundamental focus on converting Filipinos to the Protestant faith, the moral patterns toward which they pushed Filipinos to conform were those that constituted white (and capitalist) America.[59] And they established a whole network of disciplinary institutions—parallel and adjunct to those established by the government—in order to re-shape the beliefs and behaviors of Filipinos: not only churches, but also "hospitals, dispensaries, orphanages, dormitories, schools, colleges, libraries, community centers, settlement houses, and social clubs."[60] Thus, in spirit, substance, and form, Protestant missionary efforts flowed with the same biopower that energized the rest of the cast of US colonizers, which becomes more apparent in reviewing some of the major planks of the US biopolitical program.

Establishing the Biopolitical Archipelago

With the decision to formally colonize the Philippines, the US shifted to a definite project of biopower. It sought to impose over the entire archipelago a grid of institutions that would re-make both the population and the territory itself. The largest-scale manifestation of this was the division of the Philippines into two main zones, fundamentally based on the distance of the people therein from Protestant identity. In the two primarily non-Christian areas of the Philippines—territories inhabited by animist ethnic groups in the north and Muslim ones in the south—the US established a regime (the Mountain and Moro "Special Provinces," respectively) that, unlike the rest of the country, would remain exclusively under military control. The rationale was that these non-Christian groups would never be able to develop the full capacities necessary for self-governance, unlike the ethnic groups, where the Catholic Church had had greater success in evangelization.[61] Resistance to Christian conversion, whether Catholic or Protestant, becomes a mark of innate inferiority. In other words, the success or failure of missionary efforts becomes a basis for determining the extent and bounds of military control.

US biopower worked on ever-finer granularities as well. Various public works and infrastructure—many of which remain in use today—facilitated military and commercial expansion all over the islands.[62] The US imposed a pyramid of administrative oversight from the barrio level up. Their aim was to disrupt patterns of local power, which had obtained for centuries in accommodation with the Spanish.[63] The Americans established a new police force and prison system. Significant grids of educational and public health institutions steadily came to encompass nearly all the territory (except the Special Provinces, which I discuss further below). A series of geological, biological, and anthropological surveys was launched both by the military and by the civilian Philippine Commission, culminating in the 1903 Philippine Census.[64] These surveys created a corpus of data by which Philippine land and organic material could be rendered into a standardized representation and thereby made more amenable to intervention by US experts. All of these endeavors were motivated by the desire for a form of administration that was "…stable, effective, and economical"—in other words, biopolitical in its essence.[65]

The "Pedagogic Invasion"

No domain of practices during the US colonization of the Philippines better demonstrates biopower's centrality than education. Military personnel, missionaries, and civilian educators all understood themselves as participating in a common pedagogical project, for which disciplinary and regulatory biopower provided the means. In McKinley's formulation, "educate" immediately follows "take."[66] The military understood its own task, at least in part, as educating Filipinos in the laws of "civilized" warfare.[67] As the civilian US administration seeped across the islands, there was, in Kramer's analysis, "virtually no state arena of Filipino-American interaction—from office clerkships to forced road labor—that was not conceived of as 'education.'"[68]

Military personnel staffed the first US-established schools. Indeed, "[o]ne of the first images of the American soldier in the Philippines was one with a 'Krag' rifle in one hand and a school book in the other."[69] Such an image powerfully epitomizes the use of sovereign power to clear the way for biopower's operations. These soldier-teachers were replaced by civilian educators from the US, who were appointed and transported by the government beginning in 1901. They thought of themselves as a "great army of instruction" making a "pedagogic invasion" of the Philippines.[70]

In addition to militarized discourse, these government-employed educators appropriated the language of religious missionaries. They often spoke of their task in terms widely used by missionaries, for example, as "regeneration" of the Filipino population, a term laden with spiritual and moral connotations (and reflective of biopower's targeting of life).[71] One prominent US manual trained teachers to think of the "school as a sacred institution. It comes next to the church in its influence upon our national life," and shares with the church the duty of re-shaping Filipino character—that is, in the work of biopower.[72]

Perhaps the most vivid symbol of how military, religious, and educational efforts interlocked to form one biopolitical mission is the USS *Thomas*. This ship bore hundreds of US teachers to the Philippines, one of whom thrilled at the prospect of "carry[ing] on the education that shall fit the Filipinos for their new citizenship." Prior to delivering the amphibious assault of the "pedagogic invasion," the *Thomas* had been bought from the British and used to transport US soldiers to Cuba, Puerto Rico, and the Philippines. Its voyage to deliver teachers was its seventh under the US flag. The educators who journeyed on the *Thomas* called themselves "Thomasites," a term that quickly came to refer to all US educators in the Philippines. Not only did this name sound like a missionary group, but, according to Kramer, it also constructed US teachers as missionaries and connected them "to much older trajectories of Protestant evangelism in Asia, while moralizing and exceptionalizing U.S. colonialism," supposedly distinguishing it from non-salvific European colonizing practices.[73]

Thomasites and their administrators rapidly covered the islands with a pedagogical grid. This grid comprised primary schools in every village, intermediate schools in major cities, and at least one secondary school for every province, along with several major institutions of higher education. These institutions included agricultural, trades, normal, nautical, and nursing schools, as well as the University of the Philippines, which were located primarily in Manila and still operate in the present. The village schools were often placed at the center and built in part with donations from local elites, thus encouraging collaboration with the US regime. Within ten years of the Thomasites' arrival, over 4000 newly built schools housed 355,722 elementary school students and 3404 high school students; by the end of the next decade, those figures had doubled.[74] The pedagogical grid even had a relay, which extended to the US. Through the *pensionado* exchange program, the US paid for hundreds of Filipino students to attend US universities, after which these students were obligated to return to the Philippines and work in the US-governed civil service.[75]

The curriculum implemented through this pedagogical grid reflected the mindset of biopower. In the textbooks written for Philippine schools, US American authors embedded within literary, historical, scientific, and mathematical lessons content that "urge[d] Filipino children to develop American values and to manifest those values through specific social and moral practices...American educators attempted to supplant Filipino culture with American social, economic, and political values...through lessons in moral conduct, spelled out in a series of positive and negative prescriptions."[76] Such an approach was a natural extension of progressive educational practices in the US at the time and a "pedagogy of convincing non-Protestants to participate in an ideology in which Protestant and Enlightenment ideas were fused and which was signaled by specific behavioral practices."[77]

Perhaps the most culturally violent tactic in this pedagogy was the imposition of English on all students throughout the Philippines.[78] This project directly advanced biopower by amalgamating various ethnic groups into a new living unit, an English-speaking Filipino nation.[79] This conversion of Filipinos into English-speakers was intended, among other things, as an affective discipline that would re-shape the social structure by re-directing the loyalties of the vast peasant majority from the Spanish-speaking *caciques*, who dominated local power structures, to the English-speaking Americans.[80] At the same time, the US wanted many of these peasants to become prepared to join an industrial workforce: self-government, wrote Philippine Commission chair William Taft, requires "not only the teaching of that people how to read, write, and figure in arithmetic, but also...how to labor."[81] The "pedagogic invasion" sought to re-make Filipinos into imperial subjects who thought, acted, spoke, and worked like Americans—even if they would never be allowed the full rights of US citizens.

Given that most of the educational institution-building by the US was undertaken by the government, the religious missionary enterprise might seem separate from the pedagogical one. However, precisely because Protestant missionaries perceived the curricula of government schools as imbued with proper Christian moral vision and aims, they understood themselves and the schools as partners in the broader mission of regeneration. After all, civilian educational leaders in the Philippines emphasized training in Protestant moral values such as "honesty, orderliness, industry" and "'rational' religion," and they sought to form in Filipinos a "character" "predicated on values that [were] understood as inseparable from both whiteness and Protestantism."[82] Missionaries in the Philippines thought that public schools there could advance the same goal as they did back home: creating a "Christian America." As Clymer notes, not having the primary responsibility for building and operating a school system left Protestant missions free to engage in other pursuits.[83] However, because of the official separation of church and state, the missionaries felt the necessity of building "a Protestant presence near the public schools in the form of kindergartens, dispensaries, social clubs, and above all dormitories," alongside the government schools.[84] In other words, missionaries erected a disciplinary infrastructure that could envelope Filipino students during all the time when they were not disciplinarily enveloped by public schools, which already promoted Protestant values, if not explicit Protestant doctrine.

The Gospel of Hygiene

Alongside education, public hygiene was another prong of the US program of biopower in the Philippines. It led to the establishment of a grid of health to cover the archipelago, in forms that resembled the distribution of military camps, local governments, schools, and Protestant missions. As with education, US disciplines of public hygiene in the Philippines began as part of military practice and later came to be administered by civilians. However, unlike education, they retained significant military involvement and a military institutional form even under civilian control. As historian of medicine Warwick Anderson demonstrates, the US occupation of the Philippines came at a time when public health was ascendant as a key to military effectiveness. According to the dominant textbook on military hygiene at the time, healthy body and mind were "the foundation upon which the whole structure of military efficiency rests."[85] Military health officers joined patterns of precise command and control with the expertise of the modern medical science in which they had been trained. Public health physicians' immersion in the mindset of biopower is evident in their "obsess[ion] with systematic documentation" and "confidence in the power of bureaucratic intervention and technology…" Anderson also detects a religious dimension: "They clung to Protestant rectitude, affirmed the manly ideals of self-mastery and restraint," and proclaimed "the gospel of hygiene."[86]

This gospel of hygiene sought to maintain purity on both levels of biopower's concern, individual bodies, and the collective body of the targeted population (whether US troops or, later, Philippine peoples): "Conditions of military life also drew attention to…the need for meticulous *group* discipline and *personal* hygiene."[87] That military life was—as Foucault has described—already structured through disciplinary biopower made it easily adaptable to the demands of the emerging field of public health. For instance, army camps were located according to minutely specified geographical factors that would minimize health risks (consistent with the medical understandings of the time). The close living conditions of army camps generated intense scrutiny to preserve collective hygiene: "Education and camp inspection was unremitting…The personal hygiene of soldiers in the line was regulated as never before." A soldier's cleanliness had become "a constant object of solicitude on the part of his superiors."[88]

Constant surveillance and correction of each individual was necessary because each was implicated in the health of a military unit as a whole: "The glands of the skin are the individuals in a regiment. Weaken the individuals and the regiment deteriorates."[89] Biopower, in both its disciplinary and its regulatory modes, is always about producing certain kinds of subjects. In the Philippines, US military leaders were concerned not only with producing obedient subjects who were skilled in the use of force, but also hygienic subjects who protected themselves and their fellow soldiers and sailors from disease.

Hygiene took on greater importance as part of military strategy in large part because of how US military personnel and policymakers perceived the environment in which they had gone to fight: one environment full of biological threats, in addition to mechanical ones. Such threats endangered Americans as a (white) race, but were dispersed so thoroughly that they could be anywhere. This perception was generated by the conjunction of racial understandings and medical understandings that prevailed among the occupiers. The physiological models of the time held that "the white race was likely to degenerate and sicken in the tropics," with vital functions drained of efficacy and bodies prone to dysfunction and disease; along with physical health, mental and moral health, calibrated to northern climes, "seemed especially likely to jangle and twang in tropical circumstances."[90] Just being in the Philippines was a threat to soldiers' health and sanity. Further, the guerilla warfare practiced by the Filipinos—which, we have seen, was understood in thoroughly racialized ways—amplified the anxiety over biological risks. Unlike engagement on a traditional (Western) battlefield, where opposing armies clashed and usually destroyed the environment through violence, guerilla warfare required the occupying forces to fight in the environment by dispersing themselves ever more deeply into it, searching for *insurrectos*.[91]

Unsurprisingly, this perception of the environment as filled with disease shaped US perceptions of Filipinos themselves as vectors of infection: "The Filipinos are never free from contagious diseases of one form or another," claimed one military hygienist; another wrote, "although it is said their bodies are washed daily, at all events, they are not microscopically clean."[92] Without considering the possibility that Filipinos had their own practices for preserving health appropriate to their cultural and ecological context, military physicians saw "countless unsanitary evils among the natives" wherever they looked; the Filipino "figured in colonial science as a dangerous and promiscuously contaminating racial type and the major threat to white health."[93] The norms of the US discourse of hygiene meant that US medical personnel could only judge Filipinos as unclean and their lifeways unsanitary; their habits could not be slightly modified but instead had to be wholly replaced. In this way, medical ideas imposed on the Philippine context provided a rationale for invasive US intervention in nearly all aspects of Filipinos' everyday practices and some of their most private bodily acts.

As the US occupation expanded in duration and geographic reach and as the military conflict transformed from conventional to guerilla warfare, the practices of military health led to the establishment of a grid of medical discipline over the entire archipelago.[94] This began with the division of the capital, Manila, into ten medical districts. Each district had a staff of inspectors whose job it was to enforce the corpus of health regulations being steadily promulgated. The sanitary grid extended from Manila in all directions, eventually encompassing 300 local health districts, all with their administrators and inspectors.[95] Beginning in 1902, US sanitary inspectors fanned out to investigate every aspect of health and hygiene in the islands: from water supply and garbage disposal to public spaces and diseases among livestock to, most significantly, "the 'customs and habits' of the people as they affected health and sanitation."[96] This last element made Filipinos, individually and communally, vulnerable to all manner of intervention by US health workers in the name of sanitation and disease prevention. At first, US military personnel staffed the public health administration, but even after it officially transitioned to being a civilian entity, military personnel played dominant roles within it.[97]

Thus, as the US military advanced, it was able to "cover new territory with a network of disciplinary structures, including a network of hygiene."[98] Everywhere in this network, scientific understandings and rules for healthy conduct were reinforced by the threat of military force. Medical officers intended "to rule with a rod of steel," referring to "sanitary squads" that by necessity "had to invade the rights of homes, commerce and parliaments"; an archetypal figure of the medical wing of the US occupation was the health inspector, who went about with "a gun on his shoulder in order to intimidate the people to make them obey sanitary laws."[99] To threaten to harm life in order to improve life (as US hygienists understood their work) is emblematic of Foucault's point that biopower does not completely replace sovereign power, but rather layers on top of it and extends its capacities. The power to take life is held in check, but its very possibility is used to motivate compliance with a biopolitical program to foster life, on certain terms and not others.

The overarching US objective in regulating the health of the Philippine populace likewise reflected a biopolitical mentality: confronting Filipino bodies, which they perceived as filthy and disease-bearing and arising from a fundamentally unsanitary environment, the US did not aim to eradicate the Filipinos, but to transform their practices in the US's own image (although many Filipinos would be killed along the way). Filipinos would be incorporated within US hygiene practices through discipline of individual behavior and regulation of collective health outcomes (primarily disease prevalence).[100] US health officials sought to instruct and correct Filipinos' practices so that their bodily functions occurred in the manner consistent with the "gospel of hygiene," which would lead to clean living, medically and morally.

US Protestant missionaries collaborated with the government in spreading this "gospel of hygiene" even more widely than their involvement in pedagogical institutionalization. Indeed, medical work was a major enough focus of missionary activity that, at times, it was necessary to justify, before donors, "using...scarce money to send a physician and finance a hospital—instead of supporting a 'regular' missionary."[101] Patients strategically received Bibles in the hospital, at times when their health situations might make them most amenable to conversion. Moreover, "having ministered to the physical needs of the people, [missionaries] had better access to their homes for more direct evangelism": medical care, that is, would extend the reach of missionaries' disciplinary biopower. Thus, public hygiene—the direct, scientific management of the bare materials of life itself—provided another opportunity to harmonize the aims of military, civilian, and religious personnel through the logic of biopower.

The US occupied the Philippines until 1946, though a neocolonial relationship persisted for several more decades. Even as the US relinquished sovereignty, however, the biopolitical archipelago established in the first decades of occupation continues to be a basis for governing Philippine society to this day. As I have endeavored to demonstrate, this archipelago consists of institutions and practices that enable governing both individual and collective bodies. The perception that Filipinos were desperately in need of such government because they were incapable of evolving into a civilized society on their own, was the result of a white (Anglo-Saxon) supremacist framework. In this framework, capitalism, Protestantism, and US social mores (among other things) were all markers defining what Filipinos should aspire to—even if they, as non-whites, could never achieve full civilization. The forms that Protestant missionary activities took during the early phases of the occupation, as well as the ways they strategized and explained those activities, were congruent with the biopolitical programs of military commanders, public health officials, educational administrators, and others. The missions themselves played a disciplinary role of inculcating behaviors that manifested Protestant norms of propriety while also turning Filipinos into docile political subjects and workers. In domains such as public health and education, they established a network of organizations, parallel to that of the US government, to further train the individual habits and collective lifeways of Filipinos. At the same time, the way government personnel, both military and civilian, commonly thought of their work as a kind of missionary task precludes any easy distinction between political and religious visions of re-making the Filipino body politic into a "little brown brother."

One hears echoes of this biopolitical mission even as recently as the ongoing US war in Iraq. Although US government officials, leading up to and during that war, did not publicly invoke the promotion of Christianity per se to the same degree as during the occupation of the Philippines, the project and rhetoric of protecting and promoting "freedom" provided an analogue to Protestant Christianity. Not only was the military mission named "Iraqi Freedom" (and later "Enduring Freedom"), but talking about freedom also became a way of articulating a vision for re-constructing Iraqi society in line with US norms and in its image. Moreover, presenting the Iraqi people as in need of freedom and the US as the provider of it allowed US officials to characterize Iraqis as weak in certain capacities, which the occupation would strengthen, without explicitly having to say so. The biopolitical enterprise of the US in the Philippines forged habits of governing another population not only through the sovereign power of racial exterminism, but also through the biopolitical formation of a docile body politic—techniques that continue to project US military force on an imperial scale.

Notes

1. The account in this section synthesizes several key works by Foucault and major explications of Foucault by Hacking, Heyes, McWhorter, Rose, and Rose and Rabinow (all listed in the bibliography).
2. In his last years, Foucault tended to refer to the con*duct*ing of *con*duct as the overall field of "government." See, for example, "The Subject and Power," in *The Essential Foucault.*
3. Foucault discusses the relationship of state and society extensively in *The Birth of Biopolitics*, in which the liberal/neoliberal imperative to *limit* the state's interference in society is, fascinatingly, construed as the necessary condition for the emergence of biopower.
4. Michel Foucault, *Discipline and Punish*, 298.
5. I am grateful to Prof. Tat-siong Benny Liew for helping me to think more carefully about the interplay of sovereign power and biopower in the context of the Philippines.
6. Paul A. Kramer, *The Blood of Government: Race, Empire, the United States, and the Philippines* (Chapel Hill, NC: University of North Carolina Press, 2006), 138–151.
7. Ibid., 89–90.
8. Ibid., 125.

9. Ibid., 129.
10. Ibid., 127.
11. Ibid., 127–128.
12. Ibid., 144.
13. Ibid., 140.
14. Ibid., 139.
15. See H.W. Brands, *Bound to Empire: The United States and the Philippines* (New York, NY: Oxford University Press, 1992), 55–59.
16. Ibid., 145.
17. See, for instance, Stuart Creighton Miller, *"Benevolent Assimilation": The American Conquest of the Philippines 1899–1903* (New Haven, CT: Yale University Press, 1982), 206–208.
18. Kramer writes that, while the "scale of its practice and the frequency of death remain difficult if not impossible to establish," there is no doubt that "U.S. soldiers not only carried out the water cure but apparently did so in a jocular manner." Furthermore, it was represented in soldiers' writings, drawings, and songs in ways that "suggested familiarity and ease." Ibid., 140. See also Paul A. Kramer, "The Water Cure: Debating Torture and Counterinsurgency."
19. Kramer, *Blood of Government,* 157.
20. Ibid., 146. This perspective on the part of US leaders was despite the fact that their own exterminist practices violated other norms of so-called civilized warfare supposedly upheld by the West.
21. Ibid., 16.
22. Miller, 14; and Kenton Clymer, *Protestant Missionaries in the Philippines, 1898–1916: An Inquiry into the American Colonial Mentality* (Champaign: University of Illinois Press, 1986), 17.
23. Miller, 14; Kramer, *Blood of Government*, 97, 109.
24. Miller, 65; Reynaldo Ileto, "The Philippine-American War: Friendship and Forgetting," in *Vestiges of War: The Philippine-American War and the Aftermath of an Imperial Dream, 1899–1999,* ed. Angel Velasco Shaw and Luis Francia (New York, NY: New York University Press, 2002), 5.
25. Quoted in Warwick Anderson, *Colonial Pathologies: American Tropical Medicine, Race, and Hygiene in the Philippines* (Durham, NC: Duke University Press, 2006), 56; Kramer, *Blood of Government*, 1.
26. Brigadier General Frederick Funston, who was linked to numerous atrocities in the war; quoted in Brands, 58.
27. Naval officer Arthur Riggs, quoted in Kramer, *Blood of Government*, 158.
28. Protestant missionaries shared in such low estimations of Filipinos' mental and moral capacities: see Clymer, 17, 66–67, 72–78, 126, 171–72.
29. *New York Times* editorial, quoted in Kramer, *Blood of Government*, 111; Major General Lloyd Wheaton, quoted in Ileto, 11.

30. *Omaha Bee* editorial, quoted in Miller, 77. See also Victor Bascara, *Model-Minority Imperialism* (Minneapolis, MN: University of Minnesota Press, 2002).
31. Kramer, *Blood of Government*, 201.
32. Ibid.
33. Cf. Bederman's argument that US notions of civilization "linked both male dominance and white supremacy to a Darwinist version of Protestant millennialism." Gail Bederman, *Manliness and Civilization: A Cultural History of Gender and Race in the United States, 1880–1917* (Chicago: University of Chicago Press, 1996), 26.
34. Ibid., 178–181.
35. The fundamental condition, of course, was that the US alone would be the judge of whether Filipinos had sufficiently advanced in their "evolution" toward American-ness; Kramer calls this "calibrated colonialism," which echoes the disciplinary and regulatory workings of biopower. See Kramer, *Blood of Government*, 191–96.
36. Susan K. Harris, *God's Arbiters: Americans and the Philippines* (New York: Oxford University Press, 2011), 5.
37. Quoted in Miller, 21.
38. Quoted in ibid., 23.
39. Quoted in ibid., 27.
40. Quoted in Harris, 25–26.
41. Quoted in ibid., 28.
42. Ibid., 24.
43. Quoted in Clymer, 3.
44. Harris, 15.
45. Quoted in Brands, 73.
46. Quoted in Miller, 17–18.
47. Quoted in Brands, 73; Miller, 19.
48. Brands, 73.
49. Quoted in Miller, 6.
50. Ibid., 18.
51. Presbyterian minister Wallace Radcliffe, quoted in Harris, 29.
52. Congregationalist minister Newell Dwight Hills, quoted in Harris, 30–31.
53. Clymer, 5.
54. Ibid., 157.
55. Miller, 248.
56. Clymer, 73, and see 66–67 and 72–83.
57. Clymer discusses this extensively in Chap. 6.
58. Clymer 8; 161.
59. See Harris, 19, 47.
60. Clymer, 18.

61. See Kramer, 208–219.
62. See, for example, ibid., 159–160.
63. Kramer, *Blood of Government*, 173–74; but see Ileto, 9–13, for an account of the complexities of Filipino accommodation and resistance to US local government.
64. Kramer, *Blood of Government*, 220–26.
65. Brands, 51.
66. See Clymer, 3.
67. See, for example, Kramer, *Blood of Government*, 136.
68. Kramer, *Blood of Government*, 201.
69. Alexander A. Calata, "The Role of Education in Americanizing Filipinos," in *Mixed Blessing: The Impact of the American Colonial Experience on Politics and Society in the Philippines*, ed. Hazel M. McFerson (Westport, CT: Greenwood Press, 2001), 89–90.
70. Kramer, *Blood of Government*, 170; Dinah Roma-Sinaturi, "'Pedagogic Invasion': The Thomasites in Occupied Philippines," *Kritika Kultura* 12 (2009), 12.
71. Kramer, *Blood of Government*, 170.
72. Harris, 94.
73. Kramer, *Blood of Government*, 168–169; and see Roma-Sianturi for a summary of recent scholarship on the Thomasites and an analysis of their pedagogical vision.
74. Brands, 69; Kramer, *Blood of Government*, 201; Calata, 91.
75. Calata, 91–93.
76. Harris, 93; see further examples at 94–103, as well as Ileto, 5.
77. Harris, 49; see also Brands, 67–70.
78. This was of a piece with Protestant missionary efforts in Latin America during the nineteenth century, as Joerg Rieger describes. I am grateful to Nami Kim for drawing my attention to this connection.
79. Calata, 94–96; Brands, 71; see also Kramer, *Blood of Government*, 201.
80. Brands, 71–72.
81. Quoted in Brands, 68; see also Calata, 93–94.
82. Harris, 36, 94, 96.
83. Clymer, 162.
84. Ibid., 165.
85. Edward Munson, *The Theory and Practice of Military Hygiene* (1902), quoted in Anderson, 27.
86. Anderson, 7, 72.
87. Ibid., 26 (emphasis added).
88. Ibid.
89. Army surgeon Joseph Guthrie, quoted in Anderson, 60.
90. Anderson, 39, 40 (and see also Anderson, Chap. 3).

91. The emerging medical understanding of bacteria was the other basis for the perception of the US occupation as a battle against biological threats, not only traditional military ones. Yet unlike guerilla soldiers, microbes could never be seen directly (other than in a laboratory). The relatively nascent state of bacteriological medicine contributed to a sense of the omnipresence of infectious agents: it was known that bacteria were the cause of various serious illnesses, yet because the precise modes of transmission were not known in many cases, multiple aspects of the environment posed unseen health risks—wetlands, decaying vegetation, damp topographies, livestock, and so on. Even one's fellow soldier could be a threat if he did not observe proper cleaning and waste disposal. See Anderson, 58–61.
92. Army physician Henry Lippincott and surgeon Joseph Guthrie, quoted in Anderson, 59.
93. Ibid., 49, 8.
94. Moreover, "the care and disciplining of white troops would come to serve as…a guide to how natives might be reformed…" Anderson, 17.
95. As the occupation persisted, local health bureaucracies came to be staffed by Filipino elites, even as the Philippines-wide authorities were US officials.
96. Ibid., 52.
97. Ibid., 49–51.
98. Ibid., 46.
99. Ibid., 66, 70, 68.
100. "Progressive American medicos imagined themselves eventually, many generations hence, producing germ-free Filipino citizens; it is in this sense that colonial hygiene became a liberal strategy of deferral, not exclusion." Ibid., 3–4.
101. Clymer, 18.

CHAPTER 6

Killing Time

Jonathan Tran

James Henry remembers the killing. And he can't sleep. Half a century later he still recalls the atrocious images, the slaughter, the brutality of America's so-called good intentions for the world. Although he'd rather get some sleep, remembering may be the only thing that separates him from animals—or more directly, remembering may be the only thing that makes Henry human. As Friedrich Nietzsche described, Henry "cannot learn to forget but clings relentlessly to the past: however far and fast he may run, this chain runs with him. And it is a matter of wonder: a moment, now here and then gone, nothing before it came, again nothing after it has gone, nonetheless returns as a ghost and disturbs the peace of a later moment."[1] Those around him—especially those for whom he killed—would rather Henry forget or at least shut up about all he remembers. Against America's demand to forget, Henry remembers, and as Nietzsche avers, this is what makes him human. Unlike the animals that live unhistorically, Henry gets to—has to—remember. All animals kill; human animals remember.

J. Tran (✉)
Religion/Baylor University, Waco, TX, USA

N. Kim, W.A. Joh (eds.), *Critical Theology against US Militarism in Asia*,
DOI 10.1057/978-1-137-48013-2_6

In the following chapter, I investigate a conception of time that I call the *slow time of boredom*. While the frenetic drive of the domino theory to contain an incessant threat compelled what we now call "the Vietnam War," its actual delivery hit the ground walking like so many grunts humping strange and dangerous lands. As the US set its sights on a new world armed with its domino theory–inspired geographical imagination, most Americans in Vietnam just wanted to get home. Although the dominos could fall at any time, the year that made up the infantryman's conscripted tour of duty could not end soon enough, sluggishly marching from moment to moment in days that stretched out like eternity. The seemingly opposite experiences of fast time and slow time are two sides of the same temporal imagination, timekeeping adrift from its eternal horizon, intensified and flattened in order to sweeten life in the far country. Throughout I attempt to arrive at some understanding of the Vietnam War using classical Christian doctrines, most specifically conceptions of time and eternity. Specifically, I turn to Augustine of Hippo and Thomas Aquinas to theologically frame Vietnam War atrocities as a theological problem. I utilize christological and trinitarian lenses not only to theorize the war's complex eventualities but also to offer alternatives, which might save us from our own baser tendencies.

I first recount Henry's story and the frightening specifics that haunt life after Vietnam. I briefly relate a history that Henry has been telling ever since. His account has been denied, investigated, and denied again because it is a re-presenting of a past that the US has tried to forget because its very iteration challenges the deployment of patriotism and commitments one holds to the nation and people. I then attempt to portray atrocity as privative of time's good use: boredom with the everyday. For human animals—that is, those for whom the world comes through language—existence subsists between potentiality and actuality, from moment to moment, vis-à-vis existence that unfolds as past, present, and future. In the tensed internecine between promise and fulfillment, boredom threatens. Rather than wait for potentiality's actuality, rather than dwell in the moments of time, boredom demands immediate satisfaction, with impatience rushing forward as the driving force of a new temporal economy. This use of time, already having given up eternity, settles in what theologian Catherine Pickstock calls "immanentist rituals," violent assertions of an unleashed will gone berserk.[2] I juxtapose this boredom with a conception of divine eternality, which places creaturely life internal to the divine life. By doing so, God's presence is evinced in the very structure of created existence. In Thomas Aquinas' densely material temporality, time unfolds between potentiality and actuality in a way that underscores divine and creaturely difference. Rather than denigrating time, this difference heralds God's cotemporaneous eternality. An enduring simultaneity sacramentalizes the ordinary and makes time a relational analog between God and creatures.

In 1994, by decree of the Freedom of Information Act, the US government declassified thousands of documents chronicling almost 800 reported incidents of what the US military considered war crimes committed by US soldiers in Vietnam. These documents, compiled in a series of reports by the wartime Vietnam War Crimes Working Group, are currently housed at the National Archives, College Park Campus. These records and their sheer volume testify to the (common) occurrence of criminal behavior among US frontline soldiers. Although each crime deserves careful attention and recognition, this chapter cannot properly attend to most of the horrendous things that occurred during the Vietnam War. Instead, I focus on a few, which unfortunately only repeats atrocity's two-fold erasure: violence followed by forgetting.[3]

I preface this chapter by iterating that atrocity is not so much unreasonable as indescribable. Any account of atrocity is at best one among many. No definitive explanation for atrocity can ever be. By its nature, atrocity defies rationality; marking the very limits of understanding. Part of the terror of atrocity is that it seeks to destroy meaning; as if to rend discourse altogether. This claim differs from characterizing atrocity as unreasonable or branding war criminals irrational. Indeed, many war crimes are frighteningly rational, devoid of the very affect that might otherwise save us from the conclusions of cold hard logic. Memories of atrocity doggedly endure because they refuse induction into framing narratives. However, the inability to theorize atrocity is very likely a good thing. We would be advised to hold on to these caveats; otherwise, we might find ourselves unwitting voyeurs entertained by the many barbarisms of our age.

Boredom and Atrocity

On February 8, 1968, James Henry's 3rd Platoon came upon 19 unarmed women and children. Operating under the directive to "kill everything that moves," the platoon turned their automatic weapons on the civilians: "It was over in a few seconds. There was a lot of blood and flesh and stuff flying around from the velocity of the M-16's at that close a range."[4] Henry later reported, "Incidents similar to those I have described occur on a daily basis and differ one from the other only in terms of numbers killed." Indeed, this civilian massacre was not even the first Henry had witnessed that day. By mid-morning, the platoon had already waylaid many civilians, raped a young woman, and murdered an older man: "He was held down on the ground and the APC [armored personnel carrier] ran him over twice. They drove over him forward which didn't kill him because he was squirming around, so the APC backed over him again." Recalling his tour, Henry testified to the following:

> We operated west of Chu Lai, and on the 8th of October 1967, we got into a fire fight. It was my first fire fight and at that time I witnessed a 12 year old boy executed for no reason by a medic. I didn't actually see the body executed. Somebody caught him up on a hill and they brought him down and the Lieutenant asked who wanted to kill him, who wanted to shoot him. Two guys, an RTO and a medic said they did. The RTO kicked the boy in the stomach and the medic took him around behind a rock and I heard one magazine go off complete on automatic. This took place during a rainstorm. At that point the Captain called up and asked what happened. The shooting was reported as a KIA. The Captain asked where the body was and they said it was going down the river. Nobody told the Captain it was a 12-year-old boy who was unarmed and didn't have anything on but shorts. After that we stayed in the field a couple more weeks and we went into base camp on Hill 488 I think. I'm not sure about the hill number. 1st Platoon went out on a night ambush from there. I was told by men of the 1st Platoon that they raped and executed five women which they caught in their ambush. Men of the other platoons later went down and saw the bodies. From there we went to LZ Baldy which was made our base camp. Of course, the company spent almost all this time in the field. We'd come in about once a month for two or three days stand down, sometimes for five days if we were lucky. Prior to Baldy I saw a man executed in a cave. 2nd Platoon had found him sleeping in his hooch. I heard the Lieutenant in charge of 2nd Platoon ask the Captain for permission to test fire a weapon which I thought was normal procedure. I was relatively new in the country. I heard the firing as I walked and I heard small arms firing, M-60 and .45 caliber fire. As I walked through the bamboo, I saw this man sitting upright against the wall of a little cave and everybody was taking pot shots at him seeing how accurate they were.[5]

How does one make sense of such behavior? According to Henry, those who murdered "are as much victims of the war as the people they have killed." For Henry, culpability lies not at the feet of the murderers or rapists, but at the feet of the war's architects, policymakers of an abstract governance.[6]

Reflecting on his adolescent thievery, Augustine writes, "I had no motive for my wickedness except wickedness itself. It was foul and I loved it. I loved the self-destruction, I loved my fall, not the object for which I had fallen but my fall itself...I was seeking not to gain anything by shameful means, but shame for its own sake." Augustine finds himself earlier "amused" by sin, depraved for the sake of depravity, thrilled by thrill. Like the young Augustine, US soldiers in Vietnam found the civilian villagers easy pickings: "The reins were relaxed to allow me to amuse myself. There was no strict discipline to keep me in check, which led to an unbridled dissoluteness in many different directions."[7]

We might call this unbridled dissoluteness boredom. Augustine interprets the misdirected appetite as being in love with being in love. For Augustine, right love desires ends appropriate to its nature. Disordered love seeks wrong things, and even worse, no thing in particular. The will that wills no thing tends toward destruction. Armed with will and being yet uninterested in their right ends, willing spins wildly out of control, going nowhere, and finally, unchecked, imploding atrociously. Empty desire breeds atrocity as assertion for the sake of assertion spawns mutation: what John Milbank describes as "an impossible quest to enact such positivity, which can in reality only unleash a bad infinite of further and further privation, since being will not permit any final solution, any finished or perfected evil."[8] The atrocities committed by Americans in Vietnam did not obtain solely by the temporal panic of their overconfident domino theory foreign policy. Rather, a different type of terror, fitted to a different temporal register, materialized in a peculiar boredom. Quoting Tim O'Brien's Vietnam War memoir:

> I remember the monotony. Digging foxholes. Slapping mosquitoes. The sun and the threat and the endless paddies. Even in the deep bush, where you could die any number of ways, the war was nakedly and aggressively boring. But it was a strange boredom. It was boredom with a twist, the kind of boredom that caused stomach disorders. You'd be sitting at the top of a high hill, the flat paddies stretching out below, and the day would be calm and hot and utterly vacant, and you'd feel the boredom dripping inside you like a leaky faucet, except it wasn't water, it was a sort of acid, and with each little droplet you'd feel the stuff eating away at important organs. You'd try to relax. You'd uncurl your fists and let your thoughts go. Well, you'd think this isn't so bad. And right then you'd hear gunfire behind you and your nuts would fly up into your throat and you'd be squealing pig squeals. That kind of boredom.[9]

In contrast to the domino theory's frenetic fast time, slow time sequesters its own brand of dangers. It stretches minutes, hours, days, weeks, months until time takes the form of infinite repetition, cycling back on itself with no end in sight. This temporal black hole seemed to extend the soldiers' DEROS (Date of Expected Return from Overseas) indefinitely. Between arrival "in country" and date of departure lay millions of chances to never get out, packing time with immeasurable perils. Thus, O'Brien speaks of a "strange boredom," the kind that "caused stomach disorders." For front-line infantrymen, death waits in time, hidden in the minute details of each moment, camouflaged in the landscape of the everyday.

The aggressive and naked boredom of Vietnam commonly issued as a desire for action. Days and weeks without facing or even glimpsing the enemy, following weeks of anticipation and months of training, heightened soldiers' appetite for battle. After predictions of "a real firefight," soldiers often felt disappointed, even depressed, when instead of NVA regulars, they found themselves face to face with water buffalo or farmers tending muddy rice paddies. M-16's ready, M-79 grenade launchers loaded, the soldiers, itching for *something* to happen, had nothing to do, no one to shoot, nothing to kill. The relief of escaping death, yet again, mixed with a habituated *thanatos*, morphing time into something else: boredom with life.

On the morning of March 16, 1968, one of the US Americal Division's highest-achieving units approached the area of Son My, nine kilometers north of Quang Ngai near the South China Sea.[10] Expecting to engage the enemy's formidable 48th Local Force Battalion, the unit was disheartened to find the hamlet Xom Lang crowded with women, elderly men, and children. With no one to fight, the soldiers took matters into their own hands. Over the next hours, members of Charlie Company would rape, torture, and murder hundreds of unarmed civilians. Consider, harrowing as they are, the following firsthand accounts:

- "Got up at 0530 and we left 0715. We had nine choppers and two lifts. We started to move slowly through the village, shooting everything in sight, children, men, women, and animals…" *Thomas Partsch, Criminal Investigations Division (CID) statement, October 21, 1969.*
- "Fragmentation grenades were tossed inside; homes were sprayed with automatic fire. Children aged only 6 or 7…asked for food and candy they had received from other American soldiers…the soldiers scythed them down." *Denis Bunning, CID statement December 7, 1969.*

- "They stood only ten feet from their hapless victims, changing magazines from time to time. The Vietnamese screamed, yelled, and tried to get up. It was pure carnage as heads were shot off along with limbs; the fleshier body parts were ripped to shreds." *Dennis Conti, CID statement, October 30, 1969.*
- "Conti found a woman aged about 20 with a 4 year old child. He forced her to perform oral sex on him while he held a gun at the child's head, threatening to kill it." *William Calley, trial transcript, p. 3818, National Archives.*
- "The Americans were rounding up the people and shooting them, not taking any prisoners. It was completely different to my concept of what war is all about." *Ronald Haeberle, personal interview.*
- "Many women were raped and sodomized, mutilated, and had their vaginas ripped open with knives and bayonets. One woman was killed when the muzzle of a rifle barrel was inserted into her vagina and the trigger was pulled. Soldiers repeatedly stabbed their victims, cut off limbs, sometimes beheaded them. Some were scalped; others had their tongues cut out or their throats slit or both…beaten with fists and tortured, clubbed with rifles, and stabbed in the back with bayonets…Other victims were mutilated with 'C Company' or the shape of an Ace of Spades carved into the chest." *Tommy Lee Moss and Sgt. Martin Fagan, testimony to Lt. Gen. William R. Peers, January 6, 1970.*
- "I went to turn her over and there was a little baby with her that I had also killed. The baby's face was half gone. My mind just went blank. The training came to me and I just started killing. Old men, women, children, water buffaloes, everything…I cut their throats, cut off their hands, cut out their tongue, their hair, scalped them. I did it. A lot of people were doing it and I just followed. I just lost all sense of direction…Do you realize what it was like killing five hundred people in a matter of four or five hours? It's just like the gas chambers—what Hitler did. You line up fifty people, women, old men, children, and just mow 'em down." *Varnado Simpson, personal interview.*[11]

Years later, this incident came to be known as the My Lai Massacre and represented for many the nature of the war itself. It was as if the Vietnam War boiled down to My Lai—young US Americans raping and torturing innocent Vietnamese civilians.

Clearly, the long shadow of the My Lai Massacre plays a role in framing certain images in the popular imagination. However, neither every act of killing that took place in Vietnam, nor even most, could be labeled atrocity. To label all the killing so mischaracterizes the moral type of the war's killing—rendering a moral universe in which all cats are gray—and, more importantly, deflates the weight of atrocity as a moral description. However, the larger ethical question such observations press is how Americans should remember the war and morally evaluate its specific acts of killing, determine whether indeed the war was unjust. If it is the case that with 20/20 hindsight, we label the American war in Vietnam unjust, then does that brand each act of killing unjust as well? Or do so many unjust acts of war render an otherwise just war unjust? Even if most of the killing that took place during the war could not be labeled atrocity, still, killing in Vietnam has taken on the weight of something like atrocity for many US Vietnam veterans, who continue to struggle with their actions during the war. Hence, Vietnam War atrocities articulate a deeper sense regarding the war in general. Not every act of killing was an act of atrocity. Yet somehow, all the war's acts of killing have come to carry the stigma of atrocity because of the murky circumstances of the war and the ambiguous status of its killing. In that sense at least, many acts in that war now feel like atrocity. So while equating Vietnam with atrocity grossly misconstrues the war, it speaks to a lingering sense of the war as recurrent memory.

Killing became a way of passing time. In a war without shape or purpose, death and dying provided a simulacrum of meaning: the arduously constructed illusion that life counted for more than pointlessly wandering over hills and through jungles. For some, even the pulse-quickening thrill of battle was not enough. They sought increasing intimacy with death and suffering, lusting after not only death, but also death up close, wanting not only to see the enemy, but also to possess him, forcing an enemy who refused to fight fair into something he could touch, hold, ravage, and even take away.

Boredom's slow time differs in significant ways from the domino theory's fast time, but both speak of time bereft of its sacramental shape. To argue that boredom necessarily produces atrocity would be ludicrous. Nonetheless, one can see atrocity as the product of a type of boredom, the intensification of the "strange boredom" that stuffs temporal panic into seemingly eternal minutes. This is not the hysteria writ large lorded over by distant civilian commanders, who devise the policies of disengaged abstractions often thought of as war policy. Rather, this hysteria inhabits the frighteningly normal, a strange juxtaposition of regular life—days, calendars, seasons, worn trails, familiar tree lines, ancestral lands—and blood-letting that is frankly awe-inspiring, the numbing transformation of normal space into so-classified free-fire zones. DEROS stretched into 365 days, broken up into 52 weeks, comprising 8760 hours, during which the combat soldier endured 525,600 minutes, living through 31,536,000 moments during which anything could happen. In each instance, the soldier would either die or survive—until the next booby-trapped second. As one soldier weighed in, "Here, death could come from anywhere at any time."[12] The sheer randomness of death—without meaning, purpose, or shape—abandoned each to his own terrifyingly slow time, making him shamefully grateful that his pal, rather than he, stepped on the indiscriminate landmine. Humping on, and on, and on. Within this frenetically barren space, anything could happen, even the unimaginable.

Political theorist Sheldon Wolin writes that "...the temporalities of economy and popular culture are dictated by innovation, change, and replacement through obsolescence. Accordingly time is not governed by the needs of deliberation but by those of rapid turnover."[13] In contrast to "cultivating, taking care of, nurturing," US temporalities "in the business of replacement" go fast. Yet, while there are helpful dichotomies drawn between temporal speeds, it would be a mistake to valorize time in ways that make fast time necessarily bad and slow time good. Rather, the question should be: what benefits and dangers do various speeds introduce? William Connolly raises this question when discussing political existence.[14] Connolly concedes that politics "takes time," as Wolin argues, and recognizes that global capitalism contracts time, as Paul Virilio does; yet he proposes speed as torsion and continuity: "Thinking, culture, identity, and ethics are stratified processes, involving relays and feedback loops between layers of being operating at different capacities and speeds."[15] Connolly resists the tendency to romanticize slow time as cover for evading uncertainty, contestation, and change. The question is how to foster these goods within every pace. Rather than focusing on slow or fast time, Connolly asks how one measures speed. Time as looping, stratifying, layering, and relaying can simultaneously speed up and slow down based on perspective and position. Reference requires constant dissonance if it is to pace life rather than death. For the engineers of the domino theory, the US military could not deploy fast enough; for many Americans, it happened all too fast. Rather than supplant fast time with slow time, or speed time up, Connolly counsels laying different speeds side by side, paralleling and intersecting so as to illumine one via the other and to mutually inform, challenge, and overcome contrasting velocities. The goal, in this vein, is not to upend linear American fast time with, say, cyclical Vietnamese ancestral time, but rather to raise alternatives and thus highlight the reality that many times and speeds remain viable possibilities for life, without which fast or slow are but apiece, a dialectical polarity that mutually robs life. In other words, speed is relative to perspective, since perception regulates temporal measure. In this way, fast and slow time can occur simultaneously. What for some seems fast might be excruciatingly slow for others, and vice versa. More importantly, fast and slow time rely on one another as frames of judgment.[16] Fast time requires the formations of slow time—what Connolly calls "the *positive* role speed can play in ventilating dogmatic identities"—to do its good work, and slow time must be driven by fast time's animating powers.[17] The question regarding the Vietnam War is, how did the quickened temporality of the domino theory pace life on the ground toward atrocity? How was the boredom that O'Brien portrays constitutive of intermingling temporalities, the complex product of a tempo both too fast and too slow for many infantry soldiers to negotiate?

DEROS unfolds in 31,536,000 ordinary moments. Yet DEROS's promised salvation made those 31,536,000 moments extraordinary. Without any guiding narrative other than escape, DEROS unraveled into what one soldier described as "just one stupid fucking thing after another," to the extent that it became increasingly difficult to differentiate un/just acts of war, necessity from entertainment.[18] Within this logic, the abstractions of fast time subtend an inherent slow time, while slow time finds shape in a fast world. No political leader or military commander would openly condone the many war crimes committed during the Vietnam War; they could not even acknowledge the war's atrocious form.[19] Yet undoubtedly, they needed on-the-ground soldiers to actualize their many machinations. If certain excesses occurred within this larger mission, so be it. The eventual details could be worked into victory's larger narrative.

While the US has always rationalized its war crimes as aberrations, the atrocities committed in Vietnam were only part of a much larger pattern of collusive behavior fostered by US foreign policy during the Cold War. As it wrapped up operations in Vietnam, the US was already mobilizing death squads in Central America, which would unleash similar acts of terror under the catchall of staving off communism.

In Max Horkheimer and Theodor Adorno's *Dialectic of Enlightenment*, the authors characterize Nazi atrocities as "a ritual of civilization," resplendent in a world "which in reality cannot exist without disfiguring human beings."[20] Violence and the like need no explanation other than a considered analysis of world spirit, which everywhere haunts the biopolitical economy. These are not, finally, alien eventualities, which dialectically confound familiarity. Rather, they are ours through and through. The fast time of the empty shell called the domino theory unfolds slowly through US war crimes on the ground. Both speeds are necessary for those Horkheimer and Adorno call "restorers of the earth," who demonize an enemy "branded as absolute evil by absolute evil."[21] The pronounced (and convenient) distance between policy pundits, who order violence, and grunts, who commit atrocity, is not so great. As Horkheimer and Adorno brazenly put it: "The respectable rackets condone it, the disreputable ones carry it out."[22]

Perhaps the primary difference between the terrors of Vietnam and those besetting us in the age of Al-Qaeda and ISIS (Islamic State of Iraq and Syria) is a new openness, which no longer requires hiding under the cover of "half-understood ideology."[23] Somehow the non-clandestine use of torture at the beginning of the twenty-first century, like the secret carpet-bombing of civilian populations in the 1960s, has become a morally feasible option for democracies like the US. Estranged from the self-giving God, the US, like all fallen creation, is doomed to a purely immanent temporality, which, in its fast and slow varieties, renders aberrant violence not only morally feasible but also, indeed, coherently responsible: "All living things become material for their ghastly duty, which now flinches at nothing. Action becomes a purpose in itself, cloaking its own purposelessness."[24]

Time and the Ordinary

Thomas Aquinas's doctrine of divine eternality lays the foundation for his, and much of Western Christianity's, central doctrines. Aquinas draws his understanding of divine eternality through the western tradition, most directly through Boethius, who followed Augustine's theological appropriation of Middle-Platonism. Discussing divine eternality as part of God's immutability ("the idea of eternity follows immutability"), Aquinas holds that God, as "pure act, without the admixture of potentiality," neither changes, nor can be changed. God remains changeless while able to change all things.[25] For Aquinas, immutability—along with simplicity, perfection, infinity, and unity—is part of the five divine essences. This, within the structure of the First Part of the *Summa*, is how God exists. Aquinas follows Boethius's argument that eternality is constituted by life, which both exists without limit and occurs "all at once." Temporal life, as Augustine showed in the concluding chapters of the *Confessions*, is a "durationless instant," which at all times encroaches upon itself. The present robs the past of being, and the being of the present surrenders to the becoming of the future. The temporal soul in this sense, as demonstrated by Augustine, can be understood as "distended" because it exists in time continuously tossed to and fro by the ravages of time's coming and going; not so with eternality. Eternality in contradistinction to time—"the measure of movement"—is determined by duration—"permanent being." It endures (*durat ultra quodcumque saeculum*).[26] Indeed, the seeming equanimity of duration—of surviving time—prompted the ancients to begin to imagine eternality as a requirement of Being. Plotinus says of eternality, "The life, then, which belongs to that which exists and is in being, all together and full, completely without-extension-or-interval, is what we are looking for, eternity."[27] By the time Aquinas presents his reiteration—that is, as eternality had become a fundamental constituent of God being God—eternality had come to designate life without limit, which, extant all at once, lacks succession.

However, this is not to say that eternality is timeless. God is time*less*. Time does not determine God. God does not occur *in* time. However, God is time*ful* in that whatever time is, time occurs *in* God. The life that is God's eternality, as eternal, abides amidst time as its all-at-once-simultaneity, according to Eleonore Stump's recent reading.[28] It is exactly this simultaneity that names temporal existence as ordinary in the creaturely sense. In relation to the eternal, time is seen as changing, and existence in time ensues relative to time's continuous change. Rather than eternity denoting a transcendent space beyond the flux of time, such that ascending the eternal achieves a type of pure gaze, eternity relativizes all such pretensions while allocating time productive of genuine difference. According to Aquinas, God as eternal is present to each moment of time, and as such can bequeath goodness on the ordinariness of time, as something declared "good." The self in time then names not a timeless sovereign subject but a creature coming to be as creature, a condition which when understood in light of the eternal becomes the occasion for alterity and the self's inexhaustible contingency. The creature at all times remains affixed to and in time (she is not eternal). Such temporality does not curse but rather sacramentally references the eternal and hence her existence as gift. As Catherine Pickstock puts it, "…there are no such pre-established givens, for everything is a never-finished work, which yet discloses what lies inevitably within the interstices of time."[29]

God's time*ful*ness (in terms of what Stump refers to as God's eternal simultaneity) provides the basis for any coherent claim of God's relations with temporal creatures.[30] Only within the grammar of a doctrinal commitment to eternal simultaneity could one meaningfully speak about God's relation with ordinary creation. As the eternal God present to time, eternally simultaneous with time, God has relations with temporal creatures. As present to time, God is present to the past, present to time's present, and present to the future. This naturally follows Augustine's claim that God's eternality evinces God's presentness to each moment in time; that eternality means time comes to God as the present of the past, the present of the present, and the present of the future. Because God endures without succession all at once, all things are present to God all at once. God lives in the world of the ordinary. Without this account of God's being present to the past, present, and future, one could make little sense of God's dealing with creatures who, as temporal, can only exist in the past, present, and future. In this way, Christianity transforms the Plotinian account of eternality and its Gnostic tendencies by avoiding time and eternity's self-reductions.

Present to, in, and ultimately as the ordinary, God relates to creatures in part by mediating creaturely relations. God becomes the condition of possibility for temporal knowing and being. Catherine Pickstock's reading of Aquinas's *De Veritate* suggests that God knows particulars more directly than can material creatures, who know only analogically. Pickstock writes, "God is much more of a country bumpkin capable of a brutal direct unreflective intuition of cloddish earth, bleared and smeared with toil. For God's mind, although immaterial, is mysteriously commensurate with matter, since God creates matter. And because he [*sic*] makes matter, so also he knows it."[31] Precisely because God is eternal and therefore cotemporaneous—eternally simultaneous—with time, God directly engages temporal things.

In contrast, temporal beings know things mediated through God's knowing and, conversely, know God through things. Divine eternality does not divorce God from the temporal, and therefore temporal creatures, but rather locates God amidst the temporal more concretely than materiality *qua* materiality. God places God's self in the midst of things. God's activity can be traced in the play of the ordinary. Thus, Pickstock asserts, "Those very things which might seem to distance our knowledge from that of God—such as its temporal nature, diversity, and material relationships—in fact draw us nearer still."[32] By participating in God's knowing do creatures know concretely. In the same way, creatures enjoy the ordinary by sacramentally enjoying God in the ordinary.

Creatures exist in time only by knowing God in time: "whilst God knows material things precisely because he [*sic*] is timelessly outside them and brings them to be from nothing, Aquinas stresses that our very timeliness is what draws us close to God's manner of knowing concrete things."[33] God's mediation in time then allows not only divine but also creaturely disclosure. Only through God do creatures finally participate in the fullness of temporal being. With John Milbank, Pickstock shows how God, fully ensconced in the ordinariness of the elements, locates depth not beyond but in time such that time evinces a cascading unveiling of the world: "The provocations of desire reveal that the truth to be known is never exhausted, but is characterized by a promise of always more to come."[34] This is not because creation *lacks* ontological relation, but because God makes God's self simultaneous with creaturely life through an abiding *mustérion* (μυστήριον), an extant "transcendent plentitude" made possible "because God is so utterly replete and self-sufficient that he [*sic*] can share without shadow of jealousy," allowing Milbank and Pickstock to boldly claim that "there can be a created exterior to God, because God's interior is self-exteriorization."[35] Thus, God becomes the correlate not only for knowledge of God but also for knowledge of anything.

Aquinas's analogical materialism affirms the temporal as the correlate for knowledge of God and knowledge of things, thereby situating God's life with creation without jeopardizing its integrity—in fact, maximally upholding it. This not only affirms creaturely life, but God's ordering of creaturely life also avouches time as the locale of the life of virtue, while resisting holding it as possession. Unable to imagine the mundane as more than dull, the ordinary must be made to entertain. In this way, boredom indicates that something has already gone wrong.

Signifying potentiality and actuality, desire denotes temporality. According to critical theorist Judith Butler:

> In order for desire to gain determinate reality, it must continually pursue an indefinite domain of alterity; the reflexive experience of desire is only possible in and through the experience of desirable things. The conclusion drawn by self-consciousness that the world of objects is not consumable in

> its entirety has an unexpected inverse conclusion: desire requires this endless proliferation of alterity in order to stay alive as desire, as a desire that not only wants life but *is living*. If the domain of living things could be consumed, desire would, paradoxically, lose its life.[36]

Cultivating the goods of time then requires careful attention to time as a field of consummated possibility. Ordinary time orders activity to ends commensurate with time as created. As creaturely being actualizes itself by participating in God, so time is never more timeful than when it tends the eternal.[37] This good use of slow time forfeits itself in boredom. Good uses of slow time can be found in the evenness of liturgical calendars, the regularity of scripture and confession, the long-haul commitment to gathering and sending, the waiting of prayer, the long-suffering of listening, the patience of friendship, and the discipline of joy. In this good slow time, God nurtures the virtues. Paul calls these virtues the fruits of the Spirit—love, joy, peace, patience, gentleness, goodness, faith, meekness, and self-control (Gal. 5:22–23).

War vitiates these virtues when it replaces desire with boredom. Before atrocity sets in, love must have already given way to indifference, joy to disappointment, peace to wrath, patience to desperation, gentleness to callousness, goodness to evil, faith to cynicism, meekness to aggression, and self-control to avarice. When one no longer desires the one replete *in se* and in creation, the unhurried and watchful discovery of a life becomes suddenly boring. Now, time must procure its own satisfaction.

Yet since only the eternal satisfies time, it betrays itself. Uninterested in its end and detached from that which gives it meaning, time thrashes about. It hastens empty desires at breakneck velocity but goes nowhere and achieves nothing. It manifests "the will to prefer the identical repetition of emptiness of rule for no purpose, but rather for its own sake, over submission to the natural superiority of the infinite which must be perceived in ever-renewing, non-identical repetition."[38] John Milbank's language here of preference is critical because privation intimates desire, but desire for its own sake. Rather than desiring the eternal (what Milbank calls "submission to the natural superiority of the infinite"), time prefers itself, as if survival—the infinite return (DEROS) of time *to itself*—were the point. When one holds the self, the end all of creaturely existence, one cannot help but find the ordinary extraordinarily boring.

The subtitle "A True Story of Men and War" of Michael Sallah and Mitch Weiss's atrocity history *Tiger Force* implies that atrocity can be explained by the unfortunate confluence of realities produced by war.[39] In one particular incident, Sallah and Weiss tell the story of Kieu Trak, who watches as the decorated American "Tiger Force" unit murders his father. Because of the delicate harvesting process and the villagers' desperate need for food, Kieu's father, Kieu Cong, passes on his son's pleas to flee the Americans. Successful rice production, upon which the whole of the Vietnamese diet depends, puts to work generations of subtle and skillful training in order to carefully negotiate a complicated matrix of seed, climate, water, seasons, humidity, sunlight, planting, harvesting, and so on. What were for Americans colorful grids ripe for carpet-bombing represented a basic yet fragile relationship between the Vietnamese and the earth. In the context of the extreme destitution created by generations of foreign colonization and war, rice often comprised not only the staple but the entirety of the village meal. There was often nothing else to eat. While rice depended on the Vietnamese, the Vietnamese equally depended on rice—the most ordinary of crops. The whole life of the village revolved around it. (So completely symbiotic was the relationship that Vietnamese villagers often used human feces to fertilize their rice paddies.)

A respected leader and expert harvester, the other villagers trusted Kieu Cong implicitly and followed him even when the dangerous American GIs patrolled frighteningly nearby. Kieu Cong, a devout and regular worshipper at the local Buddhist pagoda, simply believed the Americans were like all people, good, and trusted that if push came to shove, they would leave the civilian farmers alone. And so he pressed on, realizing the delicate timing of the season and the importance of this particular harvest for the survival of the village. After several hours of work, Kieu Trak implored his father to abandon the rice because he risked too much exposure, but his father chose to continue harvesting lest the crop fail.

Kieu Cong directed his son to keep watch at the perimeter of the field, against the edge of the foothills. As Kieu Trak watched and waited, to his horror, a US helicopter approached. He started to run to his father, but Kieu Cong waved him off, ordering him to remain hidden from view. His father could not hide with Kieu Trak without giving away Trak's position. After identifying the farmers as elderly men and women, the elite unit opened fire, which was joined eventually by the helicopter's large-caliber automatic machine guns. Kieu Trak watched as soldiers massacred his father and other villagers. To survive, he had to bury his head in his hands so that no one could hear him cry.[40] Later, as Kieu Trak and his wife carefully prepared their father's body for burial, they were joined by others torn between wanting to weep aloud and stay alive. The rice field filled with muffled cries.[41]

Notes

1. Nietzsche, Friedrich, *Untimely Meditations*, ed. Daniel Breazeale (Cambridge: Cambridge University, 1997), 61.
2. Catherine Pickstock, *After Writing: On the Liturgical Consummation of Philosophy* (Oxford: Blackwell, 1998), xiv.
3. See Heonik Kwon, *After the Massacre: Commemoration & Consolation in Ha My & My Lai* (Berkeley, CA: University of California, 2006). Regarding the many forgotten atrocities of the war, few today remember the war crimes committed by South Korean soldiers during the war. Indeed, most do not even know that South Korea sent 300,000 soldiers to Vietnam or that America's payments for those soldiers led to the economic revitalization that has hitherto propelled the hugely successful South Korean postwar economy. See also Charles K. Armstrong, "America's Korea, Korea's Vietnam," *Critical Asian Studies* (Routledge) 33, no. 4 (December 2001): 527–539. The South Korean government has often fought against the public disclosure of these events. On the one hand, their ongoing grievances with Japanese war crimes require the presentation of purity. On the other hand, South Korea has recently become one of Vietnam's most important trading partners. The desire to leave these atrocities behind evinces what Charles Armstrong calls a "doubly forgotten event," where forgetting needs to be continuously reenacted.
4. Henry reported the incident, along with others, in an official report to the US military's Criminal Investigations Division (CID), dated February 28, 1970.
5. From "Witness Statement AR 195-10TB PMG 3," dated February 28, 1970.
6. Arnold R. Isaacs, *Vietnam Shadows: The War, Its Ghost, & Its Legacy* (Baltimore: The John Hopkins University, 1997), 22–23. Arnold Isaacs observes, "Just as the burden of national failure was largely displaced from the national leadership onto the soldiers, so was the burden of guilt; unfairly showing them…as murderers seemed a way of escaping a responsibility that properly belonged to America's leaders and to American society as a whole. The movies that made a cliché of atrocities drove another wedge between the country and its soldiers."
7. Augustine, *Confessions*, trans. Henry Chadwick (Oxford: Oxford University, 1998), 29. Susan Faludi, "Gone to Soldiers, Every One: The Vietnam War That No One Dodged," in *Stiffed: The Betrayal of the American Man*, 291–358 (New York, NY: Perennial, 2000). Thirty years after starring in the

largely unsuccessful prosecution of the My Lai Massacre, Michael Bernhardt reflected on the US military's response to the war crime: "I had hoped the army would come out of this with a sense of purpose, knowing why and what we are doing. That a change in culture would begin where we started rewarding officers who acted out of responsibility instead of careerism. But they studied this particular group of soldiers like they lived in a vacuum. They never found out the why part" (347). Marilyn McCord Adams, *Horrendous Evils & the Goodness of God* (Ithaca, NY: Cornell University, 1999). In *Horrendous Evils & the Goodness of God*, Marilyn McCord Adams suggests that what has become in recent years philosophical problems regarding evil presses theological questions and concludes that while coming to terms with evil—Bernhardt's "why"—one may begin with challenges to the US military's corps leadership (as Bernhardt hoped) or with analytical clarity about divine omnipotence (as philosophers like J.L. Mackie hoped), but confessional theology must be engaged if we hope to work through horrors like My Lai. This is not to say that theology provides answers to what are finally impossible questions (exactly because these are not questions but raped, tortured, and murdered persons), but that whatever Christian theology is, it begins and ends in places like My Lai.

8. John Milbank, *Being Reconciled: Ontology & Pardon* (London: Routledge, 2003), 3.
9. Tim O'Brien, *The Things They Carried* (New York, NY: Broadway Books, 1990), 34.
10. Lt. Gen. W. R. Peers (Ret.), *The My Lai Inquiry* (New York, NY: W. W. Norton & Company, 1979), 41; and Tim O'Brien, *In the Lake of the Woods* (New York, NY: Houghton Mifflin/Seymour Lawrence, 1994), 137. O'Brien's account offers a riveting fictional depiction of My Lai's long shadow of moral failure.
11. Michael Bilton & Kevin Sim, *Four Hours in My Lai* (New York, NY: Viking, 1992), 116, 113, 120, 124, 129, and 130–131. Appreciation to Brandon Morgan for engaging this research.
12. Sallah & Weiss, 93.
13. Sheldon. S. Wolin, "What Time Is It?" *Theory & Event*, vol. 1, no. 1, 1997. See "The Time of the Political" in the same online issue http://muse.uq.edu.au/journals/theory_and_event/toc/tae1.1.html. My distinctions here regarding slow and fast times can be construed along with Wendy Brown's "a time of events" contrasted to "the time of The Event."
14. William E. Connolly, *Neuropolitics: Thinking, Culture, Speed* (Minneapolis, MN: University of Minnesota, 2002).
15. Ibid., 159. Connolly describes his larger project both in contrast to and in continuity with Wolin: "The question for me, then, is not how to slow down, but how to work with and against a world moving faster than heretofore

to promote a positive ethos of pluralization" (160). Paul Virilio, *Speed & Politics* (New York, NY: Semiotext(e), 2007).

16. See Richard Smith, "The Brain Is the Milieu: Speed, Politics & the Cosmopolitan Screen," *Theory & Event*, vol. 7, no. 3, 2004, http://muse.uq.edu.au/journals/theory_and_event/v007/7.3smith.html.
17. Connolly, 195 (emphasis original).
18. Jonathan Shay, *Achilles in Vietnam: Combat Trauma & the Undoing of Character* (New York, NY: Scribner, 1994), 19. Regarding just and unjust acts of war, contemporary just war reasoning harbors a paradox that may be too obvious to elicit much analysis. If just cause requires sacrifices to stave off greater evils, then how can one delineate *in bellum* stipulations? In other words, if *ad bellum* circumstances require and justify war, do not those circumstances override all other considerations? Just war proponents say no, arguing that in war, moral decorum must be maintained if the war is to remain just; that unjust fighting disqualifies just cause. Yet the *ultima ratio* of immanent sacrifice intimates a disconnect between *ad* and *in bellum* considerations precisely because the very claim of necessity renders exacting *in bellum* criteria rather arbitrary. For an example, see Bao Ninh, *The Sorrow of War: A Novel of North Vietnam*, trans. Phan Thanh Hao (New York, NY: Riverhead Books, 1993). In Bao Ninh's war novel, a female infantry scout sacrifices her body to a brutal gang rape in order to buy time for comrades to escape certain death. Is sacrificing one's body to rape internal to the larger sacrifice that war claims to be? If not, why not? Bao's story raises just war's implicit paradox because in this case, what is sacrificed is not a man's life but a woman's body, which traditional just war thinking, for obvious reasons, does not anticipate. Thus, the question arises: which sacrifices count? For this woman, sacrifices were necessary in this specific situation and for the general cause of the war itself. Can we say that women soldiers submitting their bodies to gang rape is part of the just war paradigm? If not, how can we distinguish between that and a man giving his body to machine gun slaughter? Does not just war reasoning claim that what needs to be sacrificed first are one's moral disinclinations toward certain kinds of acts, such as killing? If so, which acts count, and if immanent necessity runs the show, how do we do the counting? (Bao, 183–193). Perhaps Bao's narrator articulates the best the just war tradition can hope for: "To win, martyrs had sacrificed their lives in order that others might survive. Not a new phenomenon, true. But for those still living to know that the kindest, most worthy people have all fallen away, or even been tortured, humiliated before being killed, or buried and wiped away by the machinery of war, then this beautiful landscape of calm and peace is an appealing paradox. Justice may have won, but cruelty, death, and inhuman violence have also won" (ibid., 193).

19. Arnold R. Isaacs, *Vietnam Shadows: The War, Its Ghost, & Its Legacy* (Baltimore, MD: The John Hopkins University, 1997). Arnold Isaacs relates how films about the Vietnam War rarely depict standard combat scenes but tend instead to focus on individual atrocities—US soldiers murdering children, raping women, collecting ears for gruesome keepsakes, and so on—as if the only killing that occurred during the war were somehow acts of a larger genocide. C.D.B. Bryan makes a similar observation in respect of what he calls the "Generic Vietnam War Narrative," regarding classics like Phillip Caputo's *A Rumor of War* or Michael Herr's *Dispatches.* C. D. B Bryan, "Barely Suppressed Screams: Getting a Bead on Vietnam War Literature," *Harpers*, 268:1609 (June 1984), 67–70.
20. Theodor W. Adorno & Max Horkheimer, *Dialectic of Enlightenment: Philosophical Fragments*, trans. Edmund Jephcott (Stanford, CA: Stanford University, 2002), 140, 138.
21. Ibid., 137.
22. Ibid., 139.
23. Ibid.
24. Ibid., 140.
25. Thomas Aquinas, *Summa Theologica* (Allen: Thomas More Publishing, 1981), I1.10.2, Ia.9.1.
26. *ST* Ia.10.4. Having already discussed divine immutability, Aquinas can say in the first article regarding eternity, "…time…is nothing else but the measure of before and after in movement. Now a thing bereft of movement, which is always the same, there is no before or after. As therefore the idea of time consists in the numbering of before and after in movement; so likewise in the apprehension of uniformity of what is outside of movement, consists the idea of eternity" (*ST* Ia.9.1). However, and this is critical for both Thomas specifically and Christian theology generally, time does "take place" in God in the sense that creation "takes place" in God. Time denotes God's accommodation for creation within the space that is God's eternal life. As such, all that occurs in time occurs in God. In this way, Aquinas's conception of divine eternality relies upon his fundamental claim of divine simplicity (i.e., that there is nothing anterior, no outside, to God as there are no parts to God not participant within God's life). As stated, in the *Summa*, Aquinas discusses divine eternality in relationship to divine immutability, not divine simplicity; though both, along with divine perfection, infinity, and unity, are part of "The Divine Essence."
27. *Enneads* iii 7.
28. Eleonore Stump, *Aquinas* (New York, NY: Routledge, 2003), 158.
29. Catherine Pickstock, "Radical Orthodoxy & the Meditations of Time," in *Radical Orthodoxy: A Catholic Enquiry*, ed. Laurence Paul Hemming, 63–75 (Aldershot: Ashgate, 2000), 64–65.

30. See also Norman Kretzmann & Eleonore Stump, "Eternity," in *The Journal of Philosophy*, 78 (1981), 429–458. For a critical analysis of Stump's notion of eternal simultaneity, see Paul Fitzgerald's "Stump & Kretzmann on Time & Eternity," in *The Journal of Philosophy*, 82 (May 1985), 260–269.
31. Pickstock, "Radical Orthodoxy & the Meditations of Time," 72.
32. Ibid., 71.
33. Ibid., 72.
34. John Milbank & Catherine Pickstock, *Truth in Aquinas* (London: Routledge, 2001), 98.
35. Ibid., 92, 85, 86.
36. Judith Butler, *Subjects of Desire: Hegelian Reflections in Twentieth-Century France* (New York, NY: Columbia University, 1987; 1999), 39 (emphasis original).
37. Ibid., 106.
38. Milbank, 8.
39. Michael Sallah & Mitch Weiss, *Tiger Force: A True Story of Men & War* (New York, NY: Little, Brown, & Company, 2006). Similarly, Phillip Caputo's *A Rumor of War* casts war crimes as "the things men do in war and the things war does to them." Phillip Caputo, *A Rumor of War* (New York, NY: Holt, Rinehart, & Winston, 1977), xi. Sallah and Weiss's *Tiger Force* chronicles a seven-month period in the Song Ve Valley, during which an elite US unit under the mandate "kill anything that moves" murdered hundreds of civilians (exactly 327 because they were the 327th Infantry). A massacre that culminated in the decapitation of a Vietnamese baby (Sallah & Weiss, 108, 209.) Winners of the Pulitzer Prize for their initial reporting of a story that took four decades to surface, Sallah and Weiss give unflinching details of crimes that only become imaginable, as they and Caputo suggest, within the larger terrors of war. But their conceptualization of events—"these things happen in war"—offers too much and too little: too much because clearly not all, or even many, soldiers commit atrocities in wartime, and too little in that war crimes speak to deeper horrors than war, of which war is but one expression.
40. Sallah & Weiss, 118–125.
41. This chapter is adopted and updated with permission from Jonathan Tran, *The Vietnam War & Theologies of Memory: Time & Eternity in the Far Country* (Wiley-Blackwell, 2010).

CHAPTER 7

The Impasse of Telling the "Moral Story": Transnational Christian Human Rights Advocacy for North Koreans

Nami Kim

Introduction

Cases of human rights violations exposed through the pictures of malnourished children in the Democratic People's Republic of Korea (North Korea), stories of sexual abuse and trafficking of North Korean female "defectors"[1] in the People's Republic of China (China), and the testimonies of those who witnessed the horrible persecution of Christians in political prisons in North Korea have drawn international attention to and advocacy for the human rights of North Koreans. The human rights situation in North Korea attracted media attention again in April 2006, when then-President of the US, George W. Bush, invited to the White House one of the families who had defected from North Korea. Soon after this, six more North Korean defectors arrived in the US through a third country, obtaining refugee status under the North Korean Human Rights Act (NKHRA) of 2004.[2]

N. Kim (✉)
Spelman College, Atlanta, GA, USA

N. Kim, W.A. Joh (eds.), *Critical Theology against US Militarism in Asia*,
DOI 10.1057/978-1-137-48013-2_7

Conservative evangelical Protestant Christians in both the US and the Republic of Korea (South Korea)[3] are among those who have been avidly involved in campaign activities that call attention to the violations of North Korean human rights in North Korea, as well as in China. US-based conservative evangelical groups have formed a "new faith-based movement," extending financial aid and support to the "deserving victims" of human rights violations. According to Allen D. Hertzke, author of *Freeing God's Children*, the new faith-based movement was initially motivated by a concern for "persecuted" Christians around the world.[4] He points out that since the early 1990s the new faith-based movement has pressed the US government to take a stronger stance against "global religious persecution."[5] One of the characteristics of this new faith-based movement is that it is focused "not on domestic grievances that have typically driven social movements of the past," but on humanitarian concerns beyond US borders.[6] And this new faith-based movement, as Hertzke puts it, has "gone forth" to address other human rights issues, including "gulags" in North Korea, a country that is considered one of the most reclusive and repressive regimes in current geopolitics, and human trafficking, especially sex trafficking of women and girls, around the globe.[7]

How has the issue of human rights become one of the mobilizing factors for conservative evangelical Christians in the US and their transnational allies to press the US government to incorporate the language of human rights into its foreign policy? Are conservative evangelical Christians in both the US and South Korea motivated to advocate for the human rights of North Koreans because they believe that it is a good mission strategy to defend the future *mission fields*? If not, do they advocate for the human rights of North Koreans and other "persecuted" Christians around the world because it is a *moral* or an *ethical* issue?

As feminist scholar Inderpal Grewal argues, human rights "as a regime of truth" is "not merely moral or ethical."[8] Rather, she contends, it "mobilizes all kinds of knowledges and practices—disciplinary, sovereign, military, and governmental," because claims of human rights abuse are made with such knowledges.[9] Grewal maintains that, in order to make judgments about who has suffered human rights violations, certain kinds of "language, bureaucratic apparatus, surveys, statistical analysis, photographic evidence, and psychological information are all required."[10] As she makes it clear, this is not to say that the use of the term *human rights* is somehow wrong or problematic, but rather that human rights uses have "contexts, histories, and circulations" that need to be examined.[11] In other words, what needs to be examined is "the knowledge formations in which human rights advocacy is mobilized."[12]

This chapter investigates the knowledge formations of the North Korean human rights issue. Such investigation does not deny the cases of human rights violations of North Koreans or underestimate their severity.[13] Rather, I am concerned with the knowledge formations under which transnational Christian human rights advocacy for North Koreans is mobilized. The knowledges regarding North Korean human rights violations have been gathered, formed, and produced in the context of the Cold War geopolitics. Although the "official" Cold War era ended in 1991 with the collapse of the Soviet Union, the Cold War continues to make enduring impacts, for it is "not only a historical period, but also an epistemology and production of knowledge," exceeding and outliving its "historical eventness."[14] As I show later, conservative Christian advocacy of human rights for North Koreans is enmeshed with anticommunism and American exceptionalism, as well as what can be called (South) *Korean exceptionalism*. In relation to this, I examine how transnational conservative Christian human rights advocacy for North Koreans functions as a platform for the regeneration of the myth of American exceptionalism and the justification of US military presence in East Asia.

In the analysis of conservative Christian politics of human rights and its discourse, which includes a set of ideas and practices of the Christian organizations for North Korean human rights, some of the guiding questions are the following[15]: How are human rights violations framed in conservative Christian human rights discourse? What kinds of languages and imagery are used in making claims of human rights violations? Who are portrayed as victims, villains, and saviors? Exploring these guiding questions, I argue that the politics of representation (i.e., representation of victim(s), villain(s), and savior(s)) is central to conservative Christian human rights discourse. A deeper question to understand this politics of representation is one that addresses the connection between the imperial logics of the Cold War manifested in anticommunism, the myth of American exceptionalism and Korean exceptionalism, and the mobilizing power of conservative Christians across national borders, on the one hand, and the gendered and raced subject of rescue and the Christian evangelizing mission expressed in the form of human rights advocacy, on the other hand.

Conservative Christian Advocacy for "Persecuted" Christians Around the World

Whereas nineteenth-century US Christian overseas missionaries used the rhetoric of (Christian) civilization to justify and promote their mission work, the new faith-based movement that began in late twentieth century has skillfully adopted the language of human rights to advance its agenda, which continues to influence US foreign policy. Although human rights has been one of the major concerns of religious communities and organizations, particularly since World War II, a new phenomenon in the arena of religious human rights activity emerged in the late 1980s.[16]

In his book *Freeing God's Children*, Hertzke discusses how US-based Christian evangelical groups, in alliance with other religious groups, including Jewish and Tibetan Buddhist groups, have launched successive campaigns and continued to press US political leaders to stand against human rights violations, especially violation of religious freedom as human rights, from the 1990s onward through US foreign policy. For instance, responding to pressure from evangelical Christians, the US Congress enacted the International Religious Freedom Act (IRFA) in 1998, which authorized the US's actions in response to violations of religious freedom abroad.[17] In its 2003 report, the US State Department declared North Korea the world's most abusive nation in regard to religious freedom.[18] North Korea, dubbed a rogue nation and as one of the *axes of evil*, is deemed as one of the most brutal violators of human rights not only in the areas of freedom of expression, freedom of speech, and freedom of movement but also in the area of religious freedom. Members of the new faith-based movement have successfully promoted the endorsement of the International Religious Freedom Act of 1998 (IRFA), the North Korea Freedom Act of 2003 (NKFA), and the North Korean Human Rights Act of 2004 (NKHRA).

Conservative evangelical Christians in the new faith-based movement have sought to highlight that the majority of the "persecuted" people in the Global South, as well as in current and former communist countries, are Christians and that this fact has been ignored by the US government. Activists in the new faith-based movement argue that autocratic and communist regimes have persecuted religious freedom, especially the religious rights of Christians, and that the US must take action against such persecutions through its foreign policy.[19] They assert that these claims are long overdue because "suffering churches" have long been overlooked by the US government due to factors such as "secular blinders," "oppositions from business sectors," a "hostile left-wing," and "skeptical liberal Protestants."[20] Anticipating possible reactions and opposition from these groups of people, Michael Horowitz, one of the key proponents for the legislation of IRFA, NKFA, and NKHRA, insisted on framing the issue of religious freedom in terms of "persecution" rather than "discrimination" by using vivid descriptions and accounts to mobilize people.[21] As Horowitz puts it, "You had to frame it in terms of what happened to the Jews…in terms of Nazi Germany."[22]

Framing human rights abuses as persecution rather than discrimination against Christians was a well-planned, strategic move by the new faith-based movement to rally conservative evangelical Christians. "Persecuted" Christians in the Global South are compared to Christians who had been persecuted under Roman rule in the New Testament period.[23] Christians in the "Old Christendom," hence, are urged to be in solidarity with Christians in the "New Christendom" who are suffering and being persecuted. The rhetoric of persecution has been powerful enough to mobilize conservative evangelical Christians, linking their view of persecution of fellow Christians with images of persecuted and martyred early Christians under the Roman Empire. As I have argued elsewhere, conservative Korean Christian churches, including some immigrant Korean churches in the US, have also adeptly deployed and appropriated the languages and images of martyrdom and persecution in their opposition to North Korea.[24] In doing so, conservative Christian human rights organizations and advocates "mastered the use of the language of religious persecution and martyrdom to deflect and defuse virtually any critique lodged by any opponents of its theocratic political project."[25] The language of persecution further helps to determine who can be legitimately admitted into the US. For instance, calling the Bush administration's acceptance of a number of North Korean refugees a "great act of compassion," US Senator Sam Brownback (Republican from Kansas), one of the cosponsors of NKHRA and a major player in the passing of the Victims of Trafficking and Violence Protection Act of 2000, urged the Bush administration to accept more refugees from North Korea.[26] Brownback stated:

> North Koreans brave enough to escape to China are not better off, as the Chinese government violates international conventions on refugee rights by repatriating them to North Korea, where they face prison and persecution. The United States has a moral obligation to provide refugee status to those

> who escape the regime, and certain defectors, who must have thoroughly vetted [*sic*], can aid the U.S. by providing valuable intelligence about the regime's illicit WMD programs.[27]

This illustrates how selective US policy on refugees is, as the US has granted asylum to those who fled from communist regimes while excluding "economic migrants who are nonwhite."[28] As Nina Glick Schiller argues, there is a direct connection between groups of people who are granted entry to the US as "legitimate refugees" and US neoconservatives who support granting refugee status to people who face religious persecution in regions that are of great interest to US foreign policy.[29] Although North Korea is neither an oil-supplying country nor one marked by Christian–Muslim tensions, North Korea is certainly an area of interest for the US due to its geopolitical significance in East Asia. Thus, it is not surprising that North Korean escapees who claim to have been persecuted in North Korea or who will face persecution if they are repatriated are a group of people whom the US deems to hold "legitimate status" as refugees. The rhetoric of persecution deployed by the new faith-based movement has been successful in galvanizing US Christians to protest against North Korean human rights violations and China's policy on the repatriation of North Koreans who fled to China. The cause of human rights mobilizes Christians across national borders, especially for rights of religious freedom in North Korea, as well as its neighboring country China. The rhetoric of persecution also promotes the image of the US as a champion of human rights.

The driving force behind the 2004 NKHRA is the North Korea Freedom Coalition (NKFC), established in 2003. The NKFC comprises individual members and more than 50 public organizations, which represents various political parties and religious faiths, including Korean Christian nongovernmental organizations (NGOs) for North Korean human rights.[30] Some of the goals of the NKFC include making human rights the key policy of all governments in dealing with North Korea, saving lives by helping rescue refugees and pressuring China to end its brutal repatriation policy, getting food aid directly to the North Korean people and ending all food aid distribution controlled by the regime; promoting information into North Korea through all forms of media, and bringing freedom, human rights, and dignity to the North Korean people.[31]

The Korean Church Coalition for North Korea Freedom (KCC, est. 2004), joined by about 2500 Korean American pastors and their churches in the US and Canada, also supported Senator Brownback's proposal, which includes "acceptance of 3500 North Koreans as refugees in refuge haven."[32] The KCC is "a non-partisan and non-profit religious organization" that aims to "bring an end to the sufferings endured by our brothers, sisters and orphans in North Korea, as well as China and other parts of the world, through non-violent means." Its two major campaigns, "STOP" and "Let My People Go," have been endorsed by Suzanne Scholte, chairperson of the NKFC and the president of the Defense Forum Foundation. Since its 2004 inaugural conference, the KCC has held prayer vigils in the US, South Korea, and even in China during the 2008 Beijing Olympics. The KCC boasts that it has "representative strongholds located in EVERY STATE and MAJOR CITY in the United States, as well as South Korea and the many parts of the world" (emphasis in original).[33]

American Exceptionalism and (South) Korean Exceptionalism

The growth of Korean Protestant Christianity must be considered in the Cold War context. During the Cold War, anticommunism was established as a major ideological weapon to bind the so-called free and morally "good" world (led by the US) in opposition to "evil" communist regimes. Although the "official" Cold War era is over, its lingering legacies remain in many sectors of South Korean society, especially among conservative Christian circles. The image of the US as a benevolent nation, a world leader, and a defender of freedom and democracy against ruthless communists persists among conservative Korean Christians, which consolidates the "pro-American" stance of conservative Korean Christianity. The idealization of "America" as the land of opportunity and freedom has also remained strong among South Koreans, including Korean immigrants resettled in the US.

American exceptionalism is a discourse that constructs "America" in two interrelated ways: America, unlike European imperial powers, is not an imperialist nation with territorial ambition but rather the champion of world peace, freedom, equality, democracy, and human rights, protecting the world from totalitarianism (World War II), communism (the Cold War), and terrorism (US War on Terror); the US is God's chosen nation. Discourses of American exceptionalism, as Jasbir Puar argues, are "embedded in the history of US nation-state formation, from early immigration narratives to Cold War ideologies to the rise of the age of terrorism."[34]

In her book *Meeting the Enemy*, Natsu Taylor Saito maintains that the narrative of American exceptionalism "presumes that human history is best understood as a linear progression toward higher stages of civilization, that Western civilization represents the apex of this history, and that the US embodies the best and most advanced stage of Western civilization, and, therefore, human history to date."[35] As Reginald Horsman points out, however, notions of the "American way of progress" and its "chosen nation" status imply Western Christian civilization and the racial ideology of white supremacy, or, more specifically, "the innate superiority of the Anglo-Saxon branch of the Caucasian race,"[36] which can be traced back to the seventeenth-century Puritan ideology of the New England colonies. According to Saito, Puritan writers made arguments in relation to "ordinary Indians" and their political leaders that the colonizers were there to "save" the indigenous people from their own tyrants, such as "sachems (political leaders) and powwows (priests)."[37] She continues that the language of manifest destiny (i.e., "the god-given mission of the Anglo-Saxon race to literally supplant all other peoples") was replaced by a framework of "international cooperation" through which the colonial powers would continue to lead "underdeveloped" or "backward" nations into civilization and progress.[38] In other words, the ideology of American exceptionalism (i.e., the US is exceptional in embodying freedom and democracy) justifies the US's direct and indirect overthrow of "dictators" in other countries for "other" people. By prolonging Cold War geopolitics, the US government positions "'America' as the site for the authoritative condemnation" of human rights violations in other places, which deflects any criticism of such violations within US national borders and therefore enables the US to claim a position of moral superiority.[39]

Furthermore, as Puar points out, American exceptionalism "feeds off other exceptionalism."[40] While Puar addresses Israel exceptionalism, South Korea has also exhibited its own "exceptional" status not as an empire but as a subordinate to US military empire. As with Israel exceptionalism, which centers on its "exceptional" national security matters in West Asia (i.e., the Middle East), South Korean exceptionalism also revolves around the issue of securing national security against potential military provocation from North Korea (backed by China). Its "exceptional vulnerability" in the face of communist military threat leads to "exceptional security needs," which are met by the US military presence in South Korea. US and South Korean state interests are defined through a joint oppositional position toward communist North Korea. South Korea, like Israel, finds itself entangled in "a cycle of perceived exceptional threats of violence."[41] Unlike Israel, which currently uses military force against Palestinian civilians, South Korea has engaged in an ideological war against communism and its perceived followers among South Koreans. At the same time that South Korea continues its joint military exercises with US military forces, it suppresses dissidents or progressive voices, in lieu of direct military force against North Korea. Consequently, South Korea and Japan, both allies of the US, spend a huge amount of money on US weaponry; this spending is only projected to increase under the two elected conservative Japanese and South Korean heads of state.[42] This spending is justified by the pretense of maintaining regional security in light of North Korea's nuclear threat.

The myth of American exceptionalism has been (and is likely to continue being) the ideological foundation of US engagement in Asia Pacific and West Asia, especially given that the US Secretary of the State declared Asia as the US's primary focus and interest for the next 60 years.[43] Similarly, South Korean exceptionalism and Israel exceptionalism are likely to persist unless peaceful coexistence among people in East Asia and West Asia becomes a regional priority.

The Legacy of Anticommunism

As In-cheol Kang demonstrates in his study of Korean Protestant Christianity and anticommunism, anticommunism is one of the ideologies that has underpinned Korean Christianity since the early twentieth century. The narrative and rhetoric of anticommunism has enabled the growth of Korean Protestant Christianity.[44] By linking communism with totalitarianism, and positioning both against "free capitalist democracy," conservative Protestant Christianity has often labeled oppositional voices or critiques as the product of "reds," "commies," or "pro-North" sympathizers. In a society where the state has declared national security from the potential military provocation of North Korea its priority, this accusation effectively immobilizes and suppresses opposition politically, socially, and theologically. In other words, the state's labeling a person or an organization as "red" or "commie" has effectively silenced the perceived "enemy" within. Accordingly, so-called progressive politicians and intellectuals are commonly accused of being pro-North sympathizers (read, unpatriotic, traitor, enemy of the nation) if they do not criticize North Korea's violations of human rights. Anticommunism as an ideological deployment legitimizes and justifies conservative evangelical Christian human rights advocacy and campaigns, which greatly helps motivate Christian participation. In particular, the rhetoric of anticommunism has been used for the following related causes: defending religious freedom, opposing persecution (both real and imaginary), and expanding Christianity to North Korea and China.

Deep-seated anticommunism has long been produced and reproduced through sermons, bible studies, theological education, church statements, and revival meetings in conservative evangelical Korean churches. Such anticommunism is shared with prominent US evangelicals like Billy Graham, whose conservative evangelical messages deeply influenced conservative evangelical Korean Christians through both direct and indirect contact during the formative years of Korean Christianity (1960s–1980s). Graham was the first US evangelical preacher to visit the war-torn city of Busan during the Korean War in 1952 and was one of the influential white US evangelical preachers who visited South Korea as a main speaker at various evangelical revival meetings in the 1970s. Graham has maintained that "the fight against communism is simply a fight of Christianity versus the anti-Christ."[45] His view of communism is that it is "master-minded by Satan…I think there is no other explanation for the tremendous gains of communism in which they seem to outwit us at every turn, unless they have supernatural power and wisdom and intelligence given to them."[46] He believes that the only way the US can be spared the "onslaught of demon-possessed communism" is through millions of Americans accepting Jesus Christ as their savior.[47]

A half-century after Graham's first visit to South Korea, this belief is still echoed by Scholte. She stated the following when she visited South Korea in 2009:

> The movement to improve North Korean human rights, led by the Defense Foundation, can be called a spiritual warfare. Pyongyang was the first region that accepted Christianity at the end of the Chosun Dynasty, and was once called the "Jerusalem of East Asia." In that sense, it is our ultimate goal to drastically improve the North Korean human rights situation so that North Koreans can freely practice their faith.[48]

For conservative evangelical Christians who experienced the Korean War and have memories of Korean churches in North Korea before the communist takeover, re-evangelizing and reviving Christianity in North

Korea has become a lifelong mission. This partially explains why a large number of conservative Christian churches in South Korea have been actively involved in advocating human rights for North Koreans, which is linked with religious freedom. These conservative Christian churches strive to expose the conditions of human rights violations in North Korea. This approach of coupling human rights and religious freedom, they believe, will hasten the collapse of what they consider an evil regime, and thus enable them to evangelize in North Korea.

Conservative evangelical Christians' concerted efforts to accelerate the breakdown of North Korea's communist regime is in sync with the North Korea Human Rights Act, which is construed as "a means of inducing mass subversion with North Korea, leading to regime change."[49] Quite a number of Christian NGOs in South Korea, as well as in the US, have sent humanitarian aid—along with missionaries—to assist North Koreans on the borders of neighboring China.[50] As I have argued elsewhere, linking human rights with religious freedom seems a necessary step toward the project of evangelizing in North Korea. Conservative Protestant Christians in both the US and South Korea believe that China and North Korea will be one of the most potentially "fertile" mission fields in coming years.[51]

Victims, Villains, and Saviors in Christian Human Rights Discourse

In his discussion of a new humanitarian agenda by the human rights NGOs, David Chandler notes some of the problems of "rights-based" humanitarianism. Rights-based humanitarianism often justifies foreign (i.e., Western) intervention into the affairs for the non-Western state (where humanitarian crises take place) on the conviction that the non-Western state is incapable of self-government. In addition, rights-based humanitarianism portrays "victims" of human rights abuses as helpless and solely dependent on outside support.[52] This victim is one of three constituent figures composing, what Chandler calls, a "fairy tale" or "moral story"; the other two being the villain and the savior. A "fairy tale" or "moral story" characterizes the way in which journalists and media editors frame a "humanitarian story": victims who are in distress, villains who cause humanitarian crises, and saviors who rescue deserving victims.[53] Such a "moral story" is certainly part of knowledge formations about human rights violations. Human rights violation cases use testimonies, photographs if available, statistics, and interviews in particular ways that help in "the creation of incapable human rights victim."[54]

The first component in the rights-based humanitarian "fairy story" involves victims in distress, who are depicted as "authentic insiders," subject to what feminist scholars call "Western myths of deserving victims."[55] Cynthia Enloe calls such victims "womenandchildren,"[56] to signify someone who is powerless, innocent, and needs outside rescue. The second component of the humanitarian fairy story is the villain. Villains are often represented by a non-Western government or state authorities that "caused famine and poverty through personal corruption or wrong spending policies or that consciously embarked on a policy of genocide or mass repression."[57] The third component is the savior, such as "the external aid agency, the international institution, or even the journalists covering the story whose interests were seen to be inseparable from those of the deserving victim."[58]

This "fairy tale" characterizes the ways in which the North Korean human rights situation is represented by journalists, scholars, reporters, and agencies, which are directly or indirectly related to organizations such as the NKFC and KCC. For instance, the KCC's "Let My People Go" campaign—inspired by the same campaign banner Jewish Americans used to protest the Soviet Union's restrictions against the emigration of Soviet Jews during the 1960s—demands that the Chinese government release North Korean escapees and end practices of human trafficking and repatriation of North Korean escapees. The campaign also demands that the Chinese government recognize the refugee status of North Koreans within its borders rather than classify them as economic migrants. In this campaign, the three components of humanitarian "fairy tales" that Chandler identifies are found. The "deserving victims" in this case are North Koreans, especially North Korean women and girls who are "still being sold into sex slavery."[59] The campaign claims that "90 percent of North Korean women with no legal protection fall prey to traffickers in China who sell them into sexual slavery, either as brides, concubines, or prostitutes, where they are raped and abused at will, many of them on multiple occasions."[60] The chief "villain" in this campaign is the Chinese government, which does not recognize the refugee status of North Koreans and instead sends them back to North Korea, knowing that repatriates are tortured, exploited, or executed in one of North Korea's many gulags. The KCC's campaign makes an interesting parallel. In its campaign, the victims are Soviet Jews and North Korean escapees; the villains are the former Soviet Union, which restricted the Soviet Jews' emigration, and China, which does not release North Korean escapees to other safe countries. The saviors are Jewish Americans, who led a successful campaign that resulted in "the release of a million Soviet Jews to Israel and 500,000 to the US,"[61] and Korean American Christians, who pray for and take action for North Korean escapees in China. Both Jewish Americans and Korean American Christians can be likened to the prophet Nehemiah, who not only "wept, fasted and prayed" for the tormenting situation of his own people, but also took action.[62]

Another example is found in *The Korea Times*' report on the Congressional Hearing of the Tom Lantos Human Rights Commission. One witness, Steven Kim, is the founder and president of 318 Partners Mission Foundation. *The Korea Times* reported that Kim testified to the great number of North Korean women who have fled to China suffer not only from human trafficking and prostitution but also cyber-porno, for which they are "forcefully mobilized"[63]:"The cyber-porno business run by ethnic Koreans in China locks up 4–6 North Korean women in one room and forces them to provide 'sexual' services in front of the web camera. The victimized women range from early teens to women in their 30s."[64] The victims in this story are North Korean women who are coerced into sexually exploiting themselves; the villain is primarily the Chinese government. The Chinese government becomes the villain because it refuses to grant refugee status to the victims of sex trafficking and instead classifies them as "economic migrants" or "illegal foreign residents." It is interesting that neither the ethnic Koreans in China who run the cyber-porno business nor the North Korean government is directly condemned. Instead, the Chinese government is pressed to act like other developed countries, which take international human rights policy seriously. The saviors are human rights activists who testified at the hearing against China's policy on North Korean escapees, members of North Korean human rights organizations, such as Scholte of the Defense Forum Foundation, and activists from the Coalitions for North Korean Women's Rights, who planned to protest China's policy on North Korean defectors in front of the Chinese embassy in Washington, D.C.[65]

A *Seattle Times* special column, "Tales of Horror Falling Mostly on Deaf Ears," written by James J. Na, also tells a story of the "unspeakable horrors of sexual slavery," which two North Korean women endured in China.[66] Like many other similar stories, the three components of the "fairy story" also structure Na's narrative. The "deserving victims" of his particular narrative are two North Korean women who were sexually and physically assaulted and abused in the process of sex trafficking in China. The villain, not surprisingly, is "the repugnant North Korean regime represented by Kim Jong-il." Na evokes the third component, the "savior," through a comparison—that is, a comparison between the indifferent US mainstream media and those who advocate for the rescue of these "deserving victims."

After briefly recounting these two women's ordeals, Na criticizes the US mainstream media for being too busy covering the cases of Harriet Miers's withdrawal from George W. Bush's Supreme Court nomination and Lewis Libby's indictment on the charge of lying to federal investigators and obstructing justice in the Central Intelligence Agency (CIA) leak investigation to report these women's stories.[67] In contrast to what he calls the "deaf ears" of the US mainstream media, which are not interested in hearing these women's ordeals, Na praises three Republican US senators and Scholte as those (saviors) who stand firm behind these urgent matters. Quoting Scholte, who criticized the media for being "more interested in bringing down George Bush than Kim Jong-il," Na advocates the encouragement of a "mass exodus" by "aiding the outflow of North Korean defectors and spreading the news of the outside world" to "bring down the repugnant North Korean regime."[68] Na ends his article by noting that Cha, one of the survivors of sex trafficking, apologized to "her dead husband for living, in order to save her children." He quotes Cha's final words of testimony: "If I ever see my husband on the other side…I want to be his wife again. I want to pray for so many girls who suffered and wasted their lives in China and other countries."[69] Notable in this conclusion is the manner in which "deserving victims" are those who conform to normative gender roles (the sacrificial wife and mother) in the context of a heterosexual marriage relationship.

Rather than challenge this neat "fairy tale" scenario, some writings by self-identifying feminists, though not directly involved with the faith-based movement themselves, reinscribe this human rights discourse of the new faith-based movement. Their writings include the three components of the moral "fairy story." An article on the sex trafficking of North Korean women escapees by Donna M. Hughes, a women's studies professor in a US university, is a case in point. The article begins with the "plea" of a female North Korean escapee who is hiding in China for access to an "underground railroad." Like most documents on North Korean escapees in China, Hughes's article does not fail to describe how women are treated in the sex trafficking world:

> The women are raped by sellers and buyers...A young woman refugee said that Chinese officials are complicit in the trafficking of North Korean women. Once a woman is sold, she is completely powerless. If she offers any protest, she is threatened with exposure to the Chinese authorities...A secret underground railroad, run mostly by Christian activists, operates to get refugees to safety. If the conductors on this railroad are caught, they are arrested and sentenced to prison in China.[70]

Hughes also describes the ordeals of those who were sent back to North Korea:

> The returnees are imprisoned in detention centers, interrogated, mistreated, and starved. Pregnant women are forcibly aborted or newborns killed to keep "foreign" blood out of North Korea.[71]

These excerpts from Hughes's article illustrate how the three components of the moral "fairy tale" are linked together: suffering victims, who include victims of sex trafficking, pregnant women in prison camps, and persecuted Christians; villains, who include ethnic Korean Chinese traffickers, complicit Chinese officials, and, the most vile, North Korean government officials who mistreat and abuse female "returnees"; and saviors, who include rescuers, such as Christian activists who run a secret underground railroad in China and other activists who operate human rights organizations, such as the NK Gulag, which is a member of the NKFC. While complicit Chinese officials are often included in the list of villains, Hughes extends her criticism to *both* China's one-child policy as one that has resulted in a deficit of women and thereby led to the kidnapping and trafficking of women, *and* China's violation of United Nations policy on the treatment of refugees, especially female refugees.[72] Hughes's article exemplifies one of many forms of what Puar calls US gender exceptionalism, according to which an "'American' feminist as the feminist subject par excellence"[73] attempts to rescue "Third World women" or "other" women from their oppressive governments and/or male counterparts. This can be viewed as a feminist rendition of "white men saving brown women from brown men," with the change of the gender of the agent.[74]

The clear distinction between savior and villain, and between good and evil allows readers and audiences of these tales of human rights violations to easily identify the good with savior; this alignment encourages them to be part of the "saving mission" for the frail, helpless victims. The images of distraught, starved, and often sexually abused North Korean women and undernourished, scrawny children are a primary signifier used to mobilize and consolidate both material and intangible support for North Korean human rights advocacy. These images provoke sympathy from advocates and potential sponsors. North Korean women and children whose dire situation is presented through images, narratives, testimonies, and media coverage are victims to be rescued from the evil North Korean regime and its conspirator, China. In the US and South Korea, both conservative evangelical Christians and those who support their agenda are the saviors at the forefront of the rescue projects. The knowledges gathered about human rights violations are also indispensable in pressing the US government to expedite adoptions of North Korean "orphans," who have been abandoned in China, and to admit more North Korean escapees to the US.

In all of this, the victims are viewed as unable to stand against evil; they can only be "rescued." As Grewal argues, this way of formulating human rights abuse cases constructs women's agency in "dichotomous terms of those who act and those who are acted upon."[75] The representation of non-Western women (e.g., North Korean women) as "those who need rescue" constructs and reinforces a story in which all that is non-Western (read, authoritarian, dictatorial, non-capitalist, or communist) is painted as "un-democratic" and "barbaric." In such a story, Christians in the US and South Korea are framed as being the primary bearers of freedom and human rights for women who meet the criteria of "deserving victims."

By relying on a framework of a "modernized First World" and its "exceptional" allies that should intervene and rescue those facing another crisis in the non-Western or Third World, conservative Christian human rights discourse imagines the non-Western world/Third World as "a region of aberrant violence."[76] In this way, as Grewal points out, the First World, as represented by the US, becomes "the authoritative and objective liberator."[77] Such representation, in turn, endorses and legitimizes strategies and foreign policies that the US government chooses to ratify and impose on the grounds that it brings freedom, peace, and democracy, which successfully maintains the myth of US exceptionalism.

In Christian human rights discourse, conservative evangelical Christians and Christian NGOs in South Korea and the US become the frontrunners of human rights, and the US becomes what Robert Bellah calls the "righteous empire."[78] This framing, in turn, justifies the new faith-based movement ideologically as focused on protecting the religious human rights of Christians in dictatorial and communist regimes. Conservative evangelical

Christians are mobilized transnationally to support the movement both directly and indirectly through giving monetary donations, participating in rallies and protests, and pressuring politicians to take actions in their policymaking. Such a movement supports the "righteous" work of the empire. And the three components of the moral "fairy tale"—victim, villain, and savior—help to sustain the tone, agenda, direction, and strategy of the movement. Christian human rights discourse lies at the heart of US political discourse about North Korea and any other regimes that the US deems an adversary.

Postscript: "The Danger of a Single Story"[79]

The trope of saving North Korean women deployed in conservative Christian human rights discourse is powerful, but it does little to assist North Korean women who have fled to China recognize and exercise their agency. North Korean women are framed primarily as victims in need of the saving hands of outside human rights organizations. Furthermore, Christian human rights NGOs' use of "bleak images of innocent victims" in their campaigns and discourse generates serious effects that can work against "future reconciliation and peace moves between the two Koreas."[80] To put it differently, "a just social integration on the peninsula," which is crucial for the stability of the region, can be impeded primarily because there is a "serious imbalance in human dignity between giver and receiver" if North Korean women's identity and experience is reduced to a "single story" of helpless victims and/or objects of sympathy.[81] However, such representations of North Korean women as victims do provoke public support and outrage against North Korea and China. This, in turn, helps US foreign policymakers define North Korea and China as violators of human rights, which justifies pressuring both countries to follow the "international" standards observed by the Western world as represented by the US.

If we reformulate the North Korean human rights issue as a necessary part of what Kuan Hsing Chen calls "de-cold-war" struggles, would it look different from the current approach, which reinforces anticommunism, American exceptionalism, and Korean exceptionalism? As Chen puts it, to "de-cold-war" means "to mark out a space in which unspoken stories and histories may be told, and to recognize and map the historically constituted cultural and political effects of the cold war."[82] To reframe and rearticulate the North Korean human rights issue in terms of a "de-cold-war" process, what would be required? It would require long-term aid and solutions that truly improve the lives of people in North Korea by eliminating the need to cross borders to China only to find food; border crossings during which many of them end up being exploited and risking their lives. It would also require that Christian NGOs and US-aided NGOs change their current rhetoric and practices, which work against moves toward reconciliation, peaceful coexistence, and self-determination in the region. It would further include challenging the figuration of North Korean escapees, especially women, solely as victims in need of deliverance by outside forces. Instead of representing these women only as victims, it would require seeing the inherent danger of repeatedly deploying a single narrative method, which defines the "other" as the one whom the US and its allies need to save, as the *only* story. Such a single-story narrative only enforces imperialist logics of the Cold War without understanding the realities that North Korean women face on the ground, and is therefore incapable of bringing about changes that are truly needed for the improvement of their lives. Moreover, the framing of the North Korean human rights issue as a work of de-cold-war would require us to see what Yen Le Espiritu calls the "complex personhood"—the "complex and oftentimes contradictory humanity and subjectivity"[83]—of North Korean people. This simultaneously necessitates a critical look at the narratives that represent North Korea *only* as an inhumane communist regime, South Korea *only* as a free democratic society, and the US *only* as a just and benevolent nation. Such a critical look compels us to tell the "other truths" behind these stories.[84] As Mikyoung Kim argues, North Korean escapees/refugee-settlers' stories are in fact counter-hegemonic for both Koreas[85]:

> [T]hey cultivate critical insights into both societies, posing a challenge to the dominant modus operandi of both. These refugees' escape constituted a powerful act of resistance against North Korea's self-aggrandizing propaganda, and their disillusionment with Southern society as a humbling perspective, pointing to the woes of rampant materialism and anti-communist indoctrination, which are detrimental to social integration of the peoples of both societies.[86]

Their counter-hegemonic narratives can also help debunk the image of the US as an ardent defender of human rights and freedom by challenging us to ask, who gets to decide what "freedom" means and what it looks like?[87] Thus, a first step toward reframing the North Korean human rights issue as part of the de-cold-war process is to refuse to tell *moral* "fairy tale" and instead tell both counter-hegemonic narratives and stories that reflect complex personhood.

Notes

1. North Koreans who flee to China or South Korea are often categorized as either defectors or refugees. The Chinese government classifies North Koreans who cross the borders of China and North Korea without proper documentation as illegal economic migrants. As such, they are thereby denied asylum, which is provided to refugees under the United Nations High Commissioner for Refugees (UNHCR). In this chapter, I use the term *escapee* to refer to North Koreans who flee to China, *refugee-settler* to refer to North Koreans who settle in South Korea, and *defector* and *refugee* when necessary.
2. Since the passing of the North Korean Human Rights Act in 2004 through June 2011, the US government resettled 120 North Korean refugees and their families. See Mikyoung Kim, *Securitization of Human Rights: North Korean Refugees in East Asia* (Santa Barbara: Praeger, 2012), 96.
3. I acknowledge that not all conservative evangelical Christians share the agenda of the "new faith-based movement" discussed by Allen D. Hertzke.
4. Allen D. Hertzke, *Freeing God's Children: The Unlikely Alliance for Global Human Rights* (Lanham: Rowman & Littlefield Publishers, 2004).
5. Ibid., 302.
6. Ibid., 337.
7. Ibid., 302.
8. Inderpal Grewal, "Foreword," in *Just Advocacy?: Women's Human Rights, Transnational Feminisms, and the Politics of Representation*, ed., Wendy S. Hesford and Wendy Kozol (New Brunswick: Rutgers University Press, 2005), viii.
9. Ibid.
10. Ibid., ix.
11. Ibid.
12. Ibid.
13. Though it is beyond the scope of this chapter, a more comprehensive understanding of the North Korean human rights situation is needed: one that neither subscribes to the politicized Right agenda and discourse nor minimizes human rights violations of North Koreans as insignificant. It has often been the case that raising the North Korean human rights issue is deemed to serve as a conservative agenda. However, dismissal or disregard of this issue as a so-called conservative concern leaves the North Korean human rights issue in the hands of right-wing politicians and

conservative evangelical Christian churches and organizations, whose approaches only reinforce the imperial logics of the Cold War. Necessary is a critical analysis of the complexity of the situation, which attends to the multiple actors—both individual and collective—who pursue first and foremost their own interests and priorities. From such an analysis, alternatives that truly improve the living conditions of people in North Korea could be suggested.

14. Jodi Kim, *Ends of Empire: Asian American Critique and the Cold War* (Minneapolis, London: University of Minnesota Press, 2010), 3. Also Heonik Kwon argues that the Cold War was not "a single monolithic phenomenon across places"; see Heonik Kwon, *The Other Cold War* (New York: Columbia University Press, 2010), 32.
15. I examine a body of writings that support, endorse, and enhance the agenda of the new faith-based movement. This body includes sermons, statements, documents, books, journals, media coverage, campaign posters, and other visual images produced and circulated by transnational organizations, such as the North Korean Freedom Coalition (NKFC), the largest alliance for North Korean human rights founded in the US in 2003, and the Korean Church Coalition for North Korea Freedom (KCC), formed in 2004.
16. In *For All Peoples and All Nations: The Ecumenical Churches and Human Rights* (Washington, DC: Georgetown University Press, 2005), John Nurser provides the context in which what is known as Article 18—the article on religious freedom in the Universal Declaration of Human Rights—had been developed. He argues that the motivation of some people, mostly Protestant Christians, to include religious freedom as a human right in the Universal Declaration, was the result of certain local governments' and local peoples' resistance to Protestant Christian missionary programs in the "mission-field."
17. Hertzke, *Freeing God's Children*, 3.
18. Ibid., 313.
19. The Center for the Study of Global Christianity estimates that "there are 467,894 Christians in North Korea and 10,592 Christian martyrs every year." See Ruth Moon, "World's Worst Persecutor," *Christianity Today* (December 2009): 19.
20. See Hertzke, *Freeing God's Children.*
21. Ibid., 168.
22. Hertzke quotes Horowitz from a paper presented by Pierre Rigoulot, "Comparative Analysis of Concentration Camps in Nazi Germany, the Former Soviet Union and North Korea." Presented at the First International Conference on North Korean Human Rights and Refugees in Seoul (1999). See Hertzke, 168.
23. See Hertzke.

24. See Nami Kim, "A Mission to the 'Graveyard of Empires'? Neocolonialism and Contemporary Evangelical Missions of the Global South," *Mission Studies* 27, no. 1 (2010): 3–23.
25. Elizabeth Castelli, *Martyrdom and Memory: Early Christian Culture Making* (New York: Columbia University Press, 2007), 199.
26. John Carpenter, "U.S. Urged to Accept More NK Refugees," *The Korea Times* (May 9, 2006), accessed April 20, 2007, http://times.hankooki.com/lpage/200605/kt2006050917260068040.htm.
27. Ibid.
28. Inderpal Grewal, *Transnational America: Feminisms, Diasporas, Neoliberalisms* (Durham: Duke University Press, 2005), 173–174.
29. Nina Glick Schiller, 2005. "Transnational social fields and imperialism: Bringing a theory of power to Transnational Studies," *Anthropological Theory* 5 no. 4 (2005): 447–448.
30. Public members of the NKFC include the Southern Baptist Convention, the Religious Freedom Coalition, the Christian Coalition, Ethics and Religious Liberty, the Family Research Council, the Israeli Jewish Committee Against the Gas Chambers in North Korea, and many more. See Public Members, North Korea Freedom Coalition, accessed August 2, 2012, http://www.nkfreedom.org/About-Us/Public-Members.aspx.
31. See North Korean Freedom Coalition, accessed June 15, 2007, http://www.nkfreedom.org/index.php?id=11.
32. Ibid.
33. "Who We Are," Korean Church Coalition for North Korean Freedom, accessed December 1, 2012, http://kccnk.org/index.php?mid=WhoWeAre.
34. Jasbir Puar, "Feminists and Queers in the Service of Empire" in *Feminism and War: Confronting U.S. Imperialism*, ed., Robin L Riley, Chandra Talpade Mohanty, and Minnie Bruce Pratt (London: Zed Books, 2008), 48.
35. Natsu Taylor Saito, *Meeting the Enemy: American Exceptionalism and International Law* (New York: New York University Press, 2010), 229.
36. Reginald Horsman, *Race and Manifest Destiny: The Origins of American Racial Anglo-Saxonism* (Cambridge: Harvard University Press, 1981), 4.
37. Charles M. Segal and David C. Stineback, *Puritans, Indians, and Manifest Destiny* (New York: Putnam, 1977). Quoted in Natsu Taylor Saito, *Meeting the Enemy: American Exceptionalism and International Law* (New York: New York University Press, 2010), 66.
38. Natsu Taylor Saito, *Meeting the Enemy*, 159–160.
39. Grewal, *Transnational America*, 150.
40. Puar, "Feminists and Queers in the Service of Empire," 51.
41. Ibid.
42. See "Han-Il, Chinmibosu Jipkwon, Mikook Moghisuchul Hoghi" ("The Window of Opportunity for the U.S. to Export Weaponry to South Korea's

and Japan's New Pro-American Administrations") *Hangyore* (January 2, 2013), accessed February 3, 2013, http://www.hani.co.kr/arti/international/international_general/568009.html.

43. Hillary Clinton, "America's Pacific Century," *Foreign Policy* (November 2011), accessed March 16, 2012, http://www.foreignpolicy.com/articles/2011/10/11/americas_pacific_century.
44. See In-cheol Kang, *Hankook-eui Kaeshinkyo-wa Bankongjueui* (*Korean Protestant Christianity and Anticommunism*) (Seoul: Joongshim, 2007).
45. William G. McLoughlin, Jr., *Billy Graham: Revivalist in a Secular Age* (New York: The Ronald Press Company, 1960), 138.
46. *U.S. News and World Report*, September 27, 1957, 72. Quoted in William G. McLoughlin, Jr., *Billy Graham: Revivalist in a Secular Age* (New York: The Ronald Press Company, 1960), 139–140.
47. M. J. Heale, *American Anticommunism Combating the Enemy Within, 1830–1970 (The American Moment)*. (Baltimore: Johns Hopkins University Press, 1990), 171.
48. Suzanne Scholte, "The Movement to Improve North Korean Human Rights is a Spiritual Warfare," *Gidok News* (May 5, 2009), accessed November 10, 2012, http://blog.daum.net/rione30/17055195.
49. Kim, *Securitization of Human Rights*, 101.
50. *Good Friends*, a Buddhist organization, is one of the non-Christian organizations very active in assisting North Koreans, as well as in documenting various resources concerning the situation of North Koreans.
51. See Kim, "A Mission to the 'Graveyard of Empires'?"
52. David Chandler, "The Road to Military Humanitarianism: How the Human Rights NGOs Shaped a New Humanitarian Agenda," *Human Rights Quarterly* 23 (2001): 690.
53. Ibid.
54. Ibid., 691.
55. Grewal, *Transnational America*, 5.
56. See Cynthia Enloe, *Maneuvers: The International Politics of Militarizing Women's Lives* (Berkeley, Los Angeles: University of California Press, 2000).
57. Chandler, "The Road to Military Humanitarianism, 690.
58. Ibid.
59. "Let My People Go," Korean Church Coalition for North Korean Freedom, accessed December 3, 2012, http://www.kccnk.org/kcceng/page_xvtT84.
60. Korean Church Coalition for North Korean Freedom, accessed December 3, 2012, http://www.kccnk.org/index.php?mid=Resolution.
61. "Let My People Go," Korean Church Coalition for North Korean Freedom, accessed December 3, 2012, http://www.kccnk.org/kcceng/page_xvtT84.
62. Ibid.

63. "Article on Press Conference and Protest at the Chinese Embassy, *The Korea Times* (September 24, 2010), accessed December 12, 2012, http://www.nkfreedom.org/UploadedDocuments/2010.09.25_KoreaTimesDC.pdf.
64. Ibid.
65. Ibid.
66. James J. Na, "Tales of Horror Falling Mostly on Deaf Ears," *The Seattle Times* (November 23, 2005), accessed June 10, 2006, http://seattletimes.nwsource.com/html/opinion/2002640498_na23.html.
67. Ibid.
68. Ibid.
69. Ibid.
70. Donna M. Hughes, "'How Can I Be Sold Like This?' The Trafficking of North Korean Women Refugees," *National Review* (July 19, 2005), accessed June 11, 2006, http://www.nationalreview.com/script/printpage.p?ref=/hughes/hughes200507190734.asp.
71. Ibid.
72. One of the charges against the Chinese government by the new faith-based movement and the US government is that Chinese officials send North Korean women back to North Korea on the grounds that they are in China not for the "political" reasons, but for "economic" reasons, despite the fact that they are aware that these women will be persecuted.
73. Puar, "Feminists and Queers in the Service of Empire," 49.
74. See Kwok Pui-Lan, "Unbinding Our Feet: Saving Brown Women and Feminist Religious Discourse" in *Postcolonialism, Feminism and Religious Discourse*, ed. Laura E. Donaldson and Kwok Pui-lan (New York, London: Routledge, 2002).
75. Grewal, quoted in Hesford and Kozol's *Just Advocacy?: Women's Human Rights, Transnational Feminism, and the Politics of Representation* (New Brunswick: Rutgers University Press, 2005), 17.
76. Ibid.
77. Ibid.
78. Robert N. Bellah, "Righteous Empire: How Does a Nation That Hates Taxes and Distrusts Big Government Launch an Empire? In a State of Deep Denial: Imperialism—American-style—The National Security Strategy—Critical Essay." *Christian Century* (March 8, 2003), accessed July 23, 2007, http://findarticles.com/p/articles/mi_m1058/is_5_120/ai_98754731.
79. Chimamanda Adichie, "The Danger of a Single Story," accessed March 10, 2010, http://www.ted.com/talks/chimamanda_adichie_the_danger_of_a_single_story.html.
80. Kim, *Securitization of Human Right*, 85.
81. Ibid., 86, 83.

82. Kuan-Hsing Chen, *Asia as Method: Toward Deimperialization* (Durham and London: Duke University Press, 2010), 120.
83. Yen Le Espiritu, "Thirty Years Afterward: The Endings That Are Not Over," *Amerasia Journal* 31, no. 2 (2005): xxi.
84. Ibid.
85. Kim, *Securitization of Human Rights*, 19.
86. Ibid.
87. See Saito, *Meeting the Enemy*, 243.

CHAPTER 8

A Thief, a Woman, a People of the Land: Exploring Chamorro Strategies of Incarnation

Michael Sepidoza Campos

When I was eight, my family moved to Guam. My father's work in a transnational company brought us to this unfamiliar Pacific outpost, oblivious to its history. The only thing we knew was that Guam was a territory of the US. And so, access to the island brought us closer to fulfilling the dream of every Filipino old enough to remember the so-called golden days of US rule. It was a strange arrival: I had expected to see pines and evergreens, only to be engulfed by groves of coconut trees. I had hoped to gain "American"—white—friends, only to realize that most Guam folks looked like me. The only thing that clued us to the island's US ties was the prevalence of English, the ubiquitous exchange of dollars, and cable access to Sesame Street.

We lived on Guam for four years. My social circle was limited to other expatriate dependents from the Philippines, Korea, Japan, and the US mainland. Like many of them, we left Guam as soon as our parents obtained new postings overseas. It would take another return—this time, as a seminarian

M.S. Campos (✉)
Emerging Queer Asian/Pacific Island Religion Scholars, San Francisco, CA, USA

N. Kim, W.A. Joh (eds.), *Critical Theology against US Militarism in Asia*,
DOI 10.1057/978-1-137-48013-2_8

and teacher—for me to be reintroduced to the island and its people. Resonating with Guam's colonial history, I acclimated to the strangeness of place.[1] *Cultural fluency flowed with my participation in Catholic ritual, practice, and devotions. I became a ubiquitous presence at village fiestas, receiving/giving* chenchule'*—the customary exchange of gifts—to indicate belonging to place and people. Over time, I noticed shifts in gait, the cadence of my speech; my sense of displacement dissipated as my accountability to land deepened. Guam became home. No longer the interloper, I encountered—after nearly a decade straddling Guam and Manila—the* taotao tano, *the "people of the land."*

Locating Bodies

In this chapter, I reflect on my relationship with Guam, its history, and the ways Chamorros[2]—Guam's indigenous people—have reincarnated selves over and again in a colonial trajectory that conflates culture, religious practice, and narratives of empire. My location as one both native/local to and foreign/other to place—an "alter-native" of sorts—laces my analysis with complicity, always compromising my support of indigenous interests.

While this chapter ostensibly traces the constitution of militarized bodies, I do so by unveiling three incarnations at the matrices of empire, economy, and religious practice. I retrieve the *ladrón* (thief) as the (1) first incarnation of Chamorro subjectivity. Imposed by the Portuguese Fernão Magalhães on Guam's indigenous people, the *ladrón* signifies strategies for/against colonial contact. The subsequent proliferation of devotion to the *Santa Marian Kamalen* (Our Lady of Camarin) confronts the *ladrón*'s narrative. Rather than undermine, this (2) second incarnation evokes similar—albeit increasingly subtle—iterations of resistance/thievery that scaffold *and* subvert the trajectory of conquest.[3] Before these two disparate iconographies of empire, Chamorros reconstitute bodies into tenuous existence. More than gestures of resistance, I suggest that these icons illuminate a (3) third incarnation that usurps and assuages the forgetting of bodies articulated within the confines of colonial time and space.

I wield *self*, *body*, and *identity* interchangeably as unstable metaphors to imperial articulations that contain/limit strategies of subject-consolidation. In a similar way, I transpose between *empire*, *nation*, and *center* to locate shifting colonial positionalities of which militarism serves as both its effect and its specter.[4] Constructed on centuries of colonial enterprise, the

"Chamorro body" hinges between invisibility and articulation. Native to Guam while enduring the alienation of colonial exile, Chamorros reconstitute an impossible body.

Militarism on Guam hedges against contemporary conceptions of statehood and citizenship. Given intermingling tropes of religion, politics, culture, and economy, militarism is intimately connected to—and I would argue, serves as an extension of—Guam's nearly five-hundred-year colonial history. As "a step-by-step process by which something becomes controlled by, dependent on, or derives its value from the military," *militarism* relies on strategies of defense and aggression to justify its existence.[5] Over time, defense narratives contour a community's sense of purpose, perpetually negotiating an imagined enemy with a defending empire.[6] This generates a worldview that muddles culture, progress, and civic obligation with military duty.[7] Over time, militarism overtakes culture as articulations of war, defense, and national integrity penetrate and permeate cultural narratives. More than a mechanism to secure geopolitical interests, therefore, militarism buttresses Chamorro history, epistemology, and bodily locations.

To the extent that colonial enterprises give birth to a people at war with itself, two icons embody Chamorro resistance to and complicity in the proliferation of empire: the *ladrón* and the *Santa Marian Kamalen*. Drawing from Vicente Diaz's theoretical maneuver to "re-position the missionary position," I wield these icons as incarnations of mis/naming that render colonizer and colonized complicit in a semiotic game to assert, control, and conform bodies. More than sites on which subjectivities are consolidated, icons "literalize the body's fragmentation...[while] suggesting a peculiar persistence of wholeness."[8] Together, the *Kamalen* and *ladrón* expand the location of Chamorro bodies.

Since their emergence onto Spanish/European consciousness, Chamorros have been maligned as troublesome thieves interrupting imperial progress. As a replenishing and military-controlled port in the Manila-Acapulco Galleon trade, Guam would endure a parade of *gobernadorcillos* tasked with subduing these crafty indigenes.[9] Only through missionary seduction would Spain satiate Chamorros, reorienting native desires toward the promise of a world to come. Early Jesuits—led by the martyr, Diego Luis de San Vitores—tamed impulses of resistance by substituting the preeminence of bodies for souls.[10] Over the course of three centuries, Chamorro Catholicism—incarnated through enduring devotion to the Kamalen—would come to serve as the hinge on which both colonized and colonizer would re/construct selfhood, assert political determination, and articulate meaning.

This dance between "thievery" and "devotion" would continue into the twentieth century, well after Spain ceded Guam to the US in 1898. With the island's entanglement in US and Japanese wrangling during the Second World War, the conflation of religious and military appetites would intensify control over native bodies. Only the annual Liberation Day Parade—commemorating the return of US forces at the end of Japan's brutal occupation of the island—would rival the level of devotion, number of attendees, resources, and pomp expended for the fiesta of *Santa Marian Kamalen*. Together, military and religious iconographies would bolster Chamorro bodies grasping for visibility. Never quite the faithful subject, but inevitably complicit in the imperial project, Chamorros would reconstruct selves to resist, assimilate, disclaim, and affirm military control over land, bodies, and souls.[11]

More than a critique of militarism, this chapter traces the incarnational strategies deployed by Chamorros to unfurl a colonized body. For a people who have had to endure an endless parade of colonial masters, this yearning to name/locate self illuminates an impossible body. Chamorros discern an unattainable becoming that interrupts the linearity of past, present, and possible future. The unwieldiness of Chamorro bodies leaves the self "…up against itself…ill at ease in [its] own skin…"[12] Fragmented, they cannot but attend to alienation, compelled to take responsibility for a self that is "other" to itself.[13]

Discerning the contours of this ephemeral body, I read subjectivity through critical lenses, referencing the kinds of bodies that John Caputo describes as "insubstantial quasi-beings like ashes and ghosts which flutter between existence and non-existence."[14] Rather than stabilize Chamorro selves, I trace theological turns in the ways bodies are incarnated beyond limits of time and place, bodies grasping at one's alienation as an intimate encounter with transcendence.

First Incarnation: The Thief's Specter

> They treat our history as fable and fiction.
> Haven't we the same right concerning that which
> They teach us as incontestable truths?
>
> Ma na'huyong kumu kado'kado' yan dinagi i fina'posta.

> Kåo ada ti mamparehu direcho-ta nu ayu siha
> i manmafa'na'gue-ta na mansenmagåhet?
>
> Chief Hurao, 1671[15]

As an "unincorporated territory" of the US, Guam remains one of world's last colonies. While the Organic Act of 1950 extended provisional citizenship to "Guamanian persons and persons of Guamanian descent," it limited possibility for full integration.[16] Citizenship was warranted by *time*: only Guam residents and their descendants from 1899 onward were granted citizenship "from birth"; others were to be naturalized. *Place* also determined limits of belonging: island residents enjoyed nonvoting congressional representation and gained voting rights for the US president only if they assumed residency in 1 of the 50 federated states. Guam's unincorporated status[17] thus alludes to jurisdictions arbitrarily established around imperial boundaries. These boundaries situate Chamorros in limbo; their history and place reduced to "fable and fiction."

Guam's position as a military outpost began in 1521 with the arrival of Magalhães, who named both the island and the archipelago, *Las Islas de los Ladrones* (Islands of Thieves).[18] Magalhães maligned and subdued Chamorros "for [their] alleged theft of iron and a skiff," leaving entire villages destroyed, inhabitants slaughtered.[19] The arrival of missionaries in 1662—particularly San Vitores, the revered "Apostle of the Marianas"—would unfold to the ominous marriage of church and state in a colonial enterprise that oriented native economy, culture, and worldview toward Catholic Spain. San Vitores' prominence signaled more than the conflation of ecclesial and temporal powers over the island. In order to cull imperial patronage, San Vitores renamed Guam—and the archipelago of which it was a part—*Las Islas Marianas*, after the reigning Queen Mariana de Austria.[20] With the stroke of a pen, he rebaptized the islands from a den of thieves to a people *chosen*, secured under the double appellation of *Mariana*, Spain's Queen Mother, and *Mary*, the Mother of God. This simultaneous loss/acquisition of name would scaffold the semiotic strategies deployed by Chamorros to stabilize selves before shifting narratives of empire.

Over the course of two-and-a-half centuries, Guam would endure the trajectory of every colonial outpost: the introduction of disease, usurpation of native leadership, restructuring of culture, and decimation of population.[21] In 1898 Guam would pass into the control of the US, a burgeoning empire eager to stretch its muscles across the Pacific.

Along with Cuba, the Philippines, and Puerto Rico, Guam found itself flirting with a nation enamored with its so-called "manifest destiny." US occupiers did not have much to do. Centuries of colonial penetration had formed a people accustomed to shifting loyalties. And so, as the island was placed under US naval jurisdiction, Guam's fealty took on tones of heroism and selfless commitment to military interests: families' "willing" abandonment of native lands for purposes of defense and the proliferation of voluntary service among Chamorros (along with the inevitable loss of lives) were nurtured by the promise of military patronage and economic access.[22] For Chamorros, life beyond the military infrastructure became incomprehensible. In a sense, "when the white man arrived…he disrupted the psychological horizon and mechanisms" of indigenous subjectivity.[23] Teetering at the edge, Chamorro self-worth was defined by one's ability to secure the porous borders of empire.

And yet, even after centuries of subjugation, the *ladrón* never completely vanished. Chamorros developed strategies of resistance that endured a parade of colonial masters.[24] They gave birth to a "creolized culture forged out of centuries of intercultural mixing as the principal form of indigenous social and cultural articulation."[25] Negotiating multiple languages, values, and worldviews, Chamorros undermined "conventional definitions of indigeneity based on presumptions about cultural purity and insularity."[26] Theirs was a body hewn on compounding imperial engagements, an unending affirmation and loss of self. In the last 50 years, a deepened imperative for self-determination emerged as a political necessity for Chamorros after Guam found itself caught beneath the devastating crossfire of the Second World War. As a colony, Guam could never fully disentangle its own interests from US interests. At the very least, it must speak as a "citizen." Rather than secede, therefore, Guam chose to turn to empire. For Vicente M. Diaz, this turn traces the very strategies of manipulation deployed by early *ladrones* to "reposition" the thrust of colonial penetration.[27]

Vivian Dames locates two moments in post–Second World War Guam that intensified the potency of this turn. The first took place in 1949 when members of Guam's congress, led by Carlos P. Taitano, negotiated US citizenship for island residents. The second occurred in 1993 when Danny Jackson, a member of the indigenous group, *I Nasion Chamoru* (The Chamorro Nation), denounced this same citizenship to protest the military sequestration of ancestral lands. For Dames, these events—occurring at the same congressional hall, separated by nearly 45 years—heighten shifts in Chamorro self-awareness. It is an awareness that began with a push for "inclusion as equal members within the American body politic" that later developed into an "indigenous rights movement [that] goes beyond the construction of 'national' as circumscribed by a nation-state."[28] For Dames, attempts to locate/name an "indigenous self" hedge against the impossibility of asserting Chamorro indigeneity without some apologetic acknowledgment of colonial patronage. At best, Chamorros conceive a self who must both deploy and resist the creeping (strategic) essentialism of any attempt at self-determination.[29]

Because of Guam's role as a military outpost, Chamorro identity rubs against imperial policies that shape geographical sovereignty.[30] As Dames asserts:

> Since the 1970s...the question, Who is Chamorro?, has been central to... the exercise of political self-determination and...the ultimate goal of decolonization. In this process of contestation over who constitutes the "self" in the right to self-determination, being Chamorro as a cultural group identity has become objectified, politicized and...now enshrined in Guam law.[31]

With language, culture, and worldview as sites of endless negotiations, land becomes a motif of stability for bodies on the verge of displacement. Calling themselves *i taotao tano* (the people of the land), Chamorros constitute subjectivity through familial history, matrilineal bloodline, and village affiliation.[32] *Place* scaffolds a collective autonomy. More than a marker of identity, place speaks of Chamorro *bodies.* But theirs is a "precarious body," which survives under threat of violence, in danger of obliteration.[33] Neither fully expelled nor incorporated, Chamorro bodies stand on shaky ground. Reduced to nothing more than a military outpost, Guam's worth overlooks native bodies that enliven land. As Lisa Natividad asserts, many know Guam's "strategic location, [but many] don't know anything about the people...what does that [say] about the value of the people"?[34] Unlike the *taotao tano* who breathed life to soil, the empire stripped the land of its spirit. Guam became dehistoricized, decontextualized, and depersonalized. Outside the military infrastructure, Chamorro bodies were negligible, sometimes even hindrances to military interests.[35]

As a twenty-first-century colony, Guam navigates a complicated codependency with the US. Like the late statesman Carlos P. Taitano (1917–2009), the late activist/politician Angel L.G. Santos (1959–2003), teacher/senator Hope A. Cristobal, scholar Lisa Natividad, and author/lawyer

Julian Aguon, Chamorros employ diverse attempts to (dis)engage empire, (dis)claiming varying levels of self-determination. Taitano is legendary among his peers, credited with the passage of the Organic Act, which resulted in congressional recognition of US citizenship to Chamorros.[36] In so doing, Taitano secured a legal identity for Guam residents. Decades later, Santos, Cristobal, Natividad, and Aguon, among many, built on this scaffolding to articulate Chamorro indigenous rights. Cristobal and Aguon, in fact, spoke before the United Nations Committee on Decolonization, affirming an identity distinct from the US body politic.[37] Akin to their *ladrón* ancestors, these indigenous leaders danced within/ outside/before imperial boundaries to secure land and body. They fostered a "third space" distinct from but inevitably beholden to colonial infrastructures.[38] Because Guam's union with the US "…was chosen for her," Chamorros could not but deploy a compromised citizenship that placed them smack in the heart of empire, always ready to fall away.[39] They remain both intimate to and alienated from land.[40] To be Chamorro, in a sense, is to confront an enduring un-incorporation; bodies unable to hold time and place before/outside colonization. Chamorros can only turn to empire, thieves of their own becoming.

Second Incarnation: A Lady Enduring

> She is Power Incarnate.
> Governors may come, and … depart …
> But Santa Marian Camalin abides
> Through all changes to cherish her peculiar people.
> She is the true…Ruler of Guam.[41]

As a young student on Guam, I was shepherded through First Communion by participating in an island-wide procession to honor the Kamalen. In receiving Christ's Body and Blood, we signified full integration into the island's religious and civic life. In our school, First Communion is always celebrated on the 8th of December, which is the feast of Mary's Immaculate Conception and her local iteration, the Kamalen. It is a government holiday that draws thousands of island residents to the Plaza de España, *bordered on opposite ends by the* Dulce Nombre de María *(Sweet Name of Mary) Cathedral Basilica and the legislature. All first communicants—dressed in Marian blues and whites—walk behind the Kamalen's carriage, alongside the archbishop and political dignitaries, leading the faithful in prayer and song.*

For Guam locals, this muddling of religious and civic engagement is not new. But there prevails a conflation of similar/contradictory bodies each time the Kamalen "walks among" her people on 8th of each December. The centrality of Christ's Eucharistic body is usurped by the prominence of her icon. The arbitrary divide between ecclesial and state/military bodies—itself a US imposition—is exposed as an artifice. Among the prayers of children and man'amko *(elderly)—uttered in Chamorro, English, and Spanish—past and present collide, intuiting the promise of an unknown future.*

More than a remnant of colonial practice, annual devotion to the Kamalen reconstitutes a Chamorro body anew. Hewn on this icon are scars attesting to centuries of public worship, political wrangling, and control over public revenues. But her mystique goes deeper; nobody knows from where she comes. The Kamalen's origins subvert the flow of colonial memory: Was she a gift of the first missionaries? Did she miraculously appear on the beach? On the backs of mythical, golden crabs? And yet, people continue to embrace her as their own. Her mysterious beginnings—and the contradictory narratives attached to her body—mirror Chamorro colonial conditions that are, themselves, suffused with gaps and inconsistencies. Amidst Chamorro strategies of constant self-repositioning, it is the Kamalen—this "thief" of history—who remains constant. With her, Chamorros locate an enduring self. She is, in a sense, both people and land incarnated.

Since the arrival of Spaniards, Chamorros have been engaged in a battle to outsmart the colonizer. The practice or custom of bartering served as a game to obtain more for less. Historical accounts by Antonio Pigafetta, scholar-companion of Magalhães, recount moments when native Chamorros furtively short-changed bedraggled Spaniards of replenishments, a strategy that endured throughout the period of the Manila-Acapulco Galleon trade.[42] Similar moments of mistranslation occurred between San Vitores and the *makåhnas* (native herbal healers) in their competition to control native souls (on the part of Spanish missionaries) and bodies (on the part of the *makåhnas*).[43] Disparagingly labeled, *ladrones*, Chamorros pushed back, expending wile and concessionary negotiations to dis/engage empire. If Spaniards fancied themselves as the rightful (Christian) lords of this tiny island, the *taotao tano* made the most of imperial hubris to expose their tenuous rule. For Diaz, these strategies typified Chamorro deployment of culture, religious practice, and language to claim a disappearing self in danger of colonial absorption.[44]

Insofar as thieves thrive in the interstitial spaces of exposure and invisibility, they require the stability of the master's house to exist. Blurring binaries of in/out, public/personal, property/common, thieves are tricksters "skilled at evading domination, disguising desire, guiding by misdirection."[45] The context of engagement is compromised by their relentless penetration of the *sanctum*, exposing its vulnerability to public gaze. Among Chamorros, nowhere is the thief most powerfully embodied than in the Kamalen, Guam's incarnation of Mary, the Virgin Mother of God. Only 28.75 inches tall and weighing a little over 48 pounds, the statue is made of ironwood, with probable origins in Mexico.[46] Its provenance is a mystery to most. Legends abound concerning its miraculous apparition, embedded in lore and myth. Some claim it to have appeared along the beaches of southern Guam, having been carried to the shore by golden crabs. Others believe it to have been found by a native fisherman, or perhaps even a young, zealous, Spanish soldier. More likely, the image is a surviving artifact of a sunken galleon that never completed its journey. Unremarkable for its craftsmanship, the Kamalen nonetheless stands closest to the Chamorro heart. Unveiling the image as a cultural signifier, Marilyn Jorgensen alludes to its potency to

> contribute to the social cohesiveness and continuity of a society with a long history of mixing of ethnic and cultural identities, of political subordination to off-island powers, and of struggles for survival brought about by the threat of large-scale extermination of the population either by conquering armies or by natural forces such as earthquakes, typhoons, or epidemics.[47]

More than an object of devotion, the Kamalen is the projection—or, a mirror, if you will—of a people and their story. She incarnates the double utterance of colonial submission and resistance. Before her countenance, Chamorros behold themselves and their ambivalent fidelities.

Karmen MacKendrick perceives an intimate encounter between relics and memory that shapes a community's ability to construct and undercut "the certainties of…identities."[48] She differentiates three kinds of memories evoked by relics: historical, communal, and sacred. I suggest that as a specific incarnation of a Chamorro self, the Kamalen engages all three to consolidate narratives of resistance and subjectivity. In a sense, sacred and historical time interpenetrate each other to name bodies into existence. Among the many stories associated with the Kamalen, there proliferate tropes of militarism, which expose Chamorro discomfort with colonial condition. The statue's discovery by an unnamed Spanish officer (and at other turns, a native fisherman) hearkens to the collusion of empire and church in the everyday lives of Chamorros. The very name, *Kamalen*—from the Spanish *camarín* (storage room[49])—references the military shed-turned-chapel that sheltered her during the height of the Spanish colonial period.[50] More recently, many attach significance to Japan's inauspicious attack of Guam on December 8, 1941, the Kamalen's feast, signaling the start of the Second World War. And the icon's miraculous rescue from a processional fire at war's end was similarly attributed to a US officer, who was conveniently on hand during the catastrophe, a parallel reference to the US's "liberation" of Guam from Japanese occupation.[51] Indeed, her annual enthronement at the cathedral features a parade of military officers in crisp, dress uniforms, extending their ceremonial sabers at her approach.

Insofar as the Kamalen personifies Chamorro engagement with empire, she witnesses to an ambiguous relationship with colonial bodies. Her simultaneous roles as protector, victor, victim, divinity, and muse blur the line between colonizer/colonized, conqueror/conquered. During the course of her research, Marilyn Jorgensen observed how Chamorros often projected the function of a moral compass onto the Kamalen. The manner in which foreigners treated her determined their worth before indigenous faithful. For example, early attempts by US colonial administrators to limit religious processions resulted in island Catholics demonizing them.[52] And yet, barely 50 years later, Guam's emancipation from Japanese occupation rehabilitated these same interlopers as liberators, resonating with the Kamalen's role as protector, her people's "power incarnate." It comes as no surprise that her later rescue from a processional fire should have been attributed to a soldier. To the same degree that Chamorros were liberated from Japanese brutality by the US military, so must the Kamalen be saved by a US soldier, a veritable incarnation of empire. Beholden to no master, she transcends the limits of colonial tropes, faithful only to her people. And just as powerfully, Chamorros maintain an enduring fidelity to this Lady who stabilizes the undulating navigations of their colonial condition. For Chamorros, the Kamalen articulates a body that endures threats of erasure. More than protector, she is "*ladrón* incarnate," a trickster who evades domination, redirects flows of power, forever repositioning the missionary's thrust. Ensconced in a niche high above the cathedral altar—superseding even the place of prominence reserved for Christ—the Kamalen looks to her people with care, wisdom, and the quiet tenacity of a thief.

Thief and Lady Reincarnated: Bodies Speaking Against Themselves

When I look to the future,
I see it in terms of one thing and that is my son.
If I can create in him a decolonized person,
A Chamorro who knows his values,
Who does not buy into the subtle—or maybe not so subtle—
Messages of racism and inferiority,
Then in his life I would have made a difference.

Lisa Natividad[53]

Et Verbum caro factum est. And the Word was made flesh.

Gospel of John 1:14.

Reflecting on post-9/11 America, Judith Butler discerns in colonial conditions the relentless dismemberment of certain bodies to affirm the existence of others. Rendered "precarious" in their mutual complicity, these bodies bear accountability in the articulation of a colonial self. To the extent that colonized bodies are bound to empire, they become sites of imperial constitution. Butler points thus to the impossible nameability of militarized bodies. For her, ethical engagement begins from the "very disjunction that makes representation impossible."[54] Indeed, Butler suggests that "for representation to convey the human…representation must not only fail, but it must *show* its failure."[55] And so, all colonial bodies are precarious insofar as they are (failed/incomplete) articulations of power. The imperative of militarized/colonized bodies lies in their drive not to stabilize selves, but to illuminate the impossibility of representation itself.

Fluttering "between existence and non-existence," how does one materialize a body dismembered—unincorporated—by mechanisms of imperial expulsion?[56] What does it mean to imagine self beyond the colonial episteme? For militarized bodies, there prevails an impossible remembering that distances one from an imagined past. One is stuck in functionalist narratives of defense/aggression, the speech of empire. There is a simultaneous forgetting of bodies dismembered by misinterpretations of names and function. Dames[57] and Natividad[58] often describe Chamorro displacement akin to a "soul wound" where loss scaffolds self. They echo Grace Cho's exploration of psychic trauma as constitutive of the *yanggongju*—"western princesses" prostituted by US military personnel during the Korean War. Among these women, Cho traces the ways "*yanggongju* [were] constituted by trauma and...erasure...[permeating] the unconscious of the Korean diaspora."[59] To the extent that *yanggongju* bodies speak narratives of empire, they haunt an unending loss. Colonized bodies—reconstituted over and again beneath the weight of military trope—are fragmented against their own failure to become.

Enduring nearly 500 years of colonial and militarized narratives, Chamorros articulate bodies that cannot but reiterate trauma. Their existence depends on the articulation of empire. To speak of an imagined enemy, a master (the "Other"), is to speak, really, of a body intimate to themselves. Such bodies require a *saving from* and a *saving into* a critical rehabilitation that leaves them both longing for and wary of subjectivity.[60] More than a strategy of resistance, Chamorro grasping for materiality illuminates both the limits of self and its incessant reaching for transcendence. It is in this gesture that I intuit theological hints of the incarnation.

In the Gospel of John, God's coming-into-body arises not so much out of the substitution of one (limited) body for another (transcendent) body. God's articulation materializes the Word. To privilege speech is to illuminate a dialogue between One who utters and One who hears. The self is articulated out of the *encounter* of speaker and listener (towing the line between solipsism and relationality, perhaps?). But to the extent that encounters facilitate apprehension of the other, they are threatened by the possibility of misapprehension. There prevails, therefore, an implicit risk in enfleshment as God speaks the Word into history. The "...speech between singular beings" teeters always on the edge of erasure.[61] The Word's coming-to-body arrives out of the potential for loss and trauma, the "unrepresentable that we nevertheless seek to represent."[62]

The transformative potency of the Kamalen—as an enduring articulation of colonial thievery—lies in her capacity to speak-into-body the impossible condition of her people. Through her, Chamorros apprehend a history beyond "fable and fiction." Finally able to read their *own* story, Chamorros engage in an ongoing dialogue with colonial history, tracing the failed reconstitution—and misrepresentation—of their bodies. Like the Kamalen, they speak in conflicting metaphors of resistance and complicity, self-determination and dependence. They stand simultaneously outside/beyond themselves, "fluttering between existence and non-existence." In recent years, this sense of loss has engendered an ethic of solidarity between Chamorro activists and other Pacific Island communities to foster scholarly, political, and economic strategies of resistance.[63] Silenced beneath colonial narratives, Chamorros rearticulate selves into existence, retrieving an imagined past, recreating memory lost through trauma.

Insofar as the Kamalen articulates Chamorro bodies, she reflects the face before and with whom Chamorros speak—towing the line between solipsism and relationality. The Kamalen calls, demanding responsibility for "a being who, in a certain sense, is *not* in relation to me…who is in relation with me only inasmuch as [she] is entirely in relation to [herself]."[64] To the extent that Chamorro devotion to the Kamalen speaks their bodies into being, they simultaneously confront belonging/alienation, intimacy/separation, immanence/transcendence. Their flesh is forever at odds with itself. For Emmanuel Levinas, the ethical demand of this face—the Other who utters the call—lies not so much in securing its own comprehensibility, as to "oblige [the Other] beyond…death." There is an implicit pull to transcendence, the "futuration of the future." This pull illuminates a transcendent turn, "the [falling] of God into meaning."[65] Gazing at the Kamalen, Chamorros "fall into meaning"—*et Verbum caro factum est*—enfleshing selves displaced by history and time, drawn closer to, but never quite, home.

Chamorros confront a loss that comes with an enduring colonization. To be *taotao tano*—people "native" to land and place—is to speak of bodies tempered by conflicting narratives of history. Neither here nor there. Bereft of—and yet grappling for—self. Indeed, for Diaz, there is *no* originary Chamorro. By derisively calling them, "thieves," Magalhães doomed the *taotao tano* to centuries of subterfuge. But he has also spoken the prophetic: alienated from land and history, Chamorros speak themselves into being. Grafting their bodies onto the Kamalen—herself a militarized body—articulates the usurpation—*theft!*—of history to assuage an enduring forgetting.[66] Akin to hosts/natives who bear an ambivalent coexistence with their guests/others, Chamorros reincarnate selves at the edge of belonging. They take what they can; thieves of their own becoming.

Alter-Native Arrivals and Articulations

As I close this reflection, plans to increase US military presence in the Asia-Pacific reoriented Guam to the empire's center once again. In response, community leaders initiated various campaigns to educate island residents of the long-term effects that a military buildup would bear on Guam's economy and environmental sustainability. While coalitions of resistance quickly formed, concerns around the buildup resurrected long-buried tensions between Chamorros and other settlers who have made Guam home.[67] Longtime Filipino residents, perhaps more than others, have found themselves in a particularly sensitive position given the Philippines' long complicity with Guam's colonial history.[68]

As one of these later "arrivals," I find myself again grappling with the dilemma of belonging. Guam is my home. But is it home "enough" for me? My father's work in the oil industry facilitated the proliferation of US military infrastructures throughout the Pacific. We benefitted much as expatriates. Will Guam's tenuous future—the inevitability of its political and geographical erasure—implicate my body in ways Chamorro bodies confront an ever-deepening trauma? More to the point, will my *alternative* voice further silence the ephemeral narratives of Chamorros, a people always at the cusp of articulation?

As teach-ins and campaigns traversed through Guam's villages, folks came out to speak to/against the buildup. At one of these community gatherings, Filipino resident John Norman Sarmiento articulated in elegant spoken word his fear of being "not quite local enough" to participate in shaping Guam's future. Echoing a friend who asked, "...why someone not indigenous to this island, cares so much about it," he named anxieties latent not only among Filipinos, but also among Chamorros, who see themselves as the ones with the most to lose.[69] While listening to Sarmiento speak the shared trauma of native and other/alter, I recalled Butler's reflections on a similar tension at play within Jewish identities:

> [T]he relation with the non-Jew is at the core of Jewish ethics, which means that it is not possible to be Jewish without the non-Jew and that, to be ethical, one must depart from Jewishness.[70]

By illuminating the fear that comes with attempting to speak one's self into existence, Sarmiento named the point at which a Chamorro self relies on the specter of a "non-Chamorro" body to articulate its own becoming. What does it mean, then, to be a people both native and other/alter to one's self? And beyond this fear, how do arrivals like me figure on an island in contention with its history? Where is this ethic that requires a "departure from self" implicit in Butler's words?

At a poignant turn in his piece, Sarmiento obligates his listeners to "respect the ancestors" as a prerequisite to call/name Guam home. For many of us who grew up on the island, these ancestors point to the *taotaomo'na*—the people before history—who live deep in the forest, skirting the edges of villages, watching over the *taotao tano*.[71] Akin to ghosts, *taotaomo'na* evoke fear and esteem. Entering their domain requires deference; one seeks permission to transgress boundaries. Haunting the past and present, flirting with exposure and hidden-ness, *taotaomo'na* illuminate bodies that flutter in between. By reaching for the ancestors, Sarmiento attempts to resurrect a time before colonial history, before the *ladrón* and the Kamalen took over incarnations of Chamorro selfhood. He repositions the past to present to articulate an originary self, to dismantle 500 years of colonial "silence." But even with this, Sarmiento deploys an ambivalent claim. He ends his piece on a defiant tone. But defiant against whom? Against the US military that threatens his island home? Against indigenous activists who question his belonging? Against Filipinos, new-comers, and other settlers who vacillate between home and exile?

Ultimately, I suggest that Sarmiento could not but betray his anxiety. My anxiety. His defiance stems from a fear that our words will never really convince—that we will always be silenced as interlopers on an island we call home. This is a space familiar to Chamorros. Articulating stories that speak against their bodies, they subvert and exacerbate imperial narratives that fetter them even more deeply onto colonial time and history. Reincarnating selves over and again through imperial icons forces a departure from self that, in a strange way, liberates Chamorros from the trap of indigeneity, standing always, at the cusp of articulation.

Notes

1. The Philippines and Guam share a colonial history under Spain (1521–1898) and the US (1898 onward). In 1946, after the Second World War, the Philippines gained independence, while Guam remained under US control.
2. The word *Chamorro* bears spelling variations. While *Chamoru* or *CHamoru* are alternatively used to reflect protocols of indigenous pronunciation, the official spelling adopted by the 22nd Guam Legislature is *Chamorro*. For further discussion on the topic, see Gina Eclavea Taitano, "Chamorro vs. Chamoru," *Guampedia*, July 9, 2014, http://www.guampedia.com/chamorro-vs-chamoru/.
3. The word *Kamalen* is often interchanged with *Camarin* and *Camalin*, reflecting shifts in Chamorro linguistic protocols.
4. *Colonialism* among Chamorro scholars is often used broadly and interchangeably with military interests—inclusive of Spain's nearly 350-year control of Guam, and the island's current status as an unincorporated territory

of the US. See Julian Aguon, *Just Left of the Setting Sun*, 1898 Consciousness Studies Series (Tokyo: Blue Ocean, 2006); and Vicente M. Diaz, *Repositioning the Missionary: Rewriting the Histories of Colonialism, Native Catholicism, and Indigeneity in Guam*, Pacific Islands Monograph Series 24 (Honolulu: University of Hawai'i, 2010).

5. Ronni Alexander, "Militarization and Identity on Guahan/Guam: Exploring Intersections of Indigeneity, Gender and Security," *The Journal of International Cooperation Studies* 21, no. 1 (July 2013): 2.
6. Judith Butler, *Precarious Life: The Powers of Mourning and Violence* (London ; New York: Verso, 2004), 14ff.
7. It is telling that as the US attempts to reconceive itself as a global economic leader, so too does it relegate military activity to the periphery of national consciousness, shifting defense work *abroad* to places like Guam, Turkey, Japan, the Philippines, and Cuba.
8. Karmen MacKendrick, *Fragmentation and Memory: Meditations on Christian Doctrine*, 1st ed. (New York: Fordham University Press, 2008), 106.
9. Guam is the southernmost, largest, and most heavily populated of the Mariana Islands. The archipelago's multilayered colonial histories resulted in clear distinctions between Guam-based Chamorros (occupied largely by Spain, Japan, and the US) and Chamorros in the Northern Marianas (occupied by Spain, Germany, Japan, and, now, the US). Current initiatives to assert Chamorro indigenous rights have been intentional about integrating these two peoples. See Aguon, *Just Left of the Setting Sun*. and Julian Aguon, *What We Bury at Night: Disposable Humanity* (Tokyo: Blue Ocean, 2008). For the purposes of this chapter, I focus on the experiences of Chamorros on Guam.
10. It is important to assert that San Vitores' martyrdom came about because of a disagreement between the value of one's body versus its soul. Resisting Chief Matapang's decree to leave his ill daughter alone, San Vitores proceeded to baptize her minutes before death. Mistaking "salvific act" with murder, Matapang kills San Vitores, unknowingly magnifying the latter's esteem before colonial and native inhabitants. This pivotal moment in Guam's colonial history illuminates the first usurpation of native bodies by colonial interests. See Alberto Risco, *The Apostle of the Marianas: The Life, Labors, and Martyrdom of Ven. Diego Luis de San Vitores, 1627–1672* (Agaña, Guam, US: Diocese of Agaña, 1970), 194–198; and Diaz, *Repositioning the Missionary*, 44–45.
11. Theologian Jonathan Blas Diaz alludes to this conflation of colonization/mission in his articulation of an indigenous Chamorro theology. See Jonathan Blas Diaz, *Towards a Theology of the CHamoru: Struggle and Liberation in Oceania* (Quezon City, Philippines: Claretian Publications, 2010).

12. Emmanuel Levinas, *Entre Nous: On Thinking-of-the-Other*, European Perspectives (New York: Columbia University, 1998), 59.
13. Levinas, *Entre Nous*, 59.
14. John D. Caputo, *The Prayers and Tears of Jacques Derrida: Religion Without Religion*, The Indiana Series in the Philosophy of Religion (Bloomington: Indiana University, 1997), 2.
15. Chief Hurao is revered among Chamorros as one of the earliest voices of resistance against Spanish colonization. He was assassinated a few months after the martyrdom of San Vitores. While this address is commonly attributed to Hurao, it is likely written by French Jesuit Charles Le Gobien, recorded in his early accounts of Spanish–Chamorro hostilities. See Francis Xavier Hezel, "Review of *Towards a Theology of the Chamoru: Struggle and Liberation in Oceania*, by Jonathan Blas Diaz," *The Contemporary Pacific* 23, no. 2 (2011): 549.
    This address was translated from French to English by Paul Daly C.P.S., from Charles Le Gobien's "History of the Mariana Islands," 1700, Paris. The Chamoru version was produced from the English language by the Chamoru Language Commission of the Government of Guam. See http://ns.gov.gu/hurao.html.
16. Citizenship provisions were based on Chapter II of the Nationality Act of 1940. The US Naval government adopted the name "Guamanian," immediately after the Second World War to distinguish Guam Chamorros from Chamorros who lived in Japanese-controlled Saipan and islands of the Northern Marianas. While the name initially referred to Chamorros, the use of "Guamanian" as a citizenship category extended to all residents since 1899 expanded its reference to non-Chamorro residents as well. See Gina Eclavea Taitano, "Adoption of 'Guamanian,'" *Guampedia: The Encyclopedia of Guam*, accessed July 4, 2014, http://www.guampedia.com/adoption-of-guamanian/.
17. A positive, albeit archaic, evaluation of these arrangements is seen in Charles Beardsley, *Guam, Past and Present* (Tokyo, Rutland, VT: Tuttle, 1964), 238–239. For a more contemporary and critical analysis, see Carlos P. Taitano, "Guam's Political Development," *Guampedia: The Encyclopedia of Guam*, accessed July 6, 2014, http://www.guampedia.com/guams-political-development/.
18. Now known as the Marianas Islands, the archipelago is composed of the main islands of Guam, Saipan, Tinian, Rota, and Aguijan. While all are currently under US control, Guam alone bears the status of an unincorporated territory, while the rest of the Marianas maintain commonwealth status.
19. Diaz, *Repositioning the Missionary*, 21.
20. Ibid., 10.

21. Robert F. Rogers, *Destiny's Landfall: A History of Guam* (Honolulu: University of Hawaii, 1995), 41–57.
22. Rogers, *Destiny's Landfall*, 214–217.
23. Frantz Fanon, *Black Skin, White Masks*, trans. Richard Philcox, 1st ed., new ed. (New York: [Berkeley, CA]: Grove Press; Distributed by Publishers Group West, 2008), 77.
24. Aguon, *Just Left of the Setting Sun*, 13–14.
25. Diaz, *Repositioning the Missionary*, 17.
26. Ibid.
27. Ibid., 3–7.
28. Vivian Loyola Dames, *Rethinking the Circle of Belonging: American Citizenship and the Chamorros of Guam* (Ann Arbor: University of Michigan, 2000), 272.
29. It is interesting to note that in recent years, interest in Chamorro genetic origins has increased. The National Geographic Society has, in fact, launched two studies that attempt to trace genetic roots of female bloodlines among native Chamorros. See Cameron Miculka, "History Written in Chamorro DNA: National Geographic Project Seeks to Trace Migration," *Pacific Daily News*, accessed October 14, 2013, http://www.guampdn.com/article/20131014/NEWS01/310140004/History-written-Chamorro-DNA-National-Geographic-project-seeks-trace-migration.
30. The role of place in one's identity formation is key to Chamorro subjectivity. Another name that native Chamorros use to describe themselves is *taotao tano*, "people of the land." See Rogers, *Destiny's Landfall*, 25–34.
31. Soon after the passage of the 1950 Organic Act of Guam, local educators and politicians engendered Pacific-wide, indigenous coalitions to define the right to self-determination. But these initiatives also illuminated the deeper imperative to stabilize what one means by "Chamorro." See Dames, *Rethinking the Circle of Belonging*, 1.
32. Vivian Dames observes that the increased usage of *taotao tano* in recent decades attests to shifts in identity consciousness—from grateful citizens of US governance to a people with distinct history, culture, experience, and, now, political aspirations. See Dames, *Rethinking the Circle of Belonging*, 273.
33. Butler, *Precarious Life*, 14–15.
34. Under Spanish rule, the island served mainly as a near-forgotten outpost, a replenishing center for galleons traversing the Manila-Acapulco route. Under the US, Guam's significance as a military outpost was measured by geopolitical necessity; one that increased with the diminishment of US military presence in Asia. See Lina Hoshino, Gwyn Kirk and Deborah Lee, *Living Along the Fenceline*, Documentary (Many Threads, 2011).

35. Certainly, this has been the case among other Pacific Island communities designated as US Trust Territories by the United Nations after the Second World War. In hauntingly painful prose, Julian Aguon traces local narratives that recount the use of populated atolls for US nuclear exercises. In some instances, people were allowed to "remain" on the island during the nuclear fallout, later to serve as guinea pigs for the study of fallout effects on human populations. See Aguon, *What We Bury at Night*.
36. James Perez Viernes, "The Organic Act of Guam," *Guampedia: The Encyclopedia of Guam*, accessed July 2, 2014, http://guampedia.com/the-organic-act-of-guam/.
37. For an excellent analysis of these diverse initiatives, see Vanessa Wahrheit, *The Insular Empire: America in the Marianas*, Documentary (Horse Opera Productions, 2009).
38. See Homi K. Bhabha, *The Location of Culture*, Routledge Classics (London: Routledge, 2004), 53.
39. Aguon refers in part to the distinct path to self-determination that the islands of Saipan, Rota, Tinian, and Aguijan—collectively known as the Commonwealth of the Northern Marianas—undertook in 1978. See Aguon, *What We Bury at Night*, 115–116.
40. Fanon asserts, "If psychiatry is the medical technique that aims to enable man no longer to be a stranger to his environment, I owe it to myself to affirm that the Arab, permanently an alien in his own country, lives in a state of absolute depersonalization." Quoted in Homi K. Bhabha, "Interrogating Identity," in *The Location of Culture*, Routledge Classics (London: Routledge, 2004), 58.
41. Marilyn A. Jorgensen, "Guam's Patroness: Santa Marian Kamalen" (The University of Texas at Austin, 1984), 54.
42. Accounts of early encounters often describe these strategies as "playful," akin to a game. There are power differentials at play between colonizer and colonized in this portrayal of native resistance. I suggest, rather, that such strategies were born out of active resistance. See Rogers, *Destiny's Landfall*, 7–9.
43. Accounts by the Jesuit historian Francis X. Hezel relate some of the cultural mistranslations confronted by San Vitores in his attempt to convert Chamorros to Christianity. The former's insistence on poverty—manifest through emaciated posture, dirty clothing, unwashed visage, and an infamously toothless grin—rendered San Vitores a curious sight before Chamorros, who valued bodily cleanliness. Throughout his work, San Vitores had to contend with *makåhnas*, who enjoyed influence for their care of the people. This conflict ended with his martyrdom—the result of misunderstood expectations around appropriate protocols of baptism over a chieftain's child. San Vitores baptized the deathly child to save her soul. The great chief Matapang saw this gesture as a usurpation of power over his

infant daughter, resulting in her death (see 9ff). See Diaz, *Repositioning the Missionary*, 123–124.

44. Describing the relevance of San Vitores in the fortification of a Chamorro religious sensibility, Diaz observes that "local investment in San Vitores can be understood as a postwar social and cultural 'alliance'...between Native culture and Catholicism against...the deleterious effects of postwar modernization under the mantle of US American forces of liberal individualism and uncontrolled materialism." Diaz, *Repositioning the Missionary*, 206.
45. Virginia Burrus, *The Sex Lives of Saints: An Erotics of Ancient Hagiography* (Philadelphia: University of Pennsylvania, 2004), 86.
46. Jorgensen, "Guams Patroness: Santa Marian Kamalen," 15.
47. Ibid., xiii.
48. Karmen MacKendrick, *Fragmentation and Memory: Meditations on Christian Doctrine*, 1st ed. (New York: Fordham University Press, 2008), 107.
49. *Camarín* bears diverse translations, depending on geographical and historical context. While it has often been used to describe the altar niche containing images of the Virgin, Orlando Espín pointed to its etymology as a closet and/or storage room attached to a bedroom.
50. Jorgensen, "Guam's Patroness: Santa Marian Kamalen," 48ff.
51. Ibid., 89.
52. During the early years of the US occupation, several attempts were initiated to limit the scope of religious processions, particularly those for the Kamalen, the largest religious event anywhere on the island. Such initiatives were met with resistance by the island's equally powerful Catholic hierarchy. See Jorgensen, "Guam's Patroness: Santa Marian Kamalen," 22.
53. Quoted from interview. See Hoshino, Kirk, and Lee, *Living Along the Fenceline*.
54. Butler, *Precarious Life*, 144.
55. Ibid.
56. Caputo, *The Prayers and Tears of Jacques Derrida*, 2.
57. Dames and Natividad draw from Native American tropes of trauma and loss. See Dames, *Rethinking the Circle of Belonging*, 281–283.
58. Lisa Natividad, PhD, Guam: Decolonization, Identity, and Demilitarization, Skype Video, July 27, 2013.
59. Grace M. Cho, *Haunting the Korean Diaspora: Shame, Secrecy, and the Forgotten War* (Minneapolis: University of Minnesota, 2008), 17.
60. Jacques Derrida, *On the Name* (Stanford: Stanford University, 1995).
61. Levinas, *Entre Nous*, 26.
62. Butler, *Precarious Life*, 144.
63. See the analysis of Diego Luis de San Vitores' canonization undertaken by Vicente Diaz, *Repositioning the Missionary*. From the field of theology, refer to the groundbreaking study of Jonathan B. Diaz, *Towards a Theology of the CHamoru*.

64. Levinas, *Entre Nous*, 33, emphasis mine.
65. Ibid., 173.
66. Judith Butler defines *usurp* as "an active verb [that] fortifies the conviction that one's survival is the cause of another's death." See Judith Butler, *Parting Ways: Jewishness and the Critique of Zionism* (New York: Columbia University, 2012), 186.
67. In recent years, migration scholarship has attended more closely to the history of pioneer/settlers, a phenomenon often associated with the so-called Wild West of the US, Canada, and Australia. The term *settler* takes on political weight in current discussions around the Israeli–Palestinian conflict. In some ways, my status as a Filipino migrant to Guam can leave me—and numerous others—categorized as a settler of sorts. This is something that I hope to explore in future writings.
68. Throughout the Spanish colonial period, Filipinos functioned to support Spain's military and missionary enterprises on Guam—as in the case of the canonized Pedro Calungsod, servant to San Vitores. Guam also served as a place of incarceration for Filipino revolutionary leaders, such as Apolinario Mabini, in the late nineteenth century. For further exposition, see Rogers, *Destiny's Landfall.*

    Recent Filipino migration to Guam increased soon after the Second World War, when labor contracts were extended to Filipinos as a means of expediting the rebuilding of the island's infrastructure. As a former US commonwealth granted independence at war's end, the Philippines proved to be a viable source of labor for the expansion of military infrastructure across the Pacific. Drawn by economic opportunity, thousands of Filipino contract workers willingly moved to Guam as early as 1946. For a moving documentary that traces these early years, see Burt S. Sardoma, *Under the American Sun*, 2009, http://vimeo.com/3568956. See also Bruce L. Campbell, "Filipino Migration to Guam 1945–1975," *Guampedia: The Encyclopedia of Guam*, accessed August 1, 2013, http://guampedia.com/filipino-migration-to-guam-1945-1975/.
69. John Norman Sarmiento, "It's My Home Too | Spoken Word," January 9, 2010, http://www.youtube.com/watch?v=RIynY9RDaqQ&feature=youtube_gdata_player.
70. Butler, *Parting Ways*, 99.
71. Robert Tenorio Torres, "Pre-Contact Marianas Folklore, Legends, and Literature: A Critical Commentary," *Micronesian Journal of the Humanities and Sciences* 2, no. 1–2 (December 2003): 12.

CHAPTER 9

Faith-Based Popular Resistance to the Naval Base in Gangjeong of Jeju: Transforming Militarized US–Korea Relations for Peace and Justice

Keun-Joo Christine Pae

Introduction

On a hot and humid summer day, a group of people gathered across the street from a construction site of a naval base in Gangjeong. Soon they would erect a simple tent and set up a communion table. This particular table was decorated with a flag, which read: "Gangjeong, you are the smallest village in this land but the peace of the entire nation will come from you." On the flag was painted a gray-haired lady dressed in traditional Korean attire and surrounded by Halla Mountain (one of the holy mountains in the Korean Peninsula located in Jeju), the sea, the sky, and the sun. She was holding a distinctive Catholic Rosary in her hands. As I meditated on the flag, waiting for an outdoor noontime mass, the words on the flag brought to my heart the biblical prophecy about Bethlehem,

K. C. Pae (✉)
Denison University, Granville, OH, USA

N. Kim, W.A. Joh (eds.), *Critical Theology against US Militarism in Asia*,
DOI 10.1057/978-1-137-48013-2_9

the birthplace of Jesus: "And you, Bethlehem, in the land of Judah, are by no means least among the rulers of Judah for from you shall come a ruler who is to shepherd my people Israel (Matthew 2:6, New Revised Standard Version)." The woman on the flag resembled Sulmoondae Halmang, the goddess creator from Jeju mythology. The flag seemed to symbolize a beautifully syncretic marriage between the Jeju mythology of creation and the Christian narrative of nativity.

Jeju is often called Korea's Hawaii. Its natural beauty, mild weather, and exotic volcano add a Hawaiian scent to Korea, just as Okinawa is referred to as Japan's Hawaii. In fact, not only Jeju's beautiful nature but also its political history can be compared to those of Hawaii and many Pacific islands. Due to its geographical importance, of being located between China, Japan, and Korea, Jeju experienced occupation by foreign armies (i.e. imperial Japan and the US military), and has survived systemic prejudices from Korean mainlanders. As a result, Jeju natives have a long history of resisting foreign occupation and the Korean central government's exploitation and oppression. The ongoing peace activism against the construction of the naval base in Gangjeong indeed shows the ordinary Jeju people's collective effort to preserve Jeju's natural beauty and community-based culture and spirituality, as well as their resistance to systemic prejudices and the militarization of the island.

What role then does religion play in "popular resistance" to the naval base in Gangjeong in Jeju? How would the modern US–Korea relations look through the lens of ordinary people's refusal to comply with the militarization of Jeju? Exploring religion's various roles in peace activism in Gangjeong, this chapter first studies the ideas of popular resistance in the historical and political context of Jeju. These ideas will further inform the analytical findings from my interactions with faith-based peace activists, especially women activists in Gangjeong. Thus, the second part of this chapter will delineate how religiously motivated popular resistance in Gangjeong can contribute to transforming militarized US–Korea relations into those strengthened by love and justice and marked by empathy and reconciliation. In other words, how can people of faith, especially Christians, be in communion with one another and with the God of love, peace, justice, and reconciliation, by redeeming the militarized US–Asia relations in the particular location of Gangjeong and beyond? I will contemplate these questions by reconstructing the theo-political meanings of the Eucharist, one of the most frequently practiced religious forms of peace activism in Gangjeong. My goal is to propose the Eucharist as the active Christian form of popular resistance to and as redemption of militarism, rather than a simply liturgical practice.

Faith and Popular Resistance

Popular resistance often begins without an organized committee or centered leadership that designs the movement in order to achieve political goals. Facing massive injustice, ordinary people (or *Minjung* in Korean) voluntarily gather and organically develop their movements for peace and justice. Therefore, popular resistance is often an issue-based movement, or forms an ad hoc committee in order to resolve the pressing issues that need immediate attention from the political power (i.e. government) being opposed.

Although Mahatma Gandhi and Reverend Martin Luther King, Jr., are the iconic figures of nonviolent popular resistance, I first encountered the systemic idea of "popular resistance" through Palestinian human rights activist and scholar Mazin Qumsiyeh. He articulates that "love" for the suffering (i.e. the poor, the oppressed, etc.) is the driving force for both individuals and society to participate in popular resistance.[1] Popular resistance can be both violent and nonviolent, although it usually takes nonviolence as the more effective method to transform an unjust society into a more just one. Before judging or blaming popular resisters for using violence, however, we should first reflect on that in our modern society, only a sovereign nation-state is relatively free from the moral blame attached to the use of organized violence (i.e. war, police brutality, the use of the armed forces, etc.), and therefore, can be the most violent human institution.

According to Qumsiyeh, Palestinians may use the phrase *muqawanma sha'biya* for popular resistance in Arabic, defined as a large number of people's steady movement in opposition to armed resistance for revolution.[2] Similarly, Mahatma Gandhi elaborated on the concept of *satyagraha*—*satya*, truth, and *graha*, steadfastness. Qumsiyeh argues that "[*satyagraha*] involves far more than persistence in telling the truth, and is considered an active willingness to sacrifice oneself in order to achieve justice"—an active form of popular resistance.[3] As Martin Luther King, Jr., and Gandhi agree, unearned suffering has power to redeem both oppressors and the oppressed. Jesus Christ is the good example of this redemptive power of unearned suffering, whose death on the cross would result in redeeming the oppressed from suffering and oppressors from committing the sin of oppression.[4] Furthermore, Gandhi's term of *ahimsa*, which is often translated as nonviolence in English, does not simply mean abstinence from violence but rather "a mix of love, honesty, non-aggression and peace."[5] Hence, Gandhi's popular resistance characterized by *ahimsa* should be understood as an action of love, peace, and justice, with power strong enough to redeem the world from violence and injustice.

It may not be an overgeneralization to say that the moral values in popular resistance, such as love, peace, justice, and nonviolence, are found across the globe, where commoners (or *Minjung* in Korean) willfully take diverse forms of resistance, including strikes, demonstrations, boycotts, marches, arts exhibits, and music concerts, in opposition to state-sanctioned violence and injustice. Qumsiyeh lists the common goals of popular resistance: (1) pressuring opponents to understand the injustice in which they engage; (2) strengthening the community, including forms of empowerment and steadfastness; and (3) achieving justice, including the right to self-determinations.[6] If (1) has something to do with the moral redemption of the oppressors or structural oppression, then (2) and (3) aim to redeem the oppressed.[7]

In the Palestinian context, popular resistance has been supported by local philosophical and religious traditions, including Christianity and Islam. Jesus, a Palestinian revolutionary, took self-sacrifice as an active way to resist imperialist violence and to reach out to both enemies and bystanders.[8] Islam, the dominant religious practice in the twenty-first-century Palestine, has also been consistent with the principles of human rights and universal justice and with popular resistance of tyranny since the time of the Prophet Muhammad. The true Muslim seeks peace with God and fellow humans by total submission to God's will, because God is the source of all goodness and purity, and with humans by doing good and spreading good deeds.[9] In Palestine, it is not strange at all for Christians and Muslims to collaborate with one another for peace and justice. They share common political goals and movements in resistance of Israeli occupation, rather than engaging in religious conflict that many Westerners may stereotypically believe Christian—Muslim relations to be in the region.

During my informal meeting with him in Bethlehem in May 2012, Qumsiyeh emphasized the importance of studying popular resistance across the globe. By exploring the varied forms of popular resistance in diverse regions, we can better analyze how the imperial ruling operates, why all human lives are interconnected in the globalized world, what actions are more effective in achieving peace and justice, and so forth.

In response to Qumsiyeh's emphasis, I now turn to popular resistance in Gangjeong village in its historical and political context. I am particularly interested in how popular resistance to the naval base in Gangjeong challenges Christians to reexamine their faith in God beyond the philosophical understandings of justice and human rights found in Christianity. More specifically, what does it mean to be people of faith in a militarized world, and how can we participate in Jesus' redemptive power for all creations (the universal) in Gangjeong (the particular)? "How to participate in Jesus' redemptive power" is precisely the type of question for Christian ethics to address because it requires a radical change in our relationships with God and with our neighbors.

Jeju, an Island of Peace and Island of Massacre: US–Korean Imperialism in Jeju

At Jeju International Airport, a gigantic billboard greets people as if it were a tour guide with a big smile and open arms: "Welcome to Jeju, an Island of Peace!" Ironically, Jeju earned this title because of the state-sanctioned bloody massacre in retaliation to the people's uprising, known as the Jeju Uprising or Jeju 4.3 (the people's uprising on the 3rd of April, 1948). Gangjeong peace activists consider the Jeju Uprising as the historical root of their peace activism.

On the dawn of April 3, 1948, Jeju became the site of a people's uprising against the US military government and Korean right-wing fundamentalists who exploited the Jeju *Minjung* and terrorized anyone who (allegedly) criticized the US military government's policy. Violently reacting to the uprising, the US–Korean joint military conducted "Operation Scorched Earth," systematically killing 25,000–30,000 Jeju civilians, or one tenth of the Jeju population, primarily between May 1948 and the spring of 1949.[10] The US–Korean joint military operation against the remnants of the Jeju Uprising was completely over by 1954.[11] The majority of victims were young men labeled as "Reds" (i.e. communists) and their family members, including women and children. Most victims were ordinary farmers, fishermen, and villagers who simply attempted to protect their families and communities from economic exploitation and military brutality, rather than being ideologically associated with communism.[12] Viewed through the Jeju Uprising, the Korean War actually began on Jeju in 1948 by mercilessly crushing ordinary people's desire for a more egalitarian society, and only ended on the island in 1954. However, the grand narrative remembers the Korean War as a three-year war (1950–1953) between North Korean–Chinese allies and South Korean–UN (United Nations) allies, or as the civil war between North and South Koreans.

Despite the complex political economy behind the Jeju Uprising, most scholars agree that the trigger was a shooting incident on March 1, 1947. This incident claimed the lives of six innocent people, including an elementary school child and a young mother with an infant.[13] After a celebration of the twenty-eighth anniversary of the March 1st Independence Movement, the Jeju *Minjung* nonviolently protested against the US military government's political economic failures and expressed their concern about the UN's decision to establish a separate government in the southern Korean Peninsula apart from the north of the 38th parallel.[14] Although these protesters were unarmed civilians, military police (the US troops and the supporting Korean police from mainland Korea) fired at them.[15] As the US military government refused to make a public apology for the shootings, on March 10, 1947, the majority of the Jeju *Minjung* started organizing a series of strikes in which government officials, native Jeju policemen, bankers, students, and many others participated.[16] In response to the Jeju *Minjung*'s strikes, the US military government immediately declared the leaders of these strikes communists.[17] Between 1947 and 1948, in order to suppress any form of popular resistance in Jeju, the US military government mobilized extreme rightists, especially North Korean expatriates, most notably the members of the Northwest Korean Youth Association (*Seo-Book Chyung-Nyun-Hwi*). These right-wing extremists interrogated, violated, and killed ordinary people under the pretext of a "Red Hunt."[18]

Although most studies of the Jeju Uprising focus on the massacre of civilians, the Uprising sheds important light on the history of the Korean *Minjung*'s popular resistance.

First, the *Minjung* voluntarily participated in the revolutionary uprising in order to reveal the injustice in which the US military government and the Korean right-wing fundamentalists engaged. During the US military occupation in the south of the 38th parallel on the Korean Peninsula (1945–1948), Koreans' distrust toward the US military government had escalated because American soldiers acted as if they had conquered Korea. Especially, when the prices of crops and daily necessities skyrocketed due to the US military government's failures in economic policy, the various groups of the *Minjung* (i.e. farmers and factory workers) throughout South Korea actively protested against economic injustice.[19] Among them was the Jeju Uprising, the most persistent popular resistance.

Compared with the *Minjung* in mainland Korea, those in Jeju had a stronger nationalist agenda, with a dream of founding a new Korea where class divisions would cease. The Jeju *Minjung*'s nationalist agenda stemmed from their experiences of Japanese imperialism. For instance, many men of Jeju were conscripted into the military–industrial complex in Japan and gained critical views on the class system intersecting with colonialism.[20] Furthermore, during World War II, the entire island was fortified for the sake of mainland Japan's security. Imperial Japan planned to use the islanders as human shields against US air strikes.[21] For Jeju natives, therefore, Korea's independence over Japan literally meant liberation from death. Since emancipation from imperial Japan's 35-year ruling was so precious to the Jeju *Minjung*, they could not be silent about the US imperial ruling that so closely resembled that of Japan.

Second, the Jeju Uprising consisted of both violent and nonviolent efforts in order to collectively deliver the *Minjung*'s political voice. In 1945, even before Korea's independence, the Jeju People's Committee (*Jeju In-min Whi-won-hwi*) had been born in preparation for a sovereign Korea by empowering ordinary men and women through public education.[22] The leaders of the Jeju People's Committee won the hearts and minds of the Jeju *Minjung* because of their well-known work for the independence movement and their selfless service for the people.[23] The series of strikes in response to the shootings on March 1, 1947, were the products of solidarity between the Jeju People's Committee and the *Minjung*.

Moreover, on April 3, 1948, when a group of local Jeju communists (i.e. the South Korean Labor Party in Jeju) and ordinary folks attacked the houses of the most notorious members of the Northwest Korean Youth Association who terrorized the lives of the *Jeju Minjung*, these attackers' main concerns were not only to punish unjust rulers but also to resist the US military government and Korean right-wing politicians' attempt to establish a South Korean–only government.[24] Thus, the major political goal was to resist the division of the Korean Peninsula. Jeju was the only place where the *Minjung* refused to participate in the first election in South Korea on May 10, 1948.[25] Although the Jeju Uprising had been recorded as communist armed guerilla warfare against the US-led democratic power, the weapons of most attackers were not sophisticated rifles or bayonets, but plowshares, knives, stones, and wood sticks.[26] With their modern weapons, the US–Korean joint military units brutally killed ordinary villagers and armed resisters until the last one was hunted down in Halla Mountain, simply because Jeju had successfully resisted the US-imposed national election.

Jeju has a long history of resisting the central government when it does not serve the common good for the *Minjung*. Since the Jeju Uprising and its following massacre, the Jeju *Minjung* has lived with the stigma of a "Red Island." Just as the US military government mobilized Korean mainlanders to abolish any form of resistance movements, so the newly founded Shyng Man Rhee's staunchly pro-American and anti-communist regime in 1948 intentionally encouraged Korean conservatives to migrate to the island. During the Korean War, the regime also forced Jeju natives to prove their loyalty to anti-communism by joining the army fighting against North Korea.[27] It was not until the late 1980s when the Cold War was perceived to be over that the survivors of the Jeju Massacre could finally break their silence about their experiences and memories of the historically tragic event.[28]

The Jeju Uprising and Massacre are not isolated events that happened on a remote island. Historically speaking, systemic terrors against (alleged) communists were commonly found in Jeju, Okinawa, and Taiwan, where the US military occupied immediately following World War II.[29] These islanders' experiences of death and violence suggest that the US succeeded Japanese imperialism in the Asia-Pacific and disciplined local people with its version of Cold War ideology in order to expand its hegemony in the region. During the Cold War period, the US saw itself as the leader of the free world and champion of freedom and democracy against an "evil system of totalitarian repression and slavery" represented by its rival, the former Soviet Union.[30] The Korean Peninsula was where the US had to retaliate against not only its rival empire Soviet Union, but China as well. Thus, what happened in the Asia-Pacific islands can be fully understood only in the historical context of U.S. Exceptionalism—its holy mission to save Asia from the evil of communism.

Jeju 4.3 and the Naval Base in Gangjeong Village

What similarities can be found between the Jeju Uprising and Gangjeong peace activism? More specifically, why does the Korean government's disapproval of popular resistance of the naval base in Gangjeong remind the activists of the Jeju Uprising? Let us now turn to these questions.

First, just as the Jeju Uprising criticized the US military government's lack of respect for Korean natives, the Gangjeong peace activists criticized the Korean government for failing to listen to the majority of Gangjeong villagers. The central government in Seoul did not democratically communicate with the villagers, whose lives would be dramatically changed by the naval base. According to the activists, therefore, the conflict between the government and the people first arose not because of controversies around the interpretations of peace, national security, and the necessity of the naval base, but because of the lack of transparency in the government's political decision-making.[31] As a matter of fact, the Korean government's top-down decision-making process disabled diverse interest groups to engage in productive dialogue on peace and security in the Korean Peninsula.

In December of 1993, the Korean government began planning to construct a naval base in Jeju and publicized its plan in 2002.[32] The majority of Jeju citizens resisted this plan because they were worried about the militarization of the island and the base's possible effects of ecological destruction. While the public debates concerning the naval base in Jeju continued, Geunmin Woo, the governor of Jeju, secretly met several leaders of Gangjeong village and called an ad hoc village council meeting on April 26, 2007. Eighty-seven out of 1900 villagers attended the meeting. Based on their votes, the governor of Jeju and the Korean Ministry of National Defense officially named Gangjeong as the chosen site for a new naval base.[33]

Because most villagers were unaware of this ad hoc council meeting, they would soon call for an official village council meeting, only to face police interruption. Nonetheless, on August 10, 2007, 970 villagers gathered for the council meeting, and 94 percent of them opposed the construction of a naval base in Gangjeong.[34]

Since then, the majority of the villagers and their allies protested against the naval base through peace concerts, story-tellings, peace marches, art shows, religious services, civil disobedience, and so on. In many cases, the protesters encountered police brutality, while the media willfully ignored the events. "Police brutality" reminded Gangjeong activists of the traumatic history of the Jeju Uprising quelled by state-sanctioned violence.[35]

For example, former senator Ae-ja Hyun said,

> "When I heard of the government's plan to construct a naval base, I immediately recalled the Jeju 4.3, which claimed the lives of my family members. We, Jeju folks, tremble whenever we hear that the troops and policemen come to Jeju from the mainland. They have never brought anything good to Jeju. Now the military police from the mainland arrest peace activists while the government ignores our voice for peace. How far should Jeju folks endure this kind of injustice?"[36]

Former senator Hyun is a longtime *Minjung* activist, especially for the rights of women farmers. When I first met her in August 2011, one month before the navy and the multinational corporation Samsung would start detonating the Gurumbi Rock, she had chained herself in front of the navy fence around the construction site. Chaining herself was her chosen method of popular resistance to deliver a message to the Korean government that the naval base would ultimately oppress all Koreans, as if they were chained by the military.

Second, according to the group of peace activists whose research primarily analyzes the US–Korean Defense Treaty (known as SOFA: Status of Forces Agreement), the future naval base is likely to cater to US military interest in the Pacific, which attempts to restrain China's rapidly growing military power.[37] Located between the Korean Peninsula and the mainland China, Jeju has great geopolitical importance for the US to consolidate its military power in East Asia. The naval base is designed for US naval vessels such as CVN-65, a model which Korea does not have or plan to have in the foreseeable future.[38] Therefore, the peace activists warn that the naval base will eventually accelerate the military and nuclear power competition between the US and China. As a result, the excessive militarization of East Asia will threaten the lives of Jeju citizens, Korean civilians, and beyond, instead of contributing to global peace. This foreseeable future only suggests that military imperialism epitomized by the naval base considers the livelihood and security of Jeju natives dispensable.

In spite of the peace activists' logical suspicion of the US involvement in constructing the naval base in Gangjeong, the US Armed Forces in Korea officially denied its participation in the Korean government's decision to construct the base in Gangjeong. Yet, the construction of the base needs to be examined with critical questions, such as why the Korean government first planned to construct a naval base in Jeju in 1993, one year after the first Gulf War, when the US began reorganizing its global military plan. By the same token, in the aftermath of the terrorists' attacks on September 11, 2001, the Korean government publicized the construction of the naval base when American military strategists identified an extensive area encompassing "North Africa through the Middle East, Pakistan, and the former Soviet republics in Central Asia to China" as their new focus for asserting US control.[39] Furthermore, the government rushed into naming Gangjeong as a site for a new naval base less than one year after Daechuri of Pyongtaek, a village 30 miles south of Seoul, had been fenced off so that a new US military complex could be constructed.[40]

What story would the rapid changes in the US global military strategies tell us about the Gangjeong base? Will this base eventually secure the US missile defense line in the Pacific, from Australia all the way to Korea? Although these complicated questions require further scrutiny, the undeniable or suspicious connection between the US military and the naval base in Gangjeong brings memories of Jeju 4.3 to the peace activists and Gangjeong villagers.

Third, the peace activists argue that the naval base will inevitably destroy Gangjeong's environment by severely interrupting the island's ecological life. Furthermore, not only its physical environment, but also the community-based village culture (i.e. spiritual environment) would be destroyed, just as the US military's Operation Scorched Earth during the Jeju Uprising destroyed small village communities surrounding Halla Mountain. In terms of physical environment, Jeju is known as a "clean island," a place where the World Conference of International Union for Conservation of Nature was held in September 2012. Gangjeong is particularly famous for its fertile soil, freshwater springs, and unique marine life, where a volcanic island like Jeju typically lacks freshwater.[41] Needless to say, would pollute the environment, transform the bucolic village into an armed military town, and more seriously, destroy the sacred Halmang-Mool (the water of a divine feminine), the freshwater spring in the Gurumbi Rock on the Gangjeong coastline. According to the folk tale of Gangjeong, the sacred had a special power to bring fertility to a barren woman.[42] This spring water in the corner of the Gurumbi Rock played an important role in gathering villagers for special rituals. Since this sacred space was demolished for the sake of the naval base in 2012, the Gangjeong villagers can no longer practice community-based spirituality. In fact, community-based culture and spirituality in Gangjeong are already being broken as the construction of the naval base has divided the villagers into those who support the base and those who resist it. The tension between the two groups has escalated since the detonation of the Gurumbi Rock, and many meaningful interactions between the two groups have been missing for a long time.[43]

Fourth, just as the Jeju Uprising was labeled as a communist rebellion against the legitimate political authority, so peace activists in Gangjeong are labeled as communists who are pro-North Korea and indifferent to national security. Due to the unique geopolitics in the Korean Peninsula, mainstream Korean society has censored any form of popular resistance or political activism through claims of military-based national security.

Those who criticize the nation's foreign policy, militarism, and pro-North Korean sentiments can easily be labeled as leftists, communists, or derogatorily called "Reds." Speaking up for peace and justice for all living beings in Gangjeong, the peace activists lament that right-wing politicians and media portray their resistance to the naval base as an ideological issue, and that leftists and professional demonstrators from mainland Korea aid in inciting innocent villagers in Gangjeong to resist the base.[44]

Feminine Faces of Faith in Gangjeong Peace Activism

Now let us explore the roles of religion in popular resistance in Gangjeong, with a focus on Christianity, especially through women's active participation. In Korea, religiously motivated women have contributed to peace activism for many years. For instance, a Christian women's group in the 1970s first adopted the term "peace activism" as characterized by active nonviolence. At that time, most social activist groups that were concerned about peace in the Korean Peninsula identified their activism in terms of a "reconciliation movement" because nonviolent peace activism was associated with feminine traits and passivity. By strategically adopting "peace activism," this Christian women's group challenged the conventional assumption of the necessity of military-based security in the highly militarized Korean society. Furthermore, the group organized anti-nuclear power activism in solidarity with Japanese Christian women. Both groups were deeply sympathetic to victims of the US nuclear bombings in Hiroshima and Nagasaki in 1945.[45]

In Jeju, known for being an island of women, women are important players in the anti-naval base peace activism. Jeju became a women's island because after the Jeju Massacre, of which the majority of victims were men, women had to rebuild their villages and take care of their families.[46] According to Sung-Hee Choi, the leader of the international team of Gangjeong peace activism, women had started, sustained, and would accomplish peace in Gangjeong, just as women resuscitated their villages in the aftermath of the Jeju Massacre.[47] Choi's comment is not an exaggeration. Without consistent support from the Gangjeong Women's Association, peace activists, especially from outside Jeju, would not have food to eat, a place to sleep in, or somewhere to go when they are sick. Furthermore, without Catholic and Protestant women, daily mass and prayer meetings in front of the construction site would be impossible.

The majority of the staff and the participants in the Gangjeong Peace March in July 2012 were also women.

Peace activism in Gangjeong is unique such that diverse people with various talents came to the village and found creative ways to contribute. Whether these people came as individuals or as members of social justice groups, as professional activists or as visitors with curiosity, or as religious or secular, they organically work together. By the same token, if one's talents have something to do with religion or if one is motivated by religion, s/he can bring her/his religious voice to the activism platform in Gangjeong. In Gangjeong, peace activism is a voluntary-based movement, just as Mazin Qumsiyeh describes one of the characters of popular resistance.

In order to present the distinctive faces of Gangjeong peace activism, I would like to highlight three portraits of women's participation interwoven with their religious and spiritual contemplation. First, some women activists see peace activism as a way of practicing their religion and spirituality, just as popular resistance of Israeli occupation in Palestine is philosophically and spiritually supported by local religions. The most visible religious group in Gangjeong is Catholic women.

Cecil Han, a lay Catholic woman who was a longtime peace activist in Gangjeong and organizer of the Catholic Peace Pilgrimage in July 2012, articulated, "Catholic holy sites in Jeju are connected to the Jeju Uprising and Massacre in 1948 as well as the current state-sanctioned violence in Gangjeong." She continued that

> "Korean Catholicism is not a religion of political domination but should be viewed as the religion of self-sacrificial martyrdom against state violence and oppression. The early Korean Catholics in the seventeenth century were exiled and executed in Jeju for the sake of their faith in God because they dreamt of a new world of equality. They are not apart from victims of the Jeju Massacre and Gangjeong villagers who try to protect their friends, families, and communities against the state-sanctioned violence."[48]

Three nuns from the Catholic Diocese of Jeju who participated in the 2012 Catholic Peace Pilgrimage said, "Solidarity with the suffering such as the Gangjeong villagers and nature is a part of monastic life." The activists from the Korean Catholic Women's Community for a New World added that although only 1 percent of Korean Catholics participated in social justice activism, the Catholic Church of Korea recognizes the freedom people have to participate in such activism.[49]

In January 2012, 18 nuns affiliated with the Association of Major Superiors of Religious Women in Korea were arrested while praying for peace in Gangjeong. The public was outraged by the police's overreaction to nonviolent nuns.[50] Later on, the Association criticized the police for arresting the nonviolent nuns, but more vehemently criticized the police authorities for detaining teenage activists for three days.[51]

Thanks to the Church's support for peace activism, Catholics might be the most active and persistent group in Gangjeong. Other religious groups and individuals are not as vocal about their religious identity as Catholics. Nonetheless, I encountered numerous individuals and groups who interpreted the Gangjeong issue through their faiths. One of the most fascinating stories that I heard in Gangjeong was from Ms. Lee, who introduced herself as a Jeju citizen and Catholic:

"The Gurumbi rock becomes the sacred symbol of Gangjeong. What is more sacred, however, is Halmang-Mool sitting in Gurumbi. Halmang-Mool is like a goddess and Gurumbi is her temple. You don't destroy St. Peter's Basilica in Vatican to build a military base. Only because the Gurumbi Rock is not a human-made architect, the navy walked in and destroyed it. We are not simply protecting nature. We are protecting our goddess and her temple."[52]

Second, through rituals, the religiously motivated activists try to create alternative spaces for anti-naval base activism. Since the Korean Navy completely fenced around the construction site of the base, any public assembly and attempts to protest at the site have been defined as illegal. When people cannot have freedom of speech and assembly, religion creates an alternative space that brings people together. For instance, every morning at seven o'clock, peace activists and visitors gather for 100 peace bows in front of the construction site. The meditative words written for the bows originated from "One Hundred Commitments to Life-Peace" by a Korean Engaged Buddhism monk Venerable Dobeop. The leading person of this morning ritual is Ms. Jeong, a lay Catholic and president of the Catholic mission chapel in Gangjeong. Many people come and go, but Ms. Jeong always begins her day with peace bows and offers a space for anyone who wants to be part of peace activism at Gangjeong. The eleven o'clock morning Catholic Mass and the three o'clock Protestant prayer meeting are also examples of religious spaces that transform ordinary Christian liturgies to embodiments of peace activism.

Furthermore, peace activism creates solidarity, sisterhood, and brotherhood beyond religious and spiritual boundaries. Interfaith solidarity in

Gangjeong activism has happened in various forms domestically and internationally. One example of such solidarity occurred in September 2011, as the Korean Navy prohibited anyone from approaching the Gurumbi Rock, about 20 religious leaders kayaked to the Gurumbi in hopes of delivering their interfaith message of peace.

Third, women's day-to-day activities often embody peace activism, as Han Gyeon-Rye, the general secretary of Korean Women Peasant Association, illustrates. When I walked with her at the Gangjeong Peace March in the summer of 2012, Han said, "When the first peace march was organized a few years ago, it was the springtime when farmers were busy planting. We had worked in the field until the marching team passed. As soon as we saw them, we fed them, walked with them for a while, and then, went back to work in our field."[53] For many women who have children and farm work to do, it is difficult to be peace activists 24 hours a day. Many women whom I met at Gangjeong were ready to apologize for not being able to contribute more to peace activism. Yet, these women also found creative ways to be part of Gangjeong peace activism.

Like Ms. Han, woman peace activist Deul-pool (*wild grass* in Korean) has tried every possible way to make Gangjeong peace activism truly popular. Praying and meditating with others on the streets, Deul-pool sews small stuffed dolphins, symbolic for the animals that used to swim around Gangjeong. Her crafts are often sold in order to support imprisoned Gangjeong activists. She also choreographed a Gangjeong dance—after every Catholic mass and peace gathering, every participant dances, following her lead. When she was imprisoned, Deul-pool wrote the "ten commandments" for arrested peace activists to fully practice their rights in prison, such as demanding the prison guards to bring newspapers and books into their cells. During my interview with her, Deul-pool was humble about her participation in peace activism. In my eyes, however, she was an exemplary figure of persistent popular resistance. Buying her crafts, reading her essays and poetry, and dancing with her, ordinary people are invited to join popular resistance to the naval base. Through her, people (i.e. visitors) have the opportunity to embody an alternative vision of peace that is not through military power but through respect for life and shared power relations among people.

Religious spaces for peace activism, religiously motivated activists' creativity, and women's spirituality embodied through peace activism in Gangjeong challenge us as Christians to critically reexamine our faith in the excessively militarized world. As it was stated earlier, the purpose of this chapter is not only to introduce popular resistance in Gangjeong but also to rethink about Christians' participation in God's redemptive power in the militarized world, more specifically the historically militarized US–Korea relations. By theo-politically reflecting on the Eucharist, let us search for the possibility to demilitarize these relations.

Eucharist as Popular Resistance: Transformation of the US–Korea Relations in Gangjeong and Beyond

So far, I have argued the similarities between the Jeju Uprising and anti-naval peace activism in Gangjeong in terms of US military imperialism and Jeju natives' popular resistance to militarism. One might argue that since the very beginning, US–Korea relations have been militarized. The General Sherman incident, the first historical and official contact between the US and Korea in 1866, resulted in the US navy's attacks on Korea in order to open its market.[54] Korea's independence over imperial Japan ended in US military occupation. The US–Korean military alliance was consolidated through the Korean War, in which American soldiers also fought. As Bruce Cummings argues, the tragedy of the Korean War is that "the war solved nothing": the Korean Peninsula has been divided, the US armed forces are stationed in South Korea for an indefinite period, and Koreans still live with the consequences of the war.[55]

It is impossible for Koreans to think about their modern identity apart from the Korean War and its consequences. Since the war turned the vibrant dream of constructing a new Korea in 1945 into a nightmare, Koreans have experienced a hard time imagining peace and security without armed forces. Yet the US military's presence in Korea reminds Koreans of the tragic war again and again, poking their deep psychic wounds. Anti-communist sentiments in Korea might be Koreans' self-defensive psychic reaction to the unfinished Korean War as they need someone to blame for their tragedy. As long as the US–Korea relations are militarized, Koreans (and Americans) will not be able to heal their trauma from the war. At the same time, the Jeju *Minjung* have lived with double traumas—the Korean War and the Jeju Massacre.

Seen through a critical theological lens, we need to ask: what alternative relations between the US and Korea can be imagined? What kind of Christian faith and theological thinking can help us imagine alternative

US–Korea relations that are free from militarism while accentuating peace, justice, and love? How can Christianity liberate the US–Korea relations from fear, callous capitalism, and triumphalism that consistently feed military projects? Liberative Christianity must be different from one that used to blindly support anti-communism, encourages American exceptionalism, and preaches about spiritual and military triumphalism. Here, I would like to contemplate liberative Christianity by theo-politically analyzing the Eucharist, in which I participated on the street in Gangjeong.

Eucharist: Liturgy of Social and Spiritual Transformation

The Eucharistic liturgy involves Great Thanksgiving to God for creating and continually redeeming humanity, "remembering" the death and resurrection of Jesus Christ, hope to be in perfect unity with God, and Christian commitment to a new life in the world. Just as womanist theologian Shawn Copeland elaborates, the Eucharistic table is a radical invitation for all Christians, who are the Christ's own flesh, to embody his love and justice by "memorializing" and participating in his death and resurrection.[56] Copeland further accentuates the mystical and transformative power of the Eucharist, which unites us with the love of God through the very presence of the Christ in the sacrament.[57] This Eucharist must be practiced through "acts of concrete compassion and solidarity in the here-and-now."[58] Based on her theological elaboration on the Eucharist, Copeland articulates "Eucharistic solidarity" that teaches us to imagine, to hope for, and to create new possibilities in a violent world (i.e. militarized world) because "Eucharistic solidarity enfolds us, rather than dismiss 'others'; we act in love rather than refuse 'others'; we respond in acts of self-sacrifice—committing ourselves to the long labor of creation, to the enfleshment of freedom."[59] Copeland's Eucharistic solidarity effectively disallows us to work only for our immediate community. She consistently challenges us to critically reflect on our own thoughts, words, and deeds and to look after those whose lives are violated by military imperialism, callous capitalism, racism, and so forth, although we may not have known them personally. Stanley Hauerwas, in a similar manner, presents the Eucharist as "the alternative to war."[60] At the Eucharistic table we face the mystical truth that we are created to be in communion with one another and not to kill one another. This Christian truth is incompatible with war.[61]

In order to stay truthful to the memory of the Christ, the Eucharist should not be privatized but be practiced in community. Vietnamese American Christian ethicist Jonathan Tran argues:

> Memory can certainly take place as a "monologue"; but truthful memory requires a community because memory and forgetting go hand in hand, with every remembering a forgetting and every forgetting a remembering.[62]

Based on his theo-ethical analysis of America's remembering of the Vietnam War, which domesticates the war in "American mythos" and willfully forgets Vietnamese people's memory of the war (i.e. America's killing of the innocent), Tran elaborates on the idea of "Eucharistic memory."[63] Eucharistic memory is active resistance to a politics of forgetfulness by intentionally remembering that Jesus identified with the victims in the past and by welcoming the unleashed ghosts of these victims of history at the present table of the Eucharist.[64]

Theological articulation of the Eucharist driven from the concrete contexts of the suffering mass such as those of Copeland and Tran unpacks the deeper meanings of the Eucharist, which Gangjeong activists have chosen as an active form of popular resistance. The first important political meaning of the Eucharist is how to intentionally "remember" or "memorialize" history's silenced victims. The militarized US–Korea relations have victimized countless ordinary people, including victims and survivors of the Jeju Massacre. The two countries' relationships cannot help but be haunted by the unleashed ghosts of history's victims, whose vengeance may be unbearable to us. At the Eucharistic table, Gangjeong activists intentionally remember history's victims by invoking their spirits, praying for their souls, and committing themselves to peace. Invoking the spirits of the dead and remembering the dead at the Eucharistic table may sound strange to modern Christians. However, welcoming the dead at the Eucharistic table was a common practice among early Christians. According to Rita Nakashima Brock and Rebecca Ann Parker, early Christians did not see the dead as being separated from the living. Rather, the dead and the living celebrate life together at the Eucharistic table—the dead even arrive at the table before the living.[65] The tragic Korean War and the willful forgetting of history's victims, however, prevent the living from celebrating life with the dead. In order to fully celebrate our past, present, and future life, we should welcome the dead (i.e. history's victims) at the Eucharistic table by intentionally exhuming their silenced stories, just as we remember the tragic death and resurrection of Jesus Christ. Celebrating the Eucharist with history's victims is to let them be fully liberated from their suffering, traumas, and deep sorrow, which are buried in "our" history, so that they can celebrate life with the living together.

Consuming bread during the Eucharist is political and spiritual at the same time. The bread sitting on the Eucharistic table in Gangjeong signifies the very presence of the Christ, whose identity is equated with the suffering and resisting mass, including both human and nonhuman entities. Great Thanksgiving given to God is a joyful expression of gratitude to the source of life whose presence is found in every living being—a dolphin swimming in the ocean, a crab walking on the Gurumbi rock, orange groves, laboring farmers, and so forth. By receiving and consuming the bread and wine, the participants empathetically embrace the suffering of living beings, remember the joy of life inscribed by God in every living being, join their resistance to violence, and renew their commitment to life.

In addition, the Eucharist in Gangjeong decentralizes power. God does not dwell only in the artificial sanctuary, but wherever the Eucharist is practiced. The boundaries between the sacred and the secular, the dead and the living, clergy and laity, us and them, and the US and South Korea are shattered when diverse people gather as the people of "peace," give Great Thanksgiving to God, and actively remember history's victims. This is similar to what Letty Russell imagined in *Church in the Round*, where the church becomes a decentralized power in the human world.[66] When the church becomes a decentralized power, it becomes a shared power that is ready to embody peace.

Militarism and the Eucharist

The Eucharist in the village of Gangjeong is resisting not simply the naval base but also normalized militarism in human society. Those who participate in the Eucharist should practice imagining and embodying an alternative world where peace does not have a militarized face because militarism is against the order of the Eucharist.

Military training, as David Grossman's groundbreaking work *On Killing* analyzes, transforms ordinary men and women into killers who consciously differentiate themselves from enemies and suppress their human nature not to kill other humans.[67] Rather than empathetically embracing "others" as the Eucharistic liturgy encourages, the soldiers must learn to systematically dehumanize others as enemies in order to kill them. Theologically speaking, if the Eucharist aims at unity between body and spirit by recognizing others in the Christ's body (e.g. bread and wine) and by receiving Christ's body with gratitude, militarism actively seeks to break this unity by portraying others as threats and by claiming God exclusively for us.

Feminist theologian Susan Thistlethwaite argues that the active military training is only possible based upon the dualistic understanding or separation between body and spirit. The military ideology of the body forces the soldiers to suppress and control their bodies as "lean, mean fighting machines."[68] Militarism is both a support for and a "product of the gnosticizing tendency in Christianity to denigrate the body and sexuality and to exclude them from the realm of the spirit."[69] As Thistlethwaite accentuates, in a world where violence and death are ubiquitous, the church must lead her people to reconstruct the separated body and spirit in Christianity toward "an integration of sensuality and spirituality."[70] The church can then actively resist the globalized militarism that alienates the human body from spirit and atomizes human beings one from another.

The Eucharist opens a mystical space where God and human beings become united in the flesh of the Christ. In order to encounter the mystery of the Christ at the Eucharistic table, we must make ourselves vulnerable to the unknown—God, others, our own selves, and so forth. This vulnerability is only possible when we strive to overcome the fear of the unknown by thoroughly trusting God, who is present in the Eucharist. According to British feminist sociologist Cynthia Cockburn, peace activism is ultimately "liberation from fear."[71] Her sociological analysis offers a theologically significant meaning. Not only Christianity but also Buddhism and other religions agree that fear, ignorance, and greed are the collective psychological roots of militarism. During the Cold War period, the US leaders incited fear of the communist military power in the public in order to consolidate US hegemony over the world. For example, when communist Chinese forces entered the Korean War, President Harry Truman declared a National Emergency on December 16, 1950. According to Truman, if communist imperialism achieved its goal to conquer the world, Americans would no longer worship their God or enjoy God's blessings of freedom. He urged Americans to make every possible sacrifice for America's triumph over communism—specifically America's victory in the Korean Peninsula.[72] The Truman regime used the Korean War era to forward much of the design for global security under US power.[73] In the twenty-first century, the political rhetoric of fear of terrorism and of losing global hegemonic power still forces the American public to allow the US to militarize the world.

The Eucharist forces us to ask ourselves where our fear comes from. Just as Dorothee Soelle says, "The worst fear of creatures (i.e. human beings) is the fear of the authorities (i.e. the military system) wherein people are kept dependent. Imprisoned in it, people cannot fear God (parentheses were added by the author)."[74]By fearing God, we humans refuse indifference to suffering caused by systemic injustice. The vulnerability before God that we experience at the Eucharistic table will eventually lead us to discern what to fear and what not to. Vulnerability humbles us by recognizing that the source of life, eternity, and security comes from God and not from military power. Namely, we should not fear military power, insecurity, and life's deep ambiguities. Rather, we should allow ourselves to be vulnerable to life's uncertainties. By generating empathy, vulnerability will eventually open doors for us to embrace others (both human and nonhuman entities). Through our own vulnerability, we can see others' vulnerability to suffering. Thus, we cannot but be in solidarity with them in their suffering and struggle for peace and justice.

Vulnerability at the Eucharist opposes the Christian triumphalism that has fed the American army for such a long time. Christian triumphalism as the American Civil Religion defines the US as a chosen people and as an instrument of the will of God in world affairs.[75] During the Cold War period, the military professionalized the Chaplains Corps as an integral part of the military system.[76] Cold War ideology offered a fertile ground for militant Christian evangelicals to fight communism, non-Christian religions, feminism, LGBTQ (lesbian, gay, bisexual, transgender and queer) rights, and so forth. As Emilie Townes correctly points out, Christian triumphalism has existed for the US to be empire by engaging in global warfare, and by forcing ordinary Americans to equate democracy with American imperialism. Yet, American empire fueled by Christian triumphalism has only increased economic and political misery among the poor, women, and people of color, domestically and globally.[77] According to Townes, Christian triumphalism is an ideology that is "meant to defeat permanent vulnerability and put celebration in the place of fear."[78] Christian triumphalism is still alive not only in American politics but also in Korean politics. At the Eucharistic table, we must re-remember the vulnerable death of Jesus, whose identity was merged into history's victims.

His message on the cross was not triumphalism through military power, but revelation of the ugliness and violence of military imperialism.

Eucharist as a Form of Popular Resistance

The most visible commonality between the Eucharist and popular resistance in Gangjeong is the empowerment of ordinariness. The Eucharist, after all, originated from Jesus' sharing of meals with ordinary people. Jesus's community turned this everyday activity into popular resistance to the political, economic, cultural, and religious status quo that denied the humanity of tax collectors, peasants, prostitutes, fishermen, and so forth in the Roman Empire. By the same token, popular resistance takes diverse forms through ordinary people's everyday activities, such as shopping, boycotting, working, striking, walking, marching, singing, dancing, and so forth. The spiritual continuity between the Eucharist and popular resistance is found in "mysticism," which allows us to simultaneously experience God's transcendence and immanence here and now. As Dorothee Soelle's study of Christian mysticism shows, mystics are nothing more than ordinary people who live in transcendence and immanence of God.[79] A transcendental God always challenges the status quo and social systems in which we live. An immanent God is always with us here and now by leading us to see the mystery and beauty in ordinariness. We can locate the transcendental and immanent God only in love shared with others, and thus are able to speak of sanctity for all.[80]

How can a transcendental and immanent God whom we encounter at the Eucharist motivate us to transform the militarized US–Korea relations into those of peace and justice free from militarism? Here are some suggestions to consider.

First, we should reanalyze what "real politics" are. In spite of his criticism of theologically influenced American Exceptionalism, Reinhold Niebuhr, a staunch Christian realist, still supported America's salvific role to save Asians from communism.[81] His support for America's military power came from his realistic approach to international politics that power struggle among superpower countries was inevitable because sinful humanity was contaminated by arrogance and will to power. As Mark Allman argues, however, what Niebuhr did not comprehend was the human capability to live with resurrected Jesus in eschatological hope.[82] In other words, although hierarchical and dominating power structures seem to be persistent realities throughout human history, as Rosemary Ruether points out, we also have realities of shared power relations, nonviolent resistance, and love-based popular resistance throughout human history.[83] We must not forget how human history has changed through popular resistance and willingness to suffer in order to overcome social sins. On the one hand, we, Christians, must take seriously Niebuhr's warnings of self-arrogance and will to power, both on an individual and on a collective level. On the other hand, we must comprehend our capabilities to live in the resurrected Christ—to be in communion with others, empathetically embrace others' suffering and joy, and to collaborate with one another.

Human history does not consist of a single narrative of power, such as domination or abusive power over others. It also has multiple stories of shared power relations that have existed at various levels in human society. The militarized US–Korea relations have been real, but a demilitarized US–Korea relation can also be real, as in the case of many American activists, including Gloria Steinem, Oliver Stone, Noam Chomsky, and many others supporting Gangjeong peace activism and visiting the village. In addition, we should not consider the militarized US–Korea relations as a permanent reality. An analysis of human reality or real politics is often prescriptive rather than descriptive. If this were the case, we should re-discover, re-remember, and re-tell the stories of ordinary Americans and Koreans, such as those from Gangjeong, who resist militarism with their whole hearts and minds. We must learn how to speak about, live in, and dream of demilitarized US–Korea relations. Living in the eschatological hope of demilitarized US–Korea relations calls us to exercise revolutionary power to challenge the status quo. So-called "real politik" tells us that powerful politicians can change the world. But "in reality," only ordinary people like you and me have the power to change the world, as we already saw in the Anti-Apartheid Movement in South Africa and the Civil Rights Movement in the US.

Furthermore, we must re-remember and re-tell the stories of history's victims. As long as the history of US–Korea relations remembers only General McArthur as the savior of South Koreans from North Korea, we cannot transform militarized relations between the US and Korea. We must learn how to listen to the untold stories of history's victims, such as the victims of the Jeju Massacre in 1948. Listening to their whispers, we can, little by little, liberate ourselves from militarized US–Korea relations, American exceptionalism, and, most importantly, Christian triumphalism.

Epilogue

My most recent visit to Gangjeong happened in early January 2014. Since my first visit there in 2011, the base is being built without interruptions. Neither have many peace activists and villagers stopped resisting the base. The noontime mass was still practiced, and the fence surrounding the construction site of the naval base was covered with messages of peace written by peace activists, visitors, global supporters, and so on. On the crossroad toward the Gurumbi Rock, lunch was served for whoever participated in Gangjeong peace activism. A simple house next to the food tent was where nuns and lay Catholics slept during their stays in Gangjeong, studying the bible together and learning the history of popular resistance in Jeju. A recently opened peace café and bookstore offered a space for ordinary people, especially children, to learn more about the various forms of popular resistance that value nonviolence, ecological preservation, local culture, and so on. Some longtime peace activists were planning to transform Gangjeong into a holy site for peace regardless of the presence of the naval base. In spite of the uncertain future of Gangjeong, residential peace activists did not stop embodying their belief in nonviolent peacemaking.

Gangjeong might be the smallest village on earth, but demilitarization between the US and Korea has begun there. Whether the naval base will finally be erected or not, the village will be remembered as a place where ordinary people share meals, dance, sing, and attend to the Eucharist, transforming and redeeming militarized US–Korea relations.

Notes

1. Mazin B. Qumsiyeh, *Popular Resistance in Palestine: A History of Hope and Empowerment* (New York: Pluto Press, 2011), 26.
2. Ibid., 11.
3. Ibid.
4. Martin Luther King, Jr., *Stride toward Freedom: The Montgomery Story* (San Francisco, CA: HarperSanFrancisco, 1958), 103. Quoted in Stanley Hauerwas, *War and American Difference: Theological Reflections on Violence and National Identity* (Grand Rapids, MI: Baker Academic, 2011), 87.
5. Qumsiyeh, *Popular Resistance in Palestine*, 12.
6. Ibid., 30. Qumsiyeh lists nine accomplishments through popular resistance, especially in Palestine, in relation to other similar movements. I list only three that seem most relevant to the movement in Gangjeong.

7. "Redemption" is part of Christian language, but this is a key concept for me to analyze how Christians bring their distinctive faith into popular resistance, while respecting other faiths and secular activists without a sense of moral superiority.
8. Ibid., 31.
9. Ibid., 33.
10. Jeong-sim Yang, *Jeju 4.3. People's Uprising: The History of Resistance and Suffering* (Seoul: Sun-in, 2008), 85; 123 (Korean).
11. Ibid., 183.
12. Ibid., 159; 165; 167.
13. Ibid., 58–63.
14. Ibid., 61.
15. Ibid.
16. Ibid., 63–65: One hundred fifty-six public organizations participated in strikes.
17. Ibid., 66–67.
    In fact, some of these leaders were associated with the South Labor Party, a communist political organization. But most participants in strikes were not involved in any political parties.
    Ibid., 62.
18. Jo-hoon Yang, "Jeju 4.3. Massacre" in *Peace and Human Rights in East Asia*, ed. Institute of Jeju 4.3. (Seoul: Yeoksa Bipyong, 1999), 266 (Korean).
19. Yang, *Jeju 4.3. People's Uprising*, 73–74.
20. Yang, "Jeju 4.3. Massacre," 263–264.
21. Ibid., 262–263.
22. Ibid., 263–264.
23. Ibid., 264.
24. Yang, *Jeju 4.3. People's Uprising*, 98; 102–105.
25. Ibid., 104.
26. Jeju April 3rd Peace Park, "Jeju 4.3. Almanac: 1948" http://jeju43.jeju.go.kr/index.php?mid=KR020502.
27. Yang, *Jeju 4.3. People's Uprising*, 193–194.
28. Ibid., 223.
29. Den Hideo, "Jeju 4.3., White Terrorism in Taiwan, and Japan's Responsibility" in *Peace and Human Rights in East Asia*, ed. Institute of 4.3. (Seoul: Yeoksa Bipyong, 1999), 31–33 (Korean).
30. Rosemary Ruether, *America, Amerikkka: Elect Nation and Imperial Violence* (Oakville, CT: Equinox, 2007), 136.
31. Human Rights Watch at Gangjeong, *A Report of Human Rights Violation While Constructing a Naval Base in Jeju: September 1st, 2011–June 30th, 2012*, 9–10 (Korean) http://issuu.com/pspd/docs/gangjeonghrv/3?e=0.
32. Ibid., 8.

33. Ibid., 9.
34. Ibid.
35. Ibid., 16–20.
36. Interview in Korean by the author, Gangjeong, Jeju, Korea (August, 2011).
37. Young-jae Yoo, "As the U.S. Armed Forces Wish" in *Don't Cry, Gurumbi, Stand Up, Gangjeong: The Voice of Peace from the Gangjeong Village of Jeju*, ed. The Network of Citizens for the Living Gurumbi Rock (Seoul: Narum Books, 2011), 25–30 (Korean).
   China is the second ranked vis-à-vis military expenditure. Although China's military expenditure is far less than that of the US, it far surpasses any of the other top five countries as regards military expenditure, including Russia, the UK, and France.
38. Human Rights Watch at Gangjeong, *A Report of Human Rights Violation While Constructing a Naval Base in Jeju*, 9.
39. Maria Hohn and Seungsook Moon, "Empire at the Crossroads?" in *Over There: Living with the U.S. Military Empire from World War Two to the Present*, eds. Maria Hohn and Seungsook Moon (Duke University Press, 2010), 401.
40. Eun-woo Lee, "Gangjeong Is Right, Daechuri Is Right" in *Don't Cry, Gurumbi, Stand Up, Gangjeong*, 185 (Korean).
41. Jeju Friends of the Earth Korea, "Where Will Sea Creatures Go?" in *Don't Cry, Gurumbi, Stand Up, Gangjeong*, 37–39 (Korean).
42. Young-ja Lee, "A Cheerful Village of Gangjeong Will Come Again" in *Don't Cry, Gurumbi, Stand Up, Gangjeong*, 85–87 (Korean).
43. Ibid., 83–84.
44. Gook-sang Kim, "Uncomfortable Truth about the Media Portrayal of Gangjeong" in *Don't Cry, Gurumbi, Stand Up, Gangjeong*, 45–46; 50–52 (Korean).
45. Young-hee Shim, "The History of Korean Women's Peace Activism and Its Future Tasks" in *Korean Women's Peace Movement: Its Unfolding and Issues*, eds. Young Hee Shim and Elli Kim (Seoul, Korea: Han Wool Academy, 2005), 29–30 (Korean).
46. Yang, *Jeju 4.3. People's Uprising*, 209–210.
47. Interview in Korean by the author, Gangjeong, Jeju (July, 2011).
48. Interview in Korean by the author, Daejeong, Jeju (August, 2012).
49. Interview in Korean by the author, Daejeong, Jeju (August, 2012).
50. Han Gye Rae Newspaper, "Nuns Were Arrested at the Naval Site: Never Happened Even during the Military Dictatorship," Han Gye Rae, January 26, 2012. (http://www.hani.co.kr/arti/society/area/514935.html).
51. The Association of Major Superiors of Religious Women in Korea, "The Declaration of 4023 Korean Catholic Nuns for No Naval Base in Jeju and for the State Authorities' Repentance"] (http://www.cbck.or.kr/bbs/bbs_read.asp?board_id=K1500&bid=13008381).

52. Interview in Korean by the author, Gangjeong, Jeju (August, 2012).
53. Ibid.
54. Bruce Cumings, *Korea's Place in the Sun: A Modern History* (New York: Norton, 1997), 96–97.
55. Ibid., 298.
56. Shawn Copeland, *Enfleshing Freedom: Body, Race, and Being* (Minneapolis, MN: Fortress Press, 2010), 108–109.
57. Ibid., 109.
58. Ibid.
59. Ibid., 127–128.
60. Hauerwas, *War and American Difference*, 69.
61. Ibid.
62. Jonathan Tran, *The Vietnamese War and Theologies of Memory* (Oxford, UK: Wiley and Blackwell, 2010), 206.
63. Ibid., 221–226; 262.
64. Ibid., 263–264.
65. Rita Nakashima Brock and Rebecca Ann Parker, *Saving Paradise: How Christianity Traded Love of This World for Crucifixion and Empire* (Boston, MA: Beacon Press, 2008), 69–72.
66. Letty Russell, *Church in the Round: Feminist Interpretation of the Church* (Louisville, KY: Westminster John Knox Press, 1993), 45.
67. Lt. Col. David Grossman, *On Killing: The Psychological Cost of Learning to Kill in War and Society*: Revised Edition (New York, NY: E-Rights/E-Reads, Ltd. Publishers, 2009), Kindle Edition.
68. Susan Thistlethwaite, "Militarism in North American Perspective" in *Women Resisting Violence: Spirituality for Life*, eds. Mary John Mananzan et al. (Eugene, OR: Wipf and Stock, 2004), 120.
69. Ibid., 121.
70. Ibid.
71. Cynthia Cockburn, *From Where We Stand: War, Women's Activism and Feminist Analysis* (New York: Zed Books, 2008), 258.
72. Harry Truman, "A Declaration of National Emergency, December 16, 1950" in Spencer Tucker, *Almanac of American Military History*, Vol. III (Santa Barbara, CA: ABC-CLO, 2012), 1938.
73. Ruether, *America, Amerikkka*, 145.
74. Dorothee Soelle, *The Silent Cry: Mysticism and Resistance* (Minneapolis, MN: Fortress, 2001), 87.
75. Ruether, *America, Amerikkka*, 146.
76. Ibid.
77. Emilie Townes, *Womanist Ethics and the Cultural Production of Evil* (New York: Palgrave McMillan, 2006), 96–97.
78. Ibid., 97.
79. Soelle, *The Silent Cry*, 14–17.

80. Ibid., 112.
81. Niebuhr, *The Irony of American History*, 41–42.
82. Mark Allman, *Who Would Jesus Kill?: War, Peace, and the Christian Tradition* (Winona, MN: St. Mary's Place, 2008), 115–116.
83. Rosemary Ruether, *Christianity and Social Systems: Historical Constructions and Ethical Challenges* (Lanham, MD: Rowman & Littlefield Publisher, 2008), 8–9.

Index

Note: Page numbers followed by "n" denote notes.

N. Kim, W.A. Joh (eds.), *Critical Theology against US Militarism in Asia*,
DOI 10.1057/978-1-137-48013-2

N